THE
RED LAMP
OF INCEST

Robin Fox

THE RED LAMP OF INCEST

An Enquiry into the Origins of Mind and Society

UNIVERSITY OF NOTRE DAME PRESS
Notre Dame, Indiana 46556

Grateful acknowledgment is made to the following for permission to quote
from copyrighted material:

"Heavy Date," *Collected Poems* by W. H. Auden, © 1945 by W. H. Auden,
Random House, Inc.

"Encore une fois sur le fleuve," *Histoires* by Jacques Prévert, © 1963 by Editions Gallimard

Library of Congress Cataloging in Publication Data

Fox, Robin, 1934–
The red lamp of incest.

Bibliography: p.
Includes index.
1. Incest. 2. Social evolution. I. Title.
GN480.25.F69 1983   306.7'77   83-16686
ISBN 0-268-01620-8

To the
memory of
ROBERT ARDREY

Time and death and the space between
the stars remain still rather larger
than ourselves

African Genesis

Contents

Preface

to the Notre Dame Edition

While *The Red Lamp of Incest* has, with a few obvious exceptions, been well received, it has not necessarily been well understood. This is partly a result of the very nature of the book. It is an ambitious attempt at synthesis, and synthesis is uncomfortable. The academic world in particular has settled down into a cozy departmental view of the partitioning of reality, and is unhappy with any intellectual effort that disregards this implicit metaphysic. For a start, no one knows how to handle it. Under what "listing" do the publishers list it? To what reviewers do the journals send it? Where does the Library of Congress catalogue it? Anthropologists have taught (and I discuss in chapter seven) the curious fact that what cultures regard as polluting, and what they regularly taboo, are *those things that offend established category distinctions.* Indeed, in my inaugural lecture for the Department of Anthropology at Notre Dame, I argued that such distinctions were in all probability physically established in the brain insofar as they took more than three years to become memorized. The task of a synthesizer is therefore almost impossible. He is fighting the synapses, not just prejudices. But there is no help for it, as the Irish would say. This book is committed to synthesis. It starts its exploration from anthropology, but ranges into psychoanalysis, brain evolution, primatology, psychology, sociology, epistemology, the philosophy of mind, the origins of language, palaeontology, and social criticism.

One knows the obvious objections, but it seems to me they are trivial. The proof of the pudding is in the proverbial eating. It is tiresome to be told that something cannot be done *en principe.*

The answer is to do it and see if it works. And if it doesn't work, to see if this is because it shouldn't have been done or because it was not done properly. My own faith is of course that it can be done; it remains to be seen if it has been done properly. But the world is not neatly partitioned according to departmental boundaries. Reality is a series of problems, and we should pursue the problems and ignore the boundaries. The advantage of anthropology in this is that it gives one, as Kroeber said, an intellectual poaching license: for what is not the science of Man? It means, of course, that the synthesizer must be willing to equip himself with expertise in several areas of knowledge. Most of my colleagues are not willing to undertake more than one process of initiation in a lifetime, and I sympathize. In many areas I am myself an autodidact, but since I see myself as an eternal student rather than anything more exalted, it is easy and pleasant for me to learn new things in new areas. On the other hand there is not much here that an old-fashioned anthropologist would regard as out of his sphere. The current fragmentation of anthropology is such that someone who aspires to a holistic view of man is regarded as a rash speculator rather than an exemplar of the true anthropological mandate. Odd.

As to the specific subject matter — incest, and its relation to social and mental origins — I have presented it chronologically rather than logically. That is, I have put it down in the order of ideas as they occurred to me over the twenty year period in question. There is a logic in this chronology, but an alternative way of presenting it would have been the *purely* logical. I have done this in brief in an article ("Les Conditions de l'évolution sexuelle," in *Communications*, P. Ariès, M. Foucault and A. Béjin eds., no. 35: pp. 2–13, 1982) but it would have been simply too exhausting to have done this in the book. I have summarized the logical order — from DNA replication to hominid assortative mating systems — and this must suffice. I had thought to rewrite the final chapter here as such a logical summary, but it seemed to me that this would be simply repetitious. So I have let the final chapter stand.

Again, I had almost been pursuaded to remove it on these grounds: that since it contained social commentary it detracted from the intellectual status of the book by diverting attention from the main intellectual argument to the peripheral tendentious opinions. To this I have two replies. One is that anyone who is genuinely interested in the argument of chapters one through seven will treat eight with the scepticism it deserves. We all have opinions which derive from our theories, but we know how to separate the one from the other. The other reply is that we have some obligation to say what we think follows from our theories if this is important to contemporary concerns. If we have theories from which nothing follows, well and good; but if there are consequential arguments we should vent them, however unpopular they may be, since otherwise others will draw their own conclusions anyway. With a theory like this one there are inescapable questions that automatically arise, and it would have been cowardly to avoid them. As I insist, I may be drawing wrong conclusions from my own theory. But it is surely more honest to draw these conclusions and to put them up for possible falsification than to pretend that "pure" science has nothing to do with the real world.

In fact, the only real criticism of these conclusions has come from feminists who seem ill-informed about what is happening in their own movement. What they fail to see is that most of the criticisms I advance have also come from *within feminism itself.* I recommend the brilliant critique by Janet Radcliffe Richards, *The Sceptical Feminist* (Routledge, Kegan Paul, 1980). My eldest daughter, a tough feminist philosopher who gave me the book for Christmas, says that what I am attacking is "soft-focus careerist feminism" which is totally passé anyway: *requiescat in pace!*

It has also been put to me that I should take account of Lovejoy's arguments concerning "Lucy" (O. Lovejoy, "The Origin of Man," *Science*, 211, Jan. 23, 1981). I could possibly reply that he takes no account of my case so I should pay him the same compliment. But really there is nothing to take account of. Lucy merely confirms the antiquity of the australopithecine line as a bipedal and small-brained hominid which remained in a state of evolutionary stagnation for several million years. If it was practicing "a kind of monogamy," then so much the worse for that kind of monogamy we might reply. It undoubtedly was — but *what* kind? This Lovejoy never addresses. Clearly during this period stabilizing selection was at work — there were no changes. But this is compatible with a competitive breeding situation, and I have suggested that, given the mosaic environment, several breeding systems could have been experimented with. What is interesting is what happened when the upsurge in brain size occurred. Stabilizing selection was knocked sideways and rapid shifts in gene frequency took over. This is the question that needs addressing. The modified competition of the long drag of australopithecine existence was suddenly intensified to the breaking point, and all the criteria of selection were shifted as well. That's when things began to happen: when the full potentials of reproductive competition were loosed and had to be tamed, finding both their potentially destructive energy and their potential for controlling it in the same source. There is nothing in the Lovejoy argument about bipedalism, carrying, and sharing that is incompatible with reproductive competition and even multiple-mating, although "a kind of monogamy" would indeed prevail for the majority as in any such system. There is everything that happened *after* about 1.8 million years B.P. that his argument leaves unexplained and to which this book is devoted.

On one other technical point, I should comment. I have stressed sexual competition as a basis for the rapidity of hominid evolution, and have also dealt with fission as a function of primate and hominid social systems. What I missed was a thread of argument that would make fission as important to rapid change as differential reproductive success. See, for example, Neel, J. V., and Ward, R. N., (1970) "Village and tribal genetic distances among American Indians, and the possible implications for human evolution," *Proceedings of the National Academy of Sciences*, 65, 323–330. This I missed; two other relevant articles appeared after I completed the book: Chepko-Sade, D. B., and Olivier, T. J., (1979) "Coefficient of genetic relationship and the probability of intra genealogical fission in *Macaca mulatta*," *Behavioral Ecology and Sociobiology*, 5, 263–278; Smouse, P. E., Vitzthum, U. J., and Neel, J. V. (1981) "The impact of random and lineal fission in the genetic divergence of small human groups: a case study among the Yanomama," *Genetics*, 98, 179–197. There may be others. But put the two arguments together — differential reproductive success and the "Sewall Wright" effects of fissioning — and much concerning the question of rapid evolution and the role of exogamy becomes clearer.

A number of items that were unpublished at the time have now been published. Of the more important I cite Paul Heyer, *Nature, Human Nature, and Society: Marx, Darwin, Biology and the*

Human Sciences (Greenwood Press, 1982), and C. Poletti and M. Sujatanond, "Evidence for a second hippocampal efferent pathway to hypothalamus and basal forebrain comparable to fornix system: a unit study in the awake monkey," *Journal of Neurophysiology*, 44: 514–531, 1980.

There is another important reason for leaving chapter eight as it is. It makes a serious point which, if right, is a challenge to a whole social science orthodoxy, and if wrong, has to be shown to be so. Let me try a metaphor: Society is a great Leviathan, and modern society a bloated, wounded, tormented, and stranded beast. Bad as its condition is, there is a resilience, there is endogenous healing power, there are antibodies and an autoimmune system. The Leviathan struggles to heal itself: struggles to restore its basic, healthy condition. This healing process is itself painful and the beast suffers much. Now the problem is that the diagnosticians of the wounded state have mistaken this for normality, and so see the pains and suffering of the healing process as pathologies! This is because they never knew Leviathan when it was whole and in its prime of health and growth. The frightening situation now reveals itself: they rush to cure what they see as pathologies, but what they are doing is hampering the healing process. Those a little more perceptive say: Leviathan had become used to the wounded state, it wouldn't have killed him, but the healing process is too dramatic; he has to learn to live with the wounds; they *are* normality now. Perhaps. I have no ready answer. I do not imagine that to recognize supposed pathologies as attempts at healing will make them any less painful—but it may change our way of dealing with them. We may be more patient, less alarmed, more willing to observe effects rather than rushing to judgment; more discriminating about what we label deviance and what "raised consciousness." I doubt it, but the point has to be made.

The metaphor breaks down of course, because we diagnosticians are part of our own Leviathan. We may even be one of the pathologies. At least this view can act as a cautionary tale: the physician may be part of the disease. Thus this book is only a contribution to a larger project, the aim of which is to jolt us into a revised view of ourselves as a species, to free us from the intellectual shackles of the Enlightenment faith in Reason, the Romantic passion for the Individual, and the nineteenth century

worship of Progress. It is therefore obviously puzzling to those
who can only deal with books that fall within the bureaucratic
limits of writing rituals appropriate to a profession. But if my
point here is correct, then there is nothing for it but to break out
from the suffocating pressures of those rituals and take a fresh
view. This particular view may not be correct, but the attempt
must be made before we — our own Leviathan — sink under the
misguided ministrations of the diagnosticians or the indifference
of petty-minded professionalism.

More important than the misunderstanding of chapter eight,
is the neglect of chapter seven. Anthropological and lay reviewers
have not known what to do with it. Philosophers complain that,
while they are interested, they cannot assess the "anthropological
content." So here we are trapped in the tyranny of disciplines
again. For what it is worth let me appeal to the philosophers who
seem to be in an impasse over the theory of mind: If you do not
quickly educate yourselves in neuropsychology and brain evolution, then the issue may pass from your hands. And this will be
a disaster because brain scientists do not understand the philosophical issues. I have a faint hope that within the synthesis I
propose here room may be found for an empirical grounding of
the question of the nature of mind. At least it deserves attention,
and if the anthropologists and neuro-scientists have to learn some
philosophy and vice-versa, so be it. The synapses can't be *that*
hardened.

There is here a theory of human social order and its pathologies as potentially productive and complex as those of Marx,
Weber, Parsons, etc. but richer in that it is grounded in a knowledge of society's origins in evolution, and in the Freudian insight
that our current social dramas are a replaying, with variations, of
the dramas of our evolutionary past. Once the nature of the relations between the three "blocks" is understood, and their dynamics
properly interpreted, then we can feed into these equations the
varying political, ecological, economic, and ideational components
to read off the results of a near fit or a wide divergence from the
basic pattern. Wide divergences themselves seem to differ in kind:
some are obviously easier to live with than others; some stretch
the pattern widely but do not break it; some result in rips and
tears that are mended with difficulty. But we have first to recog-

nize, as we have seen, that the ripped and torn pieces are not themselves the basic pattern!

People want prognosis and advice. I have no reliable prognosis and only vague advice: we do not know the ultimate limits, but we can see the obvious pathologies; when in doubt it can't help to stay close to the basic pattern. This will not result in Utopia —but it may make our sufferings human and understandable, rather than inhuman and unthinkable.

A final word on style since some puritanical reviewers seem to think that a serious book must be, of its nature, a dull book. This is to confuse the serious with the solemn, as Russell Baker so delightfully reminds us. For me ideas, while wholly serious, are exciting, playful, dramatic. I could have written this as a two-volume tome by incorporating all the footnote material in the text and cutting out the "plot." I would have died from boredom before volume two.

R.F.

ONE

The Lighting of the Lamp

. . . plongé d'un seul coup
dans la bienfaisante chaleur animale et tropicale
de la misérable promiscuité familiale
Et le lampion rouge de l'inceste
en un instant prend feu. . . .

> Jacques Prévert
> "Encore une fois sur le fleuve"
> *Histoires*

Jacques Prévert describes the sun passing over Paris where, with a Whitmanesque generosity, it excludes nothing. The worst thing the sun has to accept is the suicide of a girl raped and made pregnant by her drunken father. This workman, shut out from the brothels, which have been closed to protect public morals, is "plunged at one swoop into the enveloping animal and tropical heat of sordid family promiscuity." It was the next line that caught my imagination—"Et le lampion rouge de l'inceste" which "en un instant prend feu." A "lampion" is a fairy light or Chinese lantern; a red lamp, small but bright, which lights up in an instant if the right switch is thrown.

The subject is incest and the fascination of incest. Why the fascination? Because it is forbidden? But why is it forbidden—or is it always forbidden? The quick answer is—not always. But at the very least, the idea of it seems to make us easily uneasy, and at

1

worst, downright hysterical. Do we forbid it, when we do, because in fact we *really* want to do it? But if we really want to do it, why don't we just go ahead? And if we don't want to do it, why do we bother to forbid it? Is there a universal horror of incest? Again, quick answer, no. But again, there seems to be a widespread unease about it. Why then are we so easily made uneasy?

Universally, there are *some* rules about it, even if they vary widely. All societies, for example, ban marriage with some close relatives; some also ban sex. But not all societies have banned all such marriages, and even those that have banned them have not always condemned incestuous sex as such. This has been a source of much confusion in the academic attempt to understand incest taboos: Arguments that explain the banning of a relatively long-term arrangement like marriage don't *necessarily* explain the reactions to what otherwise might be very short-term sex between close relatives—either before marriage or outside marriage.

Academic confusion is not news. All teenagers understand the difference between sex and marriage, but academics, perhaps understandably, are not so well informed. It would simply be amusing were it not that far-ranging theories of human nature and behavior have been erected on the basis of this confusion, and sometimes, unfortunately, people act on academic theories. We are going to look then, at this two-sided fascination: the lay fascination—that of everyman with the forbidden, and the academic fascination—that of scientists with the incest taboo as the origins of everything distinctively human.

It was the pursuit of the idea of incest as the root problem of social evolution that linked Freud and the anthropologists. It was as if the idea glowed for them too, like a red lantern in the murk of social theory. What I want to argue here is that they were right to keep their gaze on the red lamp, but not always for the reasons they thought, because they were as bemused by the prospect of incest as the drunken father of the poem. But of all the gazers and searchers, Freud was the nearest to the truth in *Totem and Taboo*.

In pursuing our own version of Freud's truth, we are going to challenge much of the conventional wisdom. The easy acceptance that we are "by nature" monogamous creatures that naturally form "nuclear families" and that incest taboos are necessary to protect these God-given institutions will take a battering. So will the equally easy academic acceptance of incest taboos as the "basic" human reality—the gulf between incestuous nature and human culture. But that is to leap ahead.

It is well to begin by putting ourselves in nature's place and asking what it is up to. It may be objected that to impute purpose to a set of processes that clearly has none is sheer anthropomorphism. Those processes have no interest, of course, in what happens to the individuals or the species they have produced. Over 90 percent of the species that have ever lived are now extinct. Before man, there was no mourning for their loss.

But if animate nature can be said to operate under any rules at all, the basic commandment must be simply, "Go forth and multiply." It sounds like a simple rule. It should be easy to follow. But the rules human beings follow, for whatever reason, are anything but simple.

Suppose that three humans, two males and one female, are all that are left of the species. They could, perhaps, survive. But they are devout Christians. The female is married to one of the males, who, in the holocaust that has left them the sole survivors, has become impotent. Nevertheless, they take the commandment "Thou shalt not commit adultery" seriously. Eventually they die. There are no more humans. The commandment, it appears, was a mistake, like the weight of the dinosaurs.

The processes that have produced the human species do not care how, or whether, we reproduce our kind—whether we compete or cooperate, struggle, hide, cheat, or gamble; whether we use teeth, claws, speed, size, or intellect. Kropotkin was right: Mutual aid will do as well as tooth and claw.[1] They are all trappings. Anything will do as long as it serves the basic breeding function. The whole of human culture in this perspective is a congeries of trappings, which either ensure that another generation survives to breed or that it is as doomed as the dinosaurs.

Consider the june bug or the thirteen- or seventeen-year cicadas or any of the many insects that appear briefly for a matter of hours or days.[2] The male june bug has only two legs, which serve him in grasping the female. He mates with her, she lays her eggs, they die. For these insects, "life" is a fluttering moment of gene transfer, followed by up to seventeen years sucking at the tree roots; but they have stayed in the game for millions of years. Their version of staying around is infinitely more efficient and economical than ours. We are wasteful blunderers by comparison. Long life, warm blood, live birth, suckled young, large brains, culture, intelligence—they may all have been a mistake in the long run, so far as staying around is concerned; less effective than the bizarre courtship of the great crested grebe.[3]

Turning from evolution and staying around in general to what happens to any species in particular, we must examine, as closely as we can, the particular way in which the species obeys the basic rule of nature: i.e., we must examine its breeding system. If this is the ultimate clue to what is happening, we should be seriously asking about how the human system of breeding evolved. We would seem, though, to be asking about anything but that. Even the so-called science of man appears to shy away from the implications of so doing. Man cannot bear very much reality—it took a poet to tell us that—and anthropologists are no different. Yet the distinctiveness of anthropology as a social science lies in its study of human kinship systems, and at the core of that distinctiveness is the question of the incest taboo.

In the mid-nineteenth century, two anthropological founding fathers, John Ferguson McLennan and Lewis Henry Morgan, set out the basic questions of kinship theory.[4] Human beings were seen as defining groups of kin as "related" (in families, clans, moieties, kindreds, etc.) and then forbidding marriage within those groups. McLennan coined a word for this—exogamy: "marriage out." Another founding father, Sir E. B. Tylor, first proposed (on biblical authority) the maxim "Marry out or be killed out."[5] Exogamy, then, was a good way of ensuring peace among groups—and only incidentally of preventing incest. Too many anthropologists since, in my opinion, have regarded exogamy and incest as indissolubly one and the same thing—writing, for example, of "incest/exogamy regulations" and the like.[6] Sometimes they are indeed the same thing: people make a rule that you cannot marry anyone from a group of kin, and *also* that you cannot have sex with them. But the two, as we have seen, need not be coterminous, and we have to grasp this distinction. Throughout the breathtaking intellectual twists and turns that lie ahead, we are going to hang onto this like leeches: *Incest refers to sex, exogamy refers to marriage.*

Moving from exogamy as a primary phenomenon in the origins of kinship systems (that is, from marriage), theorists became obsessed with incest taboos as the psychosocial center of human institutions (that is, with sex). Everything went back ultimately to the incest taboo. Before it, there was raw nature; after it, there was culture. Incestuous man was truly in a state of nature; post-incestuous man was man removed "d'un seul coup" from nature. But the possibility of incest always lurked, like the red lantern of Prévert's poem, to tempt him back into his cultureless, natural state.

It is perhaps too easy to say that McLennan and Morgan were lawyers, and that since the "rules of exogamy" were usually explicit and codified, as in Roman law, they appealed to them more than did murky sentiment or taboos. But there is something in it. The shift toward a primary concern with the incest taboo as the explanation of everything came with Sir James Frazer and Sigmund Freud—two men who had been reared in the grip of Victorian sexual repression and who were (each for his own reasons) more concerned with sentiments than legalities. McLennan had introduced the idea of totemism as the basis of all religion, but it was Frazer—in *Totemism and Exogamy*—who linked it to both exogamy and magic, and through magic to taboo—the "negative magic" of the human mental scheme. Totems were taboo (one could not eat them, for example); totems were shared by members of the same kinship group who could not marry one another; totems were therefore linked with exogamy; members of the same group were taboo to each other sexually. The buildup was inexorable. It was, of course, easy to say that this all had to do only with savages—this "grisly horror of incest" and the accompanying taboos.

Freud shattered that comfortable shelter from the glare of the red lamp. The life of savages and the life of contemporary neurotics was not, he said, all that different. (And neurotics were only slightly exaggerated versions of the normal.) Indeed, obsessional neurosis and taboo were more or less the same thing. Most of the trappings that developed, in savage culture and in the modern neurotic, were defenses against the wish to commit incest. This was the most primary of all primary wishes and also the most feared. Totems and exogamy and all the rest were defenses against the possibility of slipping back into a state of nature.

Freud, in *Totem and Taboo,* brilliantly took Frazer's scheme and his own experience with the psychoanalysis of patients and wove from them a theory that, though much reviled, remains challenging. We shall deal with it in detail later. All that needs to be said here is that in the jungle of social theory, the red lamp of incest shone more strongly for anthropologists than for any other social scientists, even as it was being abandoned by psychoanalysts as an embarrassment. When anthropological theorists ran out of steam on the subject, it was largely because each explanation they gave was about as good as any other.[7] And they were all alike in pointing out what disastrous things would happen either to the individuals concerned or to societies as a whole *if incest taboos did not exist.* This is remarkably like the reasoning of the "savages" themselves: When asked why they have a taboo on incest, they usually cite some natural disaster that would follow if they didn't. The problem with such explanations, of course, is that short of getting rid of the taboo and seeing what follows, there is no way of knowing whether they are right or not. The social sciences have, after all, a hard enough time trying to explain why people *do* the things they do. With incest, we are trying to explain why people do *not* do something. But to point to possible dire consequences, from a scientific point of view, scarcely constitutes an adequate explanation.

In saying that humans have a rule or taboo against some action, we are surely stating something unique about them. But what is unique, it is important to notice, is the *rule,* not the necessity of doing or not doing the thing itself. Both animals and human beings, under some circumstances, avoid killing their own kind. But only humans have rules against it.

This point is very important in getting the question right—and according to my contention, the trouble anthropologists have had with the question of incest has been that they did not get the question right. Too often it is grotesquely begged. Consider, for example, the question of why there is "a universal grisly horror of incest." Answer: There isn't. In some cultures there may indeed be horror; but in others there is mere embarrassment, in still others indifference, and in a certain few there may be positive encouragement. So this can't be the right question. At the last count, there were at least ninety-six societies with some evidence of permitted sexual relations among family members, including full marriage. In at least two—certain periods during the history of Iran and of Egypt—there is evidence that brother-sister marriage was the norm.[8] Sweden has threatened to join the list just recently by considering the abolition of the brother-sister ban.[9] Half-brothers and half-sisters have often been allowed or encouraged to marry. So to ask about a *universal* taboo against incest is likewise to beg the question.

There is a natural urge in anthropology to look for universals—things that are true for the species as a whole. Frequently, however, such universals do not exist at the substantial, institutional level, where they are usually sought. The nuclear family, for example, has long since crumbled as a universal; but the bonding processes on which it is based and of which it is one possible outcome, are certainly universal. The moral from the study of universal grammar is clear: Attempts to find substantial grammatical universals have failed—the universals are at the level of *process*.

The same is then probably true for incest: *Something* is universal (or "species-specific," as we are learning to say), but what? Not horror, not taboo. What then? Let us start with a question based on facts: *Why do human beings not commit much incest?*

This could be construed as belonging to the same logical order as, Why do human beings not commit much murder? In each case, the thoughtless reply might be, because they would be punished. But is this true? There are many tribes and nations—as the next chapter will show—that do not effectively punish either, but that are not overwhelmed with incest or murder.

The questions appear to assume that we would, if not restrained by third parties, engage freely in both incest and murder. But again, is the assumption justified? Do we, in fact, go around harboring incestuous and murderous thoughts, which we fail to put into practice simply because of our fear of punishment? Perhaps. There is incest, and there is murder, and we make laws or raise sanctions against both. But to believe that we are at base a society of murderous, lecherous, and incestuous villains runs counter to common sense. Better to change the question so as to take account of what appears at face value to be true, and ask rather:

Why do human beings not want to commit incest all that much?

It seems as if they don't. People say they don't. There doesn't seem to be all that much committing of incest in proportion to total numbers. Some people do it, but not so very many. Those who insist that we are nevertheless riddled by incestuous desires would counter that it is odd to have invented all these laws, taboos, and sanctions against incest if those desires aren't there, however. So we must ask yet another question:

If human beings don't want all that much to commit incest, why are they hard on those who do commit it?

Well, we are hard on murderers even though there are proportionately very few of them. We need not assume that we have laws against murder because we all have murderous natures, but only because *some* murder occurs and we don't like that. Considering murder in this way, we can see that the question is usually put backwards with regard to incest: that is, we do not usually ask why people do *not* commit murder. We assume that most people won't, most of the time. We ask, rather, why those who commit murder do it. Similarly with incest, we could ask—and indeed many practical social workers do just this—what has caused a breakdown in the normal, non-incestuous situation? This question assumes that people will be tempted and goes on to inquire why some, like the father in Prévert's poem, succumb, and others not.

If, when left to their own devices, human beings commit very little incest (and this is obviously our suspicion), then why *do* we pursue, however mildly, those who do? (In passing, we might note that the assumption hazarded here makes the existence of many instances of institutionalized incest quite plausible: It is not naturally desired, but it can be taught.)

Returning to the analogy with murder, it may be observed that although murder is generally thought to be wrong, often very little is done about it in societies, for example, that lack a state apparatus. With the advent of statehood, murder appears to become more commonplace; furthermore, the state resents this intrusion on its right to decide who shall and shall not die. Similarly with incest: In many societies it is treated as a rarity, and either ignored or dealt with ritually in some mild way. With the advent of the state, again, the interference with individual sexuality increases, and what was once a minor offense becomes a capital crime.[10] As far as sanctions are concerned, societies that are heavily down on incest usually tend to be down on other forms of sex, and for various reasons.

What emerges from all this is that, by and large, the human species (a) doesn't engage in very much incest (but does some); (b) doesn't like it much (but sometimes allows it); (c) varies in responding to it (but always responds in some way).

Thus the basic question becomes: *Why, by and large, don't human beings like it much?* Why, in the vast majority of societies, do they take *some* trouble, however vague, to discourage incestuous unions, even though most human beings are probably not going to

indulge in such unions? Why we do not like murder much is perhaps obvious; but why should we not make love with those we love
most? At the least, the notion makes us uneasy—but we might
sanction it for a privileged few or a favored caste; at worst, it fills us
with horror. *Unease* and *avoidance* seem to be the common denomi-
nators—not fierce desire held in check by even fiercer sanctions or
lust reined in by the power of taboo. The universal root phenomenon appears to be the *ease with which it rouses our unease*. But why the
unease to begin with? Does red indeed mean danger?

Patience. Whether or not we are ever to get a good answer, it
is the gist of what has gone before that we must get the right question. What we should know in the meantime is what the assumptions are that have led to the current confusion on the subject of
incest.[11] That taboos on incest are universal; that they are uniquely
human; that incest is universally horrifying; that incest is coterminous with nature, and avoidance of incest is coterminous with
culture; that there is a universal desire to commit incest; that
taboos and strong sanctions are what prevent it from occurring;
that without them there would be dire consequences—to all of
these assumptions, anthropologists (among others) have sub-
scribed, to a degree that each of these propositions might have
been taken as self-evident.

Yet every single one of them can be challenged as, if not
wholly wrong, at least in need of severe qualification. Take the orthodox assertion—that we need incest taboos to avoid the dire
consequences that would follow. For example: (1) People would
become fixated on their primary sex choices—parents—and never
would want sex outside the family; (2) there would be an intolera-
ble level of competition for women within the family, bringing on
fierce intrafamilial strife; (3) there would be deleterious genetic effects for the group; (4) there would be a failure to form wider social
ties, again to the detriment of the species; and so on. Note, however, that dire consequence number 4—popularly called the "sociological" explanation—is really an explanation of exogamy, not of
incest taboos. My old teacher, the late Maurice Freedman, always
used to ask his class, "Why can't we have a sexual free-for-all
within the family and still marry out of it?" Thus (4) needs something like (1) before it will work as an explanation of incest avoidance or taboo, and then it would be superfluous. But even (1) is
factually doubtful. Such evidence as we have of incestuous esca-

pades (where the parties are not mentally ill in some way) suggests that we *can* indeed have incest (typically father-daughter or brother-sister), then marry out.[12]

Note further that like the conundrum of the Cretan liars, if (1) is true ("the more we lie together the merrier we will be"), then (2) can't be ("the more we lie together the nastier we will be"). At least in favor of dire consequence (3), it may be granted that some genetic consequences after all can be seen, and that if they are indeed bad then there might be a reason for banning incest. Some proponents of this argument reason that *long ago* people saw what those consequences were, but by now have forgotten them (since they don't occur anymore) and so put forward other "dire consequence" rationalizations. This all assumes, of course, that people were able to make the necessary connections. Other arguments suggest that even if they were not so able, customs that for any reason prevented incestuous mating would survive anyway, because they prevented bad genetic consequences.

Counterobjections are also made: that inbreeding of domestic animals can be seen, on the contrary, to produce *better* stock; that in small inbred communities, birth defects occur in children who are not incestuously conceived, so why should the incestuous be singled out? It is also argued that the bad effects of deleterious genes would be wiped out fairly quickly in the course of a few generations, after which the population would settle down to a new equilibrium; and that, no matter how high the "inbreeding load" may become in a small population, one or two bouts of outbreeding every few generations would rapidly offset this and reintroduce variation.[13] Close inbreeding cannot be condemned in a blanket fashion. It sometimes even helps. Consider the perfect adaptation of certain tree lice to the underside of the bark of the particular tree on which they live. They do not, as it were, want this perfect adaptation disturbed either from the outside or from inside themselves. They do not want variation, they want certainty; and in arriving at that certainty they have evolved a totally incestuous system of brother-sister matings, which continues generation after generation and thus ensures their genetic equilibrium and stability. They become virtually clones.[14]

But if you are not tree lice and you live in an uncertain or changing environment, *genetic variation* becomes useful if not vital in the business of survival and adaptation. Too much inbreeding leads to a loss of variation and, in the long run, can limit your adaptability. We do need variation as a consequence of our being a sexually reproducing species in a changing environment, so we should avoid *too much* close inbreeding. In this, however—a thought to be held onto—we are not unique: *The same is true for all sexually reproducing species,*[15]

Which brings us to the problem of nature and culture. Many anthropologists—Claude Lévi-Strauss and George P. Murdock among the most recent and most forceful—have contended that the incest taboo amounts to nothing less than the breakthrough from nature to culture. According to Lévi-Strauss, the rule against incest is no less than culture saying to nature, "Thus far and no further!" As for the reason for the taboo, he refuses to derive it from such explanations as have been given here. He dismisses the idea that there is an instinct against incest or that aversion develops naturally—ideas to which we shall return. Looking for the phenomenon behind "marriage out," he finds it in the process of "exchange." More positively than most anthropologists, he argues that we overcome nature (seen as disorderly and promiscuous) by instituting taboos on "own" in order that we may exchange "own" with "other." It is not only women, but also goods, services, and even information that are involved. An incestuous man is compared with a miser or a man who will talk only to himself: What he denies are the possibilities of any social relationships at all.

In a sense, then, Lévi-Strauss is deriving our explanation (1) of the incest taboo from (4), concerned with exogamy. Following Marcel Mauss, he derives it from the "urge" (if he will forgive the term) to exchange "own" for "other," and the derivation of this "urge" is the weakest point in his beautifully constructed argument. He needs must, like his forefather Durkheim, derive it from society: that is, we must learn it. We shall return later to the difficulties raised by this proposal when we discuss the evolution of mind (chapter 7). If Lévi-Strauss had stayed with exogamy, as McLennan did, his argument might have stuck, since the business of exchange is indeed vitally important to understanding exogamy.

And this distinction *is* important so we must emphasize it yet again. We can perhaps find an explanation for exogamy; that is, we can explain why most societies ban *marriages* with some close (or distant) relatives. But this does not necessarily explain why they should, or should not, taboo sexual relations with such relatives. The other way round it works: If you ban sex, then there is not much point in marrying. But there are countless examples of relatives forbidden in marriage with whom sex is not forbidden, or is not regarded with any more horror than fornication generally, or is considered a peccadillo, or is even encouraged. We are certainly going to see that exogamy and incest *are* linked, but they are linked as Freud thought they were linked—*in the processes of evolution.* And that is a different matter. We could not have had exogamy—our peculiarly human form of breeding system—if we had not evolved the means—the brain—to control the "incestuous" processes. But the incestuous process—as "sexual selection"—itself produced the brain. This is certainly to link incest and exogamy, but to link them in the human head, not in a sociological formula. The argument of the book will be a detailed spelling out of this point.

But the red lamp still glares for Lévi-Strauss. The forbidding of familial sex, the taboo on incest, is what he sees as the rule of rules, the universal, the leap across the abyss between man and animal. We can grant him the rule. We recognize that there is an abyss. But why the rule against incest, which, even if widespread, is not universal? Why not grammar, whose rules—à la Chomsky— are by definition universal? After all, everyone speaks a language. But there is a more serious weakness. He assumes nature to be unordered and incestuously promiscuous. It is not. We are different from the animals in having rules, yes—but we probably do not differ all that much in the actual incidence of incest.

Although rumbles concerning this had been coming from the primatologists, it was a comparative psychologist from Germany, Norbert Bischof, whose work made this point forcibly enough to shake the anthropological citadel.[16] He starts from the premise already stressed here—that sexually reproducing species can't afford to lose too much of the genetic variation they gain by being sexually reproductive in the first place. We would therefore expect to find, especially among the larger and slower-breeding animals, mechanisms for avoiding too much close inbreeding.[17]

Some of these mechanisms are quite simple, as when, for example, the young are simply dispersed once they are capable of fending for themselves. They are thus not likely to mate with their parents, and the possibility of sibling matings is at least randomized. Many ungulates have a system of separate sex groups for most of the year, with the males in one set of groups and the fe-males and dependent young in others. During the relatively brief mating season, the males compete for the various groups of fe-males. If a young male leaves his own mother's group, joins a male group, and then has to face stiff competition before getting to mate with some group of females, his chances of ending up with his mother and sisters are slim.

Among our near relatives we find various devices, which will be described in some detail in a later chapter. Chimpanzee females seem to leave the males of their groups and go off to mate else-where, often returning when the baby is born. Among baboons and macaques, there is much transfer of males between groups. Thus, once again, the chance of incestuous matings is reduced or randomized. Such matings do occur, but in relatively small num-bers. If we ignored rules and taboos, in other words, and simply looked at what actually went on, we would probably find no more actual incest in these mammalian populations than in their human counterparts. We may have some unique mechanisms, but we are not unique in our avoidance of close familial inbreeding. Accord-ing to Bischof's own interpretation of the human taboos, we be-come uneasy about those who, for whatever reason, do what those in the general population tend not to do, and the invention of taboos is the result. Culture here is not in any way saying no to na-ture; it is saying, in effect, okay.[18]

As is often stated, however, humans have a particular prob-lem: Their young stay socially immature long after they have be-come mature sexually. The consequent need to stay in the family thus causes incest problems. The subject is still being debated, but it can be argued that in most primitive human groups, girls are married off at puberty and boys begin their manhood tasks not long afterward. Dispersion, one of Bischof's commoner mecha-nisms, may have been, in this sense, the rule. An elegant and origi-nal theory has been proposed by Mariam Slater—that under very primitive conditions, the average life is short (thirty to thirty-five years), infant mortality is high (up to 90 percent), and birth spac-ing consequently wide.[19] If one looks at the population structure of the small hunting bands that characterized our ancestors until very recently, it would appear that for more than 99 percent of our history, the chances for the occurrence of incest would have been slight. Take brother and sister: With wide birth-spacing resulting from all those infant deaths (not counting abortion, infanticide, and the effects of prolonged lactation on ovulation), the chance that a brother and sister would be sexually mature at the same time in the same place would have been slim. Older sisters would have been married off at puberty, before their younger brothers had time to catch up, and the older brother would be already well into his family-building process by the time his sisters were mature. Between father and daughter, there would have been, as among other animals, somewhat more opportunity and more occurrence (the taboos are noticeably less stringent here); but even so, this would hold only for the eldest daughter in most cases. Slater's own theory concerning the taboos is that they came in after the neolithic revolution, when the demographic structure opened up, the life span lengthened, and incest became an ever-present possibility. By then, she argues, we had been non-incestuous for so long that we felt uneasy about reversing the tendency, hence the brake on it, although not in all societies all the time.

According to these theories, then, human beings are "naturally" non-incestuous, and this is the reason why we don't easily approve of the practice. I think they are right and that they give the death blow to the notion of incest taboos as the great gateway and bridge to culture, and so on. But I think there is more to it than that. They do not explain the peculiarly human systems of incest avoidance. They have not, for me, totally extinguished the red lamp. We may demote its importance, but we must not take our gaze off it altogether. It does concern the human passion for rules, which is no small matter. It concerns the evolution of the control of sex and aggression, and that is no small matter. It concerns the power relations between the generations and the sexes, and that is no small matter either. If we can just ask the right questions and avoid asking the wrong ones, we may find that it can still shed light on the origins of our humanity.

TWO

Between Brother
and Sister

*Chick souleva le couvercle de son pick-up a deux plateaux et mit deux
disques différents de Jean-Sol Partre. Il voulait les ecouter tous les
deux en même temps, pour faire jaillir des idées nouvelles du choc de
deux idées anciennes.*

Boris Vian
L'écume des jours

*The test of a first-rate intelligence is the ability to hold two opposed
ideas in the mind, at the same time, and still retain the ability to
function.*

F. Scott Fitzgerald

We have to start somewhere. Chick, in our opening quotation,
hoped to generate a new thought from the simultaneous playing of
two different speeches by his beloved philosopher Jean-Sol Partre,
while contemplating some of the latter's relics—notably a pair of
trousers. We too, but without benefit of philosophical trousers,
shall juxtapose two declarations on the same subject, but not by
the same person. They are, however, from the same age and from
persons strangely of a kind, despite one being a Nordic Swede and
the other a Viennese Jew. They are from that bearded, tight-col-
lared claustrophobic age, when the ways of savages seemed so remote from the certainties of European civilization. It was an age of
stuffy parlors, heavy bourgeois familism, repressed sex, the over-

15

flow of public prostitution: the eternal fascination with the red lamp in all its forms, and particularly with incest.

It is not always so. Rattray Taylor, in his neglected but interesting book *Sex in History,* points out that the fascination is not constant.[1] Only in "matrist" phases of history do we get it rising obsessively; in "patrist" phases, the real obsession is with homosexuality. In either case, one can be keen on the topic or down on it—but in any case, obsessed. And the strange thing is that one seems usually to be afraid of that with which one is obsessed. The Elizabethans—predominantly matrists (and it does not matter much now what that is)—were both obsessed with and down on the brother-sister possibility: forbidden, yes, but all the sweeter for the interdiction. We had to wait for Poe and—although for half-measures with a half-sister—Byron, before we got another poet of the grisly horror to match, for example, Webster. The Duke Ferdinand, in *The White Devil,* despite his obsessive devotion to his sister's chastity and his final torment and murder of her, was her lover in thought and word if not in deed.

It took John Ford to put the question openly. It is rarely put openly. Shelley dithers with innuendo in *The Cenci,* but that is about father and daughter anyway. Ford took it out onto the Elizabethan stage in a blaze of poetic protest against the restriction. Why, he asked, should a brother and a sister not be lovers, spouses? His title rings with both the condemnation and the passion: *'Tis Pity She's a Whore.* The innocence of his sibling lovers—contrasted with the civil and ecclesiastical wickedness around them—is so touching that it forces itself upon us more strongly than the thick choking lust of Ferdinand. Giovanni asks his horrified confessor, in all innocence and anguish:

> *"Shall a peevish sound*
> *A customary form, from man to man,*
> *Of brother and of sister, be a bar*
> *'Twixt my perpetual happiness and me?*
> *Say that we had one father; say one womb—*
> *Curse to my joys!—gave both us life and birth;*
> *Are we not therefore each to other bound*
> *So much the more by nature? nay, if you will have't,*
> *Even of religion, to be ever one,*
> *One soul, one flesh, one love, one heart, one all?"*

The good friar is suitably appalled:

> *"Have done, unhappy youth! for thou art lost."*

But Giovanni persists:

> *"Shall, then, for that I am her brother born,*
> *My joys be ever banished from her bed?*
> *No, father; in your eyes I see the change*
> *Of pity and compassion; from your age,*
> *As from a sacred oracle, distils*
> *The life of counsel: tell me, holy man;*
> *What cure shall give me ease in these extremes?"*

But Giovanni is mistaken if he thinks the representative of the church is going to have any spiritual counsel except prayer and repentance. The only practical advice the good father can offer is certainly non-incestuous, though not strictly exogamous within the meaning of the act:

> *"Look through the world,*
> *And thou shalt see a thousand faces shine*
> *More glorious than this idol thou ador'st:*
> *Leave her, and take they choice, 'tis much less sin;*
> *Though in such games as those they lose that win."*

In other words, if marriage is marginally preferable to fornication, the latter is much to be preferred to incest. There are sins and sins: play around if you want, but for God's sake not with your sister. Well, the impeccably exogamous Romeo and Juliet fared no better than Giovanni and his Annabella, and it has not always been that the advantages of outbreeding were so obvious.

Various Egyptian pharaohs—as we know—all called Ptolemy, variously married sisters and nieces all called Cleopatra, until the last of that name began the swing back to exogamy with a vengeance—and with Romans to boot. Evidence shows that this tendency to "marry in," even to full sisters and daughters, was common enough around that part of the Mediterranean, even, for example, during the Roman colonization of Egypt. After all, Abraham married his half-sister Sarah, and Lot's daughters seduced him in his drunken sleep lest they be left childless. That great fabulist William Golding—who can always delightfully turn the seemingly obvious on its head—imagines the time in a pocket kingdom along the pre-pharaonic Nile, where non-incestuous liaisons were not only unknown, but when contemplated were considered obscene and hence titillating.[2] Pretty Flower, the princess, who has failed to rouse her father's sexual interest (which has condemned him to the tomb and immortality) confesses also that she finds her eleven-year-old brother unappetizing, but that she finds the Liar—a non-relative who tells the truth about exogamous foreigners—attractive. The old priest hears *her* confession; he asks:

> "How did you justify yourself to yourself?"
> "I pretended to myself that he was my brother."
> "Knowing all the time that he was—a stranger, as in the fantasies of white men."
> Her voice came, muffled through her palms.
> "My brother by the God is only eleven years old. And the fact that the Liar was—what you said—*can* I tell you?"
> "Be brave."
> "It put a keener edge on my love."
> "Poor child! Poor twisted soul!"
> "What will happen to me? What *can* happen to me? I have shattered the laws of nature."

The old priest is suitably shocked himself. The brother is admittedly immature and does not like, as he puts it, "bouncing up and down" on his sister. But, adds the priest:

> "And all this, this—stood between you and your lawful desire for your father."
> She said nothing. He spoke again, his voice raised and indignant.
> "Can you wonder that the river is still rising."

Choose your favorite disaster: but this time for *not* committing incest! But we can extract two lessons from our examples: That which is both familiar and forbidden is tempting, and while there is no automatic desire for sex with a sibling, it can develop.

This takes us back to the end of the last chapter and our theoretical unease about the actual unease that seems to accompany the thought of sex with sisters. For despite the pharaohs and their neighbors, it is more common for people to be down on it than in favor. Thus, it can go either way, but it is more likely to go against than for. The human organism seems "primed" to receive anti-incest instructions; but if it does not receive them, then it will not necessarily resist incest. (And it is the resistance—the avoidance— we are concerned with, not the punishments or rules, which may or may not have anything to do with what people *feel,* as we have seen.)

This is the essence of the interactionist position on behavior and on the nature-nurture issue: There is not necessarily an anti-incest instinct (which has sometimes been proposed); nature assumes a certain learning environment in order that the avoidance can indeed be learned. This is not left to chance; that is, it must be an environment that is pretty common early in the life cycle. It does not have to be 100 percent effective—nature is concerned with probabilities, not certainties.

But if there is a mechanism built into the life cycle, what is it? How does it work? Why does it go wrong sometimes? These are our questions, and we may or may not be satisfied with the final answer. The one I try out here seems even a little dated to me. It was thought up largely under the inspiration of that genial genius Professor John Whiting of Harvard, and was much in tune with its time, being based on stimulus-response theory and, therefore, "causal" and not post facto. I am no longer so sure of its truth, but I am fond of it so I shall repeat it with a cavil. Fresh evidence since that time supports the general conclusion, but is not necessarily any nearer the heart of the mechanism (or mechanisms). The neatness of my own conclusion lies in its generation of the beautiful paradox: Cultures which essay to prevent incest between siblings often manage to promote precisely the feelings they aim to inhibit, thus making the prevention more difficult and yet more necessary, in a never-ending vicious circle—a kind of parody of human good intentions.

Freud and the Westermarck effect

We glanced at two opposed schools of thought on childhood experience and incest in chapter one: The first held that familiarity bred contempt, while the second insisted that incestuous love

choices were the first and most intense. Because of a seeming logical flaw in the familiarity argument, and because of the rise to
power of psychoanalysis, "familiarity" had, until I picked it up in
the late fifties, a rotten press. Its main supporter (who can say
who originated it?) was Edward Westermarck, the Swede I have
already mentioned. His opponent was the Viennese Jewish master Sigmund Freud. In the early twenties they slugged it out, and
Freud was reckoned to have got the better of the argument. Sir
James Frazer pronounced for him, and Lévi-Strauss recently
clinched the issue in his favor. But as so often happens in these
high academic debates, the two sides seem to be talking past each
other. Let us take a lesson from Boris Vian's Chick, and play the
two records side by side to see if they really conflict, or if one new
idea cannot be distilled from the vapor of the two old and steamy
ones.

Here is Westermarck summing up his position—we shall play
this on the left-hand turntable:

> Generally speaking, there is a remarkable absence of erotic feelings
> between persons living very closely together from childhood. Nay
> more, in this, as in many other cases, sexual indifference is com-
> bined with the positive feeling of aversion when the act is thought
> of. This I take to be the fundamental cause of the exogamous pro-
> hibitions. Persons who have been living closely together from
> childhood are as a rule near relatives. Hence their aversion to sex-
> ual relations with one another displays itself in custom and in law
> as a prohibition of intercourse between near kin.[3]

He uses "exogamous" when "incest" would have been more accurate, but note that he realizes nature's rule-of-thumb approach in
only demanding that those "living together from childhood" be
subject to aversion—these are *likely* to be kin. It is probabilities
that are at issue. But let us leave the details and concentrate on the
structure of the melody. It seems to go in a causal progression like
this:

childhood propinquity ⟶ positive aversion ⟶ prohibitions

The criticism has concentrated on the second link. Here is the
counter melody from Freud on the right-hand turntable:

The most preposterous attempts have been made to account for this horror of incest: some people have assumed that it is a provision of nature for the preservation of the species, manifesting itself in the mind by these prohibitions because inbreeding would result in racial degeneration; others have asserted that propinquity from early childhood has deflected sexual desire from the persons concerned. In both these cases, however, the avoidance of incest would have been automatically secured and we should be at a loss to understand the necessity for stern prohibitions, which would seem rather to point to a strong desire. Psychoanalytic investigations have shown beyond the possibility of doubt that an incestuous love-choice is in fact the first and the regular one, and that it is only later that any opposition is manifested towards it, the causes of which are not to be sought in the psychology of the individual.[4]

"And so say all of us," have chorused, explicitly or implicitly, most other commentators. If people don't want to do it, why do they forbid it? Well, in the last chapter we went through that one and followed Westermarck himself in suggesting that rules and laws often have an origin and persistence that has little to do with what people actually feel. Or even that they may forbid it precisely because they don't want to do it and hence don't like those who do. But it would be much better if we left the problem of sanctions and prohibitions at the margins; it is not the central issue really, and this is where much of the debate has gone astray. What we want to do now—and unfortunately retaining the debate on prohibitions because it is there—is to see whether or not our two records are playing cacophonous or harmonious music when properly listened to.

What after all, is the causal chain that Freud, with such smug confidence, is proposing as the universal and only one? It is this:

strong desire ⎯⎯⎯⎯→ stern prohibitions

Let us play them side by side, concentrating on the logical progressions rather than on the noisy side effects, and see if we cannot achieve harmony:

Westermarck
childhood propinquity ⎯⎯→ positive aversion ⎯⎯→ ( ) prohibitions

Freud
(   ) ⎯⎯→   strong desire ⎯⎯→ stern prohibitions

This raises the intriguing possibility that they might just be singing versions of the same tune if we fill in the blanks that would make the arguments complementary:

childhood propinquity $\longrightarrow$ positive aversion $\longrightarrow$ (lax) prohibitions
(childhood separation) $\longrightarrow$ strong desire $\longrightarrow$ stern prohibitions

Could it be then, that instead of each one talking about universally valid and hence completely contradictory processes, they are really talking about two different and complementary processes; two different routes that the socialization of children can take? Or even, for that matter, two extreme cases, between which the various cultures of the world may lie, neither provoking too much strong desire nor wholly instilling positive aversion? In other words, these two causal sequences could describe two possible modes of socialization that do not conflict at all, but relate the range of possibilities open to the species in its handling of the problem.

Pretty Flower's aversion to her brother was obvious enough, but was there less "propinquity" between Giovanni and Annabella? What constitutes propinquity for these purposes? How averse is "positive aversion," and can there be "weak desire" that is indistinguishable from it? What is it about "separation" that provokes desire? It is to these questions that we must address ourselves with such evidence as we can muster. First, let us ask about the variables.

CAUSE OF THE EFFECT. One thing is obvious, and that is that we are right to bracket off the brother-sister case from the parent-child—and even with the latter we may find that the two possibilities (mother-son and father-daughter) merit very different analysis. As Westermarck himself put it:

> What I have here spoken of is lack of inclination for, and a feeling of aversion associated with the idea of, sexual intercourse between persons who have lived in a long-continued intimate relationship from a period of life when the action of sexual desire, in its acuter forms at least, is naturally out of the question.[5]

Naturally. Or at least it's much less likely, and his quaintly discreet language hides an important insight into which we shall inquire later. But let us first admit that this "lack of inclination" is what is most widely reported between brothers and sisters who have grown

up together. It is the commonest reaction by far, at least in my experience and across many and varied cultures: not horror, not
shame, but just a simple lack of inclination—a puzzlement, an indifference. Why, then, should this not be taken at face value? Answer: because of the sanctions; and around we go again.

For the moment, let us ignore the sanctions for all the reasons
stated and concentrate on another factor that enters into the cal-
culations: When is the "sister" married? In the vast majority of the
world's societies, both at present and throughout human—even
hominid—history, girls have been married off at puberty or before.
Thus, when it came to the point that the incestuous relationship
might be consummated, the sister would already be the wife of another man. At this point then, intercourse with the sister would
come under the laws against adultery. There is no necessary reason
why the interference with a husband's rights by his brother-in-law
should be more heinous than interference by any other man. In
any case, it is often true that much wealth has changed hands between the brothers-in-law, and a very special relationship exists
between them. This is often the reason cited by savages against incest, in effect: It would wreck the good relations between brothers-
in-law. But my point is that here we need no *special* sibling-incest
sanctions as opposed to adultery sanctions. It has been argued that
the incest taboo among Malinowski's Trobriand Islanders (we will
be back to them) "guards against conflict among the brothers for
the sexual services of the sisters," thus preserving the unity of the
matrilineage.[6] But, again, this is a "favorite disaster" type of argument, since if the girls are married at puberty, adultery laws
should be enough. If any society feels it necessary to punish as a
special case (and it often does) intercourse between adult siblings,
then there has to be a special reason.

Again, this may or may not be connected with how people
feel, which is what we are interested in—but in looking for examples we should note when girls are married. It could be that if they
are kept around in the family after puberty and not married off
until later, some special sanctions might be needed, assuming that
one wanted to prevent incest and that the girls would want to
practice it.

But what is there about the relationship of brother and sister
during sexual immaturity that might make for a strong or weak
sexual reaction between them after puberty? Propinquity and sep-

aration are our clues, and evidence exists from animals, moths, and birds that shows that opposite-sex creatures reared together during immaturity copulate less readily than strangers when mature.[7] Familiarity, as some wag put it, not only breeds contempt, it does not breed at all. And we must note that this is not the same as the lessening of desire between adult partners that has often been noticed in both man and animals. The seven-year itch is a different matter and is probably just a result of sheer boredom: The man who keeps sending his wife out to have a new hairdo is reacting to what we can hide under the jargon term of "stimulus saturation." But our brothers and sisters are not tired of sex with each other, they haven't had any. So to what are they averse (or not)? Here we are in the area of intelligent guesswork, but let's try a few ideas.

Assume that propinquity means constant and free physical interaction—not just being in the same household, for example, but rough and tumbling, bathing, touching, sleeping, etc., together for most of the time. This would be one extreme of propinquity and is not that uncommon around the world. Anyone who has watched such interaction between opposite-sex children (and it was Whiting who first pointed it out to me) will know how extremely excited the children become. In fact, they can become so excited that uncomfortable parents often feel the need to separate them, although they cannot often say just why. There is something perhaps too embarrassingly sexual about this sheer physical stimulation. But in most cases, although there is heightened sexual excitement, this is rarely consummated by successful intercourse. The frustration engendered by the lack of detumescence—in the male particularly—will often lead to anger and aggression, and the episode which began as fun will end in tears.

Since this was pointed out to me, I have seen it over and over again. Exactly why the sexual play is not consummated is arguable, with some saying it is simply not possible in children since the little boy's penis cannot achieve penetration. This is not always true, and intercourse between seven year olds is not unknown. But it is very rare. Whether or not it is possible anatomically, for many reasons—ignorance of technique being an obvious one and parental intervention another—it does not happen. Very often, the children don't even know it is supposed to happen. They are not playing their intensely sexual game to this end. But for whatever reason, it is frustrating.

Now imagine this happening over and over again in the life of some particular boys and girls. They are free to indulge in as much tactile interaction as they wish, and in the early stages this is clearly pleasurable in the extreme. But if carried through, the result is pain, frustration, tears, and anger. If this happens very often, year in and year out, the other-sex children will become objects of a strange mixture of love and hate, of approach and avoidance, of promise and disappointment—for reasons unknown to the participants. What is happening is, in the jargon of learning theory, negative reinforcement. One is not being reinforced—or perhaps we can just say encouraged—for intensive physical interaction with these opposite-sex people. With the advent of sexual maturity and the possibility of consummation, the latter becomes devoutly not to be wished with those people of the other sex who seem to provoke only pain and frustration. One looks elsewhere; one looks to those from whom one need not expect a painful experience.

There are problems with this. Why is not the experience generalized to all members of the opposite sex, leading to a universal avoidance? I suppose one can assume that the sex drive will be strong enough to send our newly matured children out looking. It is simply a matter of where they will look, and if they have been through the aversion experience, they will not want to look to siblings, or at least to those other children with whom they had the painful experience. Of course this could include people other than siblings—but remember nature's rule-of-thumb approach: Among those with whom one has had this experience, there is a high probability that the siblings will be included.

Consider now the polar opposite. Actually, the true polar opposite would be no contact whatsoever during childhood, in which case the siblings would really be no different than strangers. But let us look at the more interesting case—since it crops up more often—where the siblings are brought up together but without the opportunities for tactile, physical contact that we have described. Here there will have been propinquity, but no chance to develop the negative reinforcement. At the approach and onset of puberty, the other-sex siblings will be there as stimulus objects, but there will be no conditioned avoidance to them. They will be objects of sexual temptation that have perhaps been tabooed and are consciously avoided, but they will not be automatically avoided. In fact, since they are in some cases the most available sex objects at this period, there may be heightened temptation. It is a very sad thought that the physical separation of children in childhood is often practiced to prevent incest, while if we are correct, it may only serve to provoke it.

Self-defeating it may be, but the category of "close but separate" needs to be looked at more closely. The amount of provocation and temptation over the sibling will depend on a number of things, not least the relative closeness of other aspects of the relationship and the availability of other sexual outlets. Giovanni and Annabella, for example, were probably brought up in the same household, but relatively segregated because of the general segregation of male and female activities. Annabella was for her brother then, in some senses, a stranger and yet emotionally very close. Pretty Flower had been "bounced on" by her younger brother and had developed a hearty aversion to the whole thing. Separation can be harsh or gentle, relative or absolute, effective or ineffective, and all these will affect the outcome. It is not simply then separation as such, but how the separation is effected, that will determine the quality, intensity, and effectiveness of the strong desire in adult life. For that matter, so will the relationship of the siblings after puberty. If they simply part and marry, it need never be an issue; if they are thrust together into some special and ongoing relationship, then there may be problems.

The same is true of our category of "propinquity," which we should now rewrite as "intense physical interaction." This too can vary a lot. Simply because some kinds of physical interaction might have the painful outcome we have described does not mean that that is the only possibility. The warmth of companionship between adult siblings is well enough known. Even if they have been through the painful process of aversion training, they may react to this later by practicing a form of warm asexual intimacy from which the anxiety-provoking factor—physical contact—is absent. Insofar as their childhood experience has left them with a general sex anxiety, the existence of a companion of the opposite sex who is *not* a sex stimulus may be comforting.

But the range of physical interaction will vary in intensity. It may well be that certain forms of low-level stimulation—soothing, stroking, petting—will not overexcite the participants and not lead to the pain and anger. This will have the opposite effect and be positively rewarding. Perhaps this can generate a desire to preserve this warm, rewarding relationship and not intrude the more excitable genital behavior into it. This would not work in isolation—none of our factors would. It would work best, for example, where the transition to genital sexuality was traumatic, causing the siblings to seek refuge in their non-genital but physical contact. But whichever way it worked out, the result would be positive aversion to the sex act itself with those opposite-sex people familiar from childhood.

The possibilities can get a little dizzying, but we must consider them because what we are thinking of here is not an either/or situation, but a continuum with many variations along the way. Hence, we should expect a great deal of variation in the way different societies with different socialization practices react to what I dubbed somewhat pompously the "incest stimulus": the thought, fantasy, dream, suggestion, or occurrence of incest. But in looking at the ends of the continuum, it is obvious that we have rewritten Westermarck's "propinquity" as "intense physical interaction." Propinquity in the sense of mere nearness, coupled with separation in the sense of no physical interaction, would on this hypothesis produce the highest incest anxiety and possibly the strongest desire of all. So we should perhaps rewrite our limiting cases—the two ends of the incest spectrum—like this:

Conditions during sexual immaturity	Resultant motivation	Associated sanctions
Intense physical interaction	Positive aversion	Lax
Physical separation plus propinquity	Strong desire	Fierce

So in the first case, we should get low anxiety about incest, a minimal interest in the subject, and fairly lax treatment of offenders who nevertheless will be pulled into line in some mild way, because it just "isn't done." At the other extreme, we should get high anxiety, an obsession both with the subject and the temptation, and a savage venting of spite on offenders who do what everybody wants to do but daren't.

Of course we are back, in the second case, to the question of why, if they have these strong desires, they do not act on them. I

doubt we can answer this if we stay within the brother-sister situation itself. The strong desire stems from the separation-plus-pro-
pinquity effect coupled with, probably, a sexually repressive atmo-
sphere generally. Societies that are down on incest, I suggest, tend
to be down on sex all round, and probably have taboos on mastur-
bation and an obsession with virginity in the bargain. If we look at
the whole thing as a system, then it doesn't much matter why it got
started, since it will be unhappily self-perpetuating. Psychologists
have found that where drives are very strong but unfulfilled, the
organism may go into a kind of self-imposed reverse. The stronger
the motive becomes, the more difficult it is to satisfy it and the
more painful frustration of it becomes.[8] Faced with this awful pre-
dicament, the psyche resorts to various mechanisms of anxiety reduction: withdrawal, conversion, and aggression are the commonest. In the first case, one just shuts off from the problem; in the
second, one rationalizes it in some way; in the third, one lashes out.
(If one is a super guilty type, one might turn the aggression against
oneself or invite it from others.)

So if, for whatever reason, the siblings in our drama are forced
into the temptation-plus-taboo situation, they may well go automatically into reverse, and by one or other of these means deny or
avoid the reality of the temptation in classical Freudian fashion,
while still, as Freud insisted, retaining the strong but unfulfillable
desire. It only needs one push to get the system started, for once
trapped in its coils, the siblings-become-parents will repeat the separation treatment, thus ensuring that their children in turn will
grow up desiring precisely what is most forbidden and being shot
through with anxiety about it. If the whole distressing process
leads to a culture riddled with obsessions, neuroses, horror, and ferocity over incest, then it is no small wonder. Its self-perpetuation
is a positive hymn to the genius of human culture for getting things
wrong. Is it too much to speculate that nature, which was so freely
invoked in the introduction to all this argument, really intended
the Westermarck effect and not the Freudian horrors? Actually
nature doesn't give a damn. Either way incest is avoided, and if
humans want to torment themselves about this when they don't
need to, well then that is just what humans do about most things
anyway. A little anxiety, plus a lot of imagination, sets cultures off
and running on a dizzy race to see who can get the most bizarre
legends, the queerest religious beliefs, the most effective magic, and

the most moving literature—to say nothing of the most refined tortures.

I am not altogether ducking the question of how such mistakes get made in the first place. I think there is an answer, "the causes of which"—as Freud has told us in the passage quoted— "are not to be sought in the psychology of the individual." We have to move further out from our gamboling siblings in their Westermarckian innocence and see what the older generation is up to and why, to answer that. But that is to jump too far ahead. Where we are now is still with the little world of sibling interaction, or the interaction of any young children socialized together, which, need we remind ourselves, has a high probability of including siblings. And this is all nature is after. Left to their own devices, we are suggesting, these children will not grow up with a strong sexual desire for one another. There will be a variety of results in adult life, depending on the precise nature of the childhood circumstances. The only way we can document this is simply to choose some anthropological accounts that are rich in a description of childhood conditions and adult attitudes and see what they turn up. To be more precise is impossible, because descriptions are so uneven that statistical methods would be inappropriate. I doubt in any case that they would add much. I am not trying to test a scientific hypothesis here, but just to illustrate the range of possibilities and show how they fall along the continuum proposed. If anyone can turn up well-documented counterexamples, fine. I haven't found any, but I haven't read everything either. All I can say is that none of the writers cited here was gathering data to prove or disprove anything. Thus the data are "naive" about our hypothesis and cannot have been biased in its favor.

VICISSITUDES OF THE EFFECT. I shall start with Spiro's description of Kiryat Yedidim, an Israeli kibbutz,[9] because it was reading this that startled me into a reconsideration of the Westermarck hypothesis as far back as 1958. Also, my putting the old Swede back on the intellectual market via the Jewish evidence from a psychoanalytical anthropologist had the side effect of alerting a number of people to the problem, with interesting results. Thus, at the end of this chapter I shall return to the kibbutzim with the latest news from the battlefront. For the moment, let us see what Spiro had to say of them in 1958.

The socialization unit (our "siblings") is the *kevutza*, a children's group that inhabits a common living and sleeping quarter.
Spiro has recorded the behavior within the kevutza group from
nursery days onward. Of children between one and five he says:

> Boys and girls sleep in the same rooms, shower together, sit on the
> toilet together, and often run around nude before getting dressed in
> the morning or after being undressed in the evening. . . . Heterosex-
> ual behaviour includes a number of quite different kinds of activi-
> ties, both within any one group as well as among groups. In group
> 11, for example (mean age two years), its most frequent expression
> consists in a simple embrace of one child by another, followed in
> frequency by stroking or caressing, kissing and touching of genitals
> (pp. 221-225).[10]

The interaction intensifies among children aged seven to
twelve.

> Heterosexual behavior has been observed by the nurse and teacher
> of the second grade, although they have never observed either at-
> tempted or actual intercourse. The nurse is confident that boys and
> girls often get into bed with each other at night, but she does not
> know how frequently this occurs, nor does she know what they do.
> These children frequently play "clinic," a game in which the boys
> "examine" the girls, who are nude. Moreover, boys and girls often
> lie on top of each other, and hug and kiss each other in public, even
> in the classrooms and in the presence of the teacher, "with no sense
> of shame." At least one boy would "kiss like a man of twenty" (p.
> 278).

However: "Sexual shame increases quite conspicuously with
age." What is more,

> The sense of shame developed by the sixth-grade girls, for example,
> was not merely a shame phenomenon. It also involved great hostil-
> ity toward the boys, and their attempt to create unisexual showers
> was, among other things, an expression of this hostility. As their
> nurse pointed out, the relationship between the sexes at that time
> was "terrible." They practically "hated" each other, would not talk
> to each other, and were constantly involved in petty altercations (p.
> 280).

These children were either pubescent or on the verge of puberty. During high school (ages twelve and over) the conflict over mixed showers continued. "Outsiders" influenced the children in the form of a city girl who refused to shower with the boys, but the "sense of shame" was already deep.

> Much of the sexual shame that led to the abolition of the mixed shower continues to characterize the attitude of some of the girls in their rooms as well. Most of the girls, for example, attempt to conceal their nudity from the boys. . . . At this age (ninth grade—fifteen) an interest in sex, restricted almost exclusively to the girls, may be observed. *Not directed toward the boys of their own kevutza whom they view as immature, hence, asexual* [italics mine], this interest is in the older students and the young unmarried males in the kibbutz (pp. 330–333).

The sibling hostility continued up to the age of fifteen and then relationships became easier, perhaps because alternative sex outlets were found, although this is not certain.

With respect to the adult (fifteen-plus) situation, Spiro remarks (Note: *Sabras* are age-mates within the kibbutz):

> There are two aspects of sabra sexuality that require comment. The first concerns the choice of sexual partner—whether for intercourse or for marriage. In not one instance has a sabra from Kiryat Yedidim married a fellow sabra nor, to the best of our knowledge, has a sabra had sexual intercourse with a fellow sabra. If, in the light of additional data the latter part of the generalization be rendered false I would be highly confident of the validity of its following reformulation: In no instance have sabras from the same kevutza had sexual intercourse with each other.
>
> The reason given by the sabras for their exogamy is interesting: they view each other, they say, as siblings. We have then an instance of a self-imposed primary group exogamy, despite the absence of any prescribed—formal or informal—incest taboo (pp. 347–348).

Spiro goes on to discuss the paradox that arises from the psychoanalytic theory that siblings have a repressed sexual interest in each other. He finds only one deviant (atypical) sabra who manifests overt interest—the rest deny it. On our theory there would be no paradox. Kiryat Yedidim is an example of a "pure" Wester-marck effect. It is interesting to note also that the sabras whom Spiro observed reacted away from the "sexual-freedom" ethic of their parents, the founders of the kibbutz. What is more, they tended to impose voluntary sexual prohibitions, thus giving us an insight into the genesis of "mild prohibitions."

Let us shift quickly to the other extreme, lest our enthusiasm for the Westermarck effect leads us to forget those examples that so delighted the anthropological myth-makers and that are indeed numerous enough to command respect: the cultures of the grisly horror. As representative as any are the Apache, the great hunter-warriors of the American Southwest, well enough known to all screen buffs and television fans. Opler's description of the Chirica-hua (pronounce it roughly "cheery-*cow*-ah") is justly regarded as a classic of Amerindian ethnography.[11]

The Chiricahua "siblings" start their lives in a nomadic, mother-daughter extended family. The typical family group will be one pair of grandparents and their unmarried children, plus the married daughters with their husbands and unmarried children.

Premarital chastity is a rule that is strictly enforced. "The girl should come to her first menses and her puberty rite a virgin." "When a girl who is about to pass through the ceremony is discov-ered to be unchaste, she is fortunate if she is not cast off to fend for herself" (p. 82). In the "old days," the man would have been killed unless he could make a good match for the girl himself. The really serious loss, in the event of the girl's defalcation, is economic.

> If sexual relations between two young people are discovered, the girl's family has suffered an economic loss. Should the young man not be considered eligible by the parents, their anger is particularly aroused, for they have probably lost a chance to marry their daughter worthily and yet cannot force a suitable match from the intrigue (p. 145).

We also learn that it is much more serious to rape an unmarried woman than a married woman.

Avoidance of sex play is inculcated from six onward for all children. Although the boys and girls play house realistically, there is no overt sexuality involved. This is because "boys rarely continue to participate in this form of amusement after the age of six or seven." Thus at this age, close contact between children of the opposite sex ceases: "An informant, when he was questioned about sexual play among children, claimed that he had never heard of children engaging in sex games, but added that if two children had been caught at 'such a thing,' the parents 'would certainly have whipped them both' " (p. 79). The avoidance training between brother and sister (the term for the latter being extended to all female relatives of the same generation) is begun early and carried to extreme lengths. "Brother and sister are so carefully trained to be reserved when they are together that any inclinations to exhibit overt sexual interest in each other are almost certain to be repressed" (p. 59). All informants stress the extreme avoidance between brother and sister. To "come where your sister is alone" brings disgrace on the whole family. "Many households where there are older children find it convenient to erect an additional shelter where the boy can stay if he should find his sister the sole occupant of the family dwelling" (p. 60).

Does not this avoidance, with the concomitant rule of exogamy, make it difficult to find a legitimate sex object? It does in many cases, especially as sex outside marriage is "illegal" with any woman, especially an unmarried one. "Young men have been known to journey far from their homes for the purpose of making contacts which could lead to marriage" (p. 62).

Incest is equated with witchcraft, thus "the gravest crime in the religious sphere and the most abhorrent act in the social realm have been combined." Informants are very emphatic about the treatment that would be meted out to an offender.

> If two persons committed incest and were found out, a crowd would gather and any headman would say, "I know those two had intercourse together; get them." Everyone considered them witches and they were burned. Incest sometimes goes before a council of people and sometimes the parents kill them outright. Usually the parents handle them (p. 250).

A striking parallel to the classic Trobriand incest story concerns the brother and sister who, when discovered, committed suicide together on the occasion of their final liaison by means of a stick pointed at both ends which they placed between them. Unlike the Trobrianders, the pair did this to escape the more terrible

punishment that would have followed their capture.[12] Punishment
for incest between distant relatives was "milder." "A person might
be whipped until he couldn't stand, but that's all."

Incest is, then, a crime at least as abhorrent as witchcraft. In
fact, some informants say that "even witches wouldn't do that."
The punishment in the case of intercourse with a near relative is
always a very painful death. Brother and sister who offend will
commit a terrible suicide rather than face the punishment that the
irate society would otherwise inflict upon them.

Back to the other extreme, with an interesting case from West
Africa: the Tallensi of what was the Gold Coast and is now
Ghana.[13] Again the description gives us what we need and is especially good, because Meyer Fortes, careful ethnographer that he is,
probed Tallensi motives on incest more than is usual. He was, of
course, a psychologist before he was an ethnographer and has always carried a banner for Freud through the inhospitable ranks of
British anthropologists. Could it be that the Tallensi attitude surprised him enough that he felt he must ask more than usual? In
any case, it is a particularly eloquent statement by a people who
not only conform to the Westermarck effect, but are quite articu-
late about it into the bargain. Of course, they never read Freud.

Tallensi social structure is based on the alliance between patrilineages and clans tracing relationship to a depth of fourteen
generations and more. Children sleep in their mother's hut and associate with the children of their co-mothers and the children of
members of the medial lineage who form a group of playmates,
siblings, half siblings, and cousins. (As with the kevutza, intercourse always takes place outside this group.)

Play groups of children of both sexes are composed of children
up to the age of eight and possibly after. Fortes noted that in these
groups there is full freedom of contact, squabbling, fighting, and
soothing being common. Brothers and sisters are together for
sleeping, playing, and eating until the age of nine or ten. It is
worth quoting in full Fortes' comment on the behavior he noted
between siblings of opposite sex:

> The psychological undercurrents of these conventional attitudes do
> not concern us here, but it might be remarked that there is proba-
> bly a strong and partly overt sexual component in the affective re-
> lation of brother and sister. I was struck by this when I once had an

opportunity of observing the behavior of Yamzooga (aged about
eleven) and his soog (real) sister (aged about nine) who were playing together in a corner of the room where I was chatting to their
father. The children, who were quite naked, stood embracing each
other, the boy with his legs round his sister's, and they twisted and
wriggled about as if they were engaged in a mixture of an orgiastic
dance and a wrestling match. They were both in a state of high excitement, panting and giggling and muttering to each other, with
obvious sexual pleasure. They seemed oblivious of their surround-
ings. This game went on for about twenty minutes, after which
they separated and lolled back as if exhausted. These children were
most attached to each other (p. 251).

There are many sex objects for the boy. These are his clan
"sisters" (related females in the patrilineal line with whom sexual
relations are permitted but between whom marriage is strictly forbidden). An unrelated woman is not a permitted object of premarital intercourse. The only possible relationship a man could
want with an unrelated woman would be marriage. There is a low
premium on the girl's virginity, and if she has a child, it is welcomed by her future husband. In adult life, there is high ritual cooperation as well as mutual affection between brother and sister.

The treatment of incest is mild in the extreme:

There are no penal sanctions against any form of incest, nor are the
culprits believed to be subject to automatic physical retribution.
Incest is so incompatible with the pattern of cooperation and the
structure of disciplinary and affective relations in the family that
this in itself serves to banish it from the field of family relationships
(p. 111).

A breach will be treated with ridicule. The man who commits it is
obviously not mature and in possession of himself. Incest with a
full sister arouses feelings of disgust but is less reprehensible than
intercourse with the wife of a member of the lineage.

Tallensi do not regard incest with the sister as sinful. When they
say it is forbidden . . . they mean it rather in the sense that it is dis-
graceful, scandalous. . . . They deny the temptation exists. "Look,"
said Sinkawol, arguing this point with me, "my sister, is she not
marriageable? And here am I, however attractive she is, I do not
even notice it; I am never aware she has a vagina; she is my sister

and someone will one day come and marry her and I will give her to him and get my cows. You and your sister grow up together, you quarrel and make it up, how can you desire to have intercourse with her?" This is a stock argument among the Tallensi (p. 250).

The children also learn conscious norms about their behavior. To play at actual coitus with their "real" sister they know is wrong. If they do it, they will be smacked by their parents and ridiculed by the other children. As we have seen, however, they are otherwise allowed complete intimacy of contact.

The "overt sexual incest" that Fortes noted here was between an eleven year old and a nine year old who were actually engaged in precisely the kind of behavior that we have suggested might ultimately produce positive aversion without great guilt or anxiety but with a feeling that sibling sex was just not done. This seems to be the case with the Tallensi; a happy example, since their notion about premarital sex—that it can only be with a related woman whom one must *not* marry—beautifully illustrates the point made in the first chapter about separating sex from marriage, incest from exogamy.

It is also superfluous perhaps to describe at length the attitudes to sibling incest of Malinowski's justly famous Trobriand Islanders. But so much in the great debate has hinged on them, and we shall have to return to them later, that it is worthwhile to remind ourselves of the more obvious facts. And in any case, as a teacher, I know that a generation has arisen that knows not Malinowski in its heart, and has forgotten, or never knew, what a bombshell his tales from Melanesia were to the savants of the thirties. Yea, even the Freudians quailed (before rallying behind the damaged complex of Oedipus), while the prophets of sexual freedom rejoiced, and believers in matriarchy even now take comfort.

The matrilineal Trobrianders, while tracing descent and clan membership in the female line, still live in nuclear families that would be familiar to us. But the growing children know that the real authority over them is not their father but the eldest brother of their mother. Her reserve and deference in his presence, his yearly *urigubu* gifts of food, which at least symbolically insist that he is her protector and caretaker, make him an awesome figure to his nephews and nieces. What is more, the boys know that when they reach puberty, and at least when they marry, they must move to his village and live under his rule. The sister is "lent away" to her husband and the children "claimed back" at puberty. This puts the brother and sister into a very special relationship from birth. The little girl growing up in the boy's hut will one day be the woman whose children he must claim and provide for: he will one day be the godlike supervisor of her and her offspring. It is not an easy or freewheeling relationship from the start.

In other matters sexual, however, the Trobrianders are the original permissive society, at least for children and teenagers. Boys and girls can, through the institution of the "bachelor house," freely experiment with sex. There is no particular premium on virginity, although illegitimate children are not approved. (There do not seem to be many, which led the Trobrianders into the heart of the adolescent sterility debate.) But we should carefully note here that there is no constraint on sex in general, and the only anxiety seems to be to keep it out of the brother-sister relationship.

Brother and sister live in close propinquity but under strict rules of separation. The degree of temptation is evidently high, since they are in close contact, but, as Malinowski describes, in *The Sexual Life of Savages:*

> Brother and sister thus grow up in a strange sort of domestic proximity: in close contact, and yet without any personal or intimate communication; near to each other in space, near by rules of kinship and common interest; and yet, as regards personality, always hidden and mysterious. They must not even look at each other, they must never exchange any light remarks, never share their feelings and ideas. . . . Thus, to repeat, the sister remains for her brother the centre of all that is forbidden (p. 440).

He rates the stringency of incest taboos in the order brother-sister, mother-son, father-daughter; while the second two are regarded as unthinkable, the same emotional intensity does not occur over them. In the case of a breach of the taboos "in the old days," the couple, or at least the man, would have committed suicide. But it is interesting to note that Malinowski seems to think that this self-punishment would occur if the couple were publicly accused and "shamed" about their conduct. If this did not happen, there would be disapproval and public ostracization; the couple might commit suicide, but they might just go away. There appears to be a certain reluctance to inflict direct punishment in the Trobriand Islands, and social control is effected by pressure of communal scorn and sorcery. Thus, it is significant that in the case of public exposure of incest, the individual will probably commit suicide.

While illegitimate children are not approved, it seems that the incidence of illegitimacy is low, possibly due to physiological reasons induced by early intercourse. Cases of actual breach of the brother-sister taboo are rare, but incestuous dreams seem common, although they affect the sister only, not the mother. In answer to his questions regarding these dreams, Malinowski records some interesting reactions:[14]

> To the question: "Do you ever dream of your mother in this way?" the answer would be a calm, unshocked negation. "The mother is forbidden—only a tonagowa (imbecile) would dream such a thing. She is an old woman. No such thing would happen." But whenever the question would be put about the sister, the answer would be quite different, with a strong affective reaction. Of course I knew enough never to ask such a question directly of a man, and never to discuss it in company. But even asking in the form of whether "other people" could ever have such dreams, the reaction would be that of indignation and anger. Sometimes there would be no answer at all; after an embarrassed pause another subject would be taken up by the informant. Some, again, would deny it seriously; others vehemently and angrily. But, working out the question bit by bit with my best informants, the truth at last appeared, and I found that the real state of opinion is different. It is actually well known that "other people" have such dreams—"a man is sometimes sad, ashamed, and ill-tempered. Why? Because he has dreamt that he had connection with his sister." "This made me feel ashamed," such a man would say. I found that this is, in fact, one of the typical dreams known to exist, occurring frequently, and one which haunts and disturbs the dreamer. That this is so, we will find confirmed by other data, especially in myth and legend (pp. 91–92).

And indeed we do. The Trobrianders are nothing if not inventive on the subject and manage what to them must seem the supreme wickedness by making the formula for love-magic derive from a legendary act of brother-sister sex: the most forbidden is the most potent. But we should also look at the contrast with the Apache. The taboos on sibling sex among the Trobrianders seem to float on a sea of sexual permissiveness quite the opposite of the grim puritanism of the Chiricahua. That the taboo-separation-proximity scheme provokes a desire for that which it is designed to prevent is clear enough here, but it does not lead to savage reprisals and burning over slow fires. The community just wants the terrible thing to go away through the couple's either physically removing themselves or committing suicide. Witch hunts and torture are not part of the Trobriand way, and we should have to classify their sanctions as "lax" while noting that, if severe, they are self-inflicted in their severity. But the feelings are easy to gauge.

Let us take a brief trip to Southeast Africa to the Pondo, to rub in the message of the Tallensi with a similar example before we return to the Far East. Monica Hunter's account is once again one of direct simplicity, which tells of the childhood situation and the adult attitude.[15]

The Pondo live in scattered groups of huts with a tendency to reside near patrilineal relatives of the same clan. The immediate set of relatives around the child will be the wives of his father and their children and the child's paternal grandparents, who are responsible for much of his upbringing.

> Own brother and sister play much together as small children and although from about six years when the boys go out to herd and both boys and girls begin to go about in gangs with those of their own age and sex from other imizi, they do not see so much of each other, nevertheless they live on intimate terms in the umzi. Often I have seen a small sister snuggling up to an older brother, keeping warm under the cover of his blanket and getting titbits from his plate. Even when grown up sisters will sit and chat with their brothers, near the Kraal. To an elder brother, who in time may be in the place of her father, a girl should show respect, but "a younger brother doesn't matter" (p. 32).

There is high indulgence of premarital sex and plenty of objects, and although virginity at marriage is the ideal, it seems rarely to be a decisive factor, and there is division of opinion over the examination of girls. The sanction against any breach is mild.

Formerly if a couple were caught in incest a beast provided by the man was killed at the girl's house, and a fire made of the pole used for closing the kraal gate. The couple were made to sit naked in the inkundla. A strip of meat was cut from "any part" of the beast killed and roasted on the fire mentioned. The meat was not nicely cooked but scorched. The pair were then made to eat the strip, each nibbling from an end until it was finished. The whole community came to look on, and the pair were sworn at, exhorted, and told, "There your filthiness has been exposed" (pp. 185–86).

The ceremony is never performed now. A supernatural sanction for a breach is found in the belief that the child of an incestuous pair will not suckle unless they confess. It would appear that the ritual eating acts as a purification. Incest and adultery are treated alike.

To the Pondo, incest is "filthiness" but only on the same level as adultery. It was more severely condemned than among the Tallensi but merited nothing more than some abuse and the eating of underdone meat—again like adultery. Indeed, with both peoples, adultery was if anything the graver of the two crimes.

Moving across to New Guinea we encounter another of the great ethnographic descriptions in the old grand manner, Margaret Mead on the Mountain Arapesh.[16] Her chronicle of their lives is in the Malinowskian mold, and she dutifully asked them for their views on incest and received their famous reply with its close resemblance to the less well known but equally emphatic declaration of the Tallensi. Let us quote her account in full:

To questions about incest I did not receive the answers that I had received in all other native societies in which I had worked, violent condemnation of the practice combined with scandalous revelations of a case of incest in a neighbouring house or a neighbouring village. Instead both the emphatic condemnation and the accusations were lacking: "No, we don't sleep with our sisters. We give our sisters to other men and other men give us their sisters." Obviously. It was as simple as that. Why did I press the point? And had they not heard of a single case of incest? I queried. Yes, finally, one man said that he had. He had gone on a long journey, towards Aitape, and there in the village of a strange people he had heard a quarrel; a man was angry because his wife refused to live with him, but instead kept returning to her brother, with whom she cohabited.

Was that what I meant? That, in effect, was what I meant. No, we don't do that. What would the old man say to a young man who wished to take his sister to wife? They didn't know. No one knew. The old men never discussed the matter. So I set them to asking the old men, one at a time. And the answers were the same. They came to this: "What, you would like to marry your sister! What is the matter with you anyway? Don't you want a brother-in-law? Don't you realize that if you marry another man's sister and another man marries your sister, you will have at least two brothers-in-law, while if you marry your own sister you will have none? With whom will you hunt, with whom will you garden, whom will you go to visit?" Thus incest is regarded among the Arapesh not with horror and repulsion towards a temptation that they feel their flesh is heir to, but as a stupid negation of the joys of increasing, through marriage, the number of people whom one can love and trust (pp. 67–68).

There is no incest anxiety evident here; in fact, there is simply indifference. "We give our sisters to other men and other men give us their sisters."

What then of childhood conditions among the Arapesh? They live in father-son extended families in clusters of three or four households, and it is obvious that the children have complete freedom of interaction:

Small children are not required to behave differently to children of their own sex and those of opposite sex. Four-year-olds can roll and tumble on the floor together without anyone's worrying as to how much bodily contact results. Thus there develops in the children an easy, happy-go-lucky familiarity with the bodies of both sexes, a familiarity uncomplicated by shame, coupled with a premium upon warm, all-over physical contact (pp. 43–44).

This then gives us a lovely example of the warm, rewarding relationship that we suggested might lie somewhere on the continuum. One of its results might well be the more or less academic interest in the consequences of incest that Mead reports, but even more interesting in some ways is its effects on the marital relationship. Children are betrothed while still very young, and the little girl of six or seven years is taken to live in the house of her "husband" where they "live together like brother and sister" for "long years" (he will be a few years older than she). During this time,

they may indulge in "overt sex expression" but not actual intercourse, much like the other "siblings" in the household. Mead's
account of the phase of the betrothal just before the girl is ready to
marry is particularly revealing and touching:

> Towards her young husband, her attitude is one of complete trust
> and acceptance. No constraining taboo marks the ease of their rela-
> tionship. He is just another older male to whom she looks up and
> upon whom she depends. She is to him another small girl, his spe-
> cial small girl, whose hand must be taken in rough places on the
> paths. He calls out to her to light his pipe, or to feed his dog. And
> all of his brothers share his attitude towards her, and she includes
> them in the circle of her affection. With the smaller ones she romps
> and plays. To all of them she becomes warmly attached. Her feel-
> ing for her husband and his father and brothers is practically iden-
> tical with her feeling for her own father and brothers. Ease of com-
> panionship, lack of taboo, lack of fear, characterize all of these
> relationships (p. 70).

Thus there has been a "sibling" relation of the warm, rewarding type between husband and wife. But, even if in our theory
this should lead to aversion, for the Arapesh there is little or no sex
outlet outside marriage. What is the result? A marked muting of
the sex relationship in marriage amounting to an unwillingness to
copulate. The sex act itself has to be slow and unexcited; no climax
is aimed at. Mead writes:

> A man must approach his wife gently, he must make "good little
> talk," he must be sure that she is well prepared to receive his ad-
> vances. Otherwise even she who has been reared by his side, on his
> food, may become a stranger, the inimical one. There is no em-
> phasis upon satisfaction in sex-relations; the whole emphasis for
> both men and women is the degree of preparedness, the complete-
> ness of the expectancy. Either man or wife may make the tentative
> advance that crystallizes a latent consciousness of the other into the
> sex act. It is as customary for the woman as for the man to say,
> "Shall I lay the bed?" or "Let us sleep." The verb "to copulate"
> may be used either with a male subject and a female object, or with
> a female subject and a male object. More often the phrase, "They
> played together" or "They slept" is used. Women express their
> preferences for men in terms of ease and lack of difficulty of sex-re-
> lationships, not in terms of ability to satisfy a specific desire. There

is no recognition on the part of either sex of a specific climax in women, and climax in men is phrased simply as loss of tumescence. The emphasis upon mutual readiness and mutual ease is always the dominant one (p. 81).

Thus, if the genital sexuality has to intrude on the warm relationship, it has to do so with great care or the wife "may become a stranger." This is extremely interesting since it shows us what happens when "aversion without hostility" is generated, but the "siblings" have to mate when mature. We should bear it in mind when looking later at the Chinese case of which much has recently been made.

Again in the great tradition of ethnographic description, we have Raymond Firth's *We, The Tikopia*, perhaps the greatest descriptive ethnography ever written.[17] Picking out the same items for examination, we get some curious results. Children are allowed great freedom of interaction. They remain unclothed for some years, and there are no taboos on bodily contact. They simulate intercourse, and there is familiarity and freedom in the relationship between brother and sister. This familiarity is taken to remarkable lengths in adult life. Although they do not mention sex matters to each other, and although there is an extremely high premium on virginity,

> Brother and sister may take part freely in all joint household affairs, tend the oven together, eat together, sit together, and even more strange, sleep side by side, covered by the one blanket. When the wife of my neighbour Pa Taitai was soon to have a child, she slept some distance away from him, while his sister lay next to him on the floor of the house. This evokes no comment from the Tikopia; it is quite normal (p. 192).

With regard to occurrences, Firth states:

> In Tikopia incest between brother and sister is abhorred, and often stated to be impossible; its occurrence is denied point-blank by most people. Sometime, however, an informant will admit that the temptation may be too much for a man, and that he may yield to an overpowering urge for sexual satisfaction. Such conduct is always represented as the fruit of his momentary sex passion, not the

attainment of a long-cherished desire. It is the presence of an accessible female that is held to be the cause of the incest, not the wish to embrace the sister as such (p. 193).

This suggestion that it is "momentary sex passion" rather than "long-cherished (strong) desire" that accounts for occurrences makes sense in our theory.

Brother-sister intimacy is, then, of a close physical nature. The sister can approach the brother in a way forbidden to anyone else:

> If a man has been fishing, for instance, he comes up to his house, removes his wet waistcloth, and covering his genitalia with his hand—a practice in which the Tikopia are peculiarly expert in preserving their modesty—hands the garment with no trace of embarrassment to his sister to wring it out for him and lay it on the sand to dry. Upon request she also brings him a fresh cloth, with no discomposure (p. 194).

But there are occurrences (for whatever reason), and the supposed sanction is suicide. What is more, the analysis of dreams shows that temptations to incest do occur. Note the Tikopia man's reaction to these dreams: "Thereupon the man who is having this dream wakes with a start and ponders it is not good." "Hence the reaction upon waking is not one of shame, but of anger mingled with fear—a man does not conceal such a dream, he curses aloud" (pp. 328–329). How different from the Trobriand reaction! The Tikopia dreamer is vociferously furious at what he considers to be a trick played by spirits in the dream—or he is reflective, he "ponders." The "temptation" in this case, we suggest, is physical. There is some "positive aversion" to the sex act as such, but constant physical proximity of two opposite sex adults during the night is bound to lead to sheer physical stimulation. As the brother does not wish to have intercourse and is largely indifferent to his sister sexually, he is annoyed or upset because the temptation arises to do something to which he is positively averse. It is a trick—somehow unfair.

The well documented Tikopia case gives us a chance to see some of the complexities of the Westermarck effect and shows how much societies may differ in detail while remaining within the bounds of our theoretical expectations.

We can now move to an example that has an intriguing difference: the author, having been alerted to the possibilities of the
Westermarck effect, actually tackled his data with it in mind and
consciously tried to frame hypotheses to test it. Arthur Wolf studied intensively a rural area of Taiwan and not only gained impressions of native attitudes but some impressive statistics to boot. He
was not the first to see the implications for the Westermarck hypothesis of the Chinese case. He quotes Tai Yen-hui, who wrote in
1943 of his own people:

> Westermarck says that when people are acquainted too closely they
> become sexually indifferent. He therefore emphasized the need for
> marriage outside of the family. If is possible that there may be
> feelings of disgust or coolness between a *sim-pua* and her intended
> husband.[18]

In 1966, Wolf elaborated on this for the anthropological public at least. The Chinese traditionally had two forms of marriage.
In the major form, the bride came to her husband's home as an
adult, in the minor form, she came as a *sim-pua:* virtually an
adopted daughter of the family who came in during childhood and
lived there until old enough to marry a designated son of the
household. Wolf describes the situation of the young betrothed
couple.[19]

> The couple's jural status reflects the fact that they are born into
> two different families, but the actual circumstances of their child-
> hood are the same as if they had been born into the one family.
> They are trained and educated by the same set of adults, and in
> their relations with other members of the community they are both
> children of the same household. From the time the girl enters the
> family, she and the boy are in contact almost every hour of every
> day. Until seven or eight years of age they sleep on the same tatami
> platform with his parents; they eat together and play together; they
> are bathed with the other children of the family in the same tub;
> and when they work or study, they work in the same fields and
> study in the same school. At the age of ten or eleven, when they
> become aware of the implications of their jural status, they may
> attempt to avoid each other, but this is not socially required of
> them. "It is just because they are embarrassed." So far as society at
> large is concerned, they are free to behave as though they were sib-
> lings until they are designated husband and wife (p. 884).

The situation is, therefore, quite like that of the kibbutz, where the sabras were expected to marry and, even more strikingly, like the Arapesh, where the "siblings" had to marry. Wolf does not mention the Arapesh, which is odd since he draws heavily on my paper of 1962, but the parallel is remarkable. The Chinese may not be the "only known human society" as he claims, where one can "adopt a daughter-in-law and marry a sister," but they do furnish a case with interesting parallels to that of the Arapesh. The latter simply toned down the marital relationship to a point of very low sexuality. The Chinese seem to have a harder time, and what Wolf does very elegantly is to contrast some outcomes for the couples in the two types of marriage (major and minor) in terms of the "satisfactory" nature of the marriage. Thus he compares how they fare in terms of divorce, adultery, resort to prostitutes, and fertility. In each case, the minor marriages come out a very bad second. Also, it was clear that the couples involved did not like these marriages at all, did not much care about their partners, avoided each other a great deal, and generally were unhappy with the arrangement. It had often been a difficult business to get them to cohabit in the first place. On the eve of the lunar New Year, the father announces to the two young people that they are now man and wife:[20]

> One old man told me that he had to stand outside of the door of their room with a stick to keep the newlyweds from running away; another man's adopted daughter did run away to her natal family and refused to return until her father beat her; a third informant who had arranged minor marriages for both of his sons described their reactions this way: "I had to threaten them with my cane to make them go in there, and then had to stand there with my cane to make them stay" (p. 508).

Not all instances were as drastic as these, but the overwhelming reluctance was there in all cases. The result, as we have seen, was extreme marital unhappiness with, for example, 46.2 percent of the minor marriages ending in divorce and/or adultery by the wife, as opposed to 10.5 percent of the major marriages. Wolf elegantly goes through all the possible alternative reasons why this should be, but is forced back on the conclusion that it is the childhood association that seems to be almost entirely responsible for this sad state of affairs: "The only conclusion justified by the data presented in this paper is that there is some aspect of childhood association sufficient to preclude or inhibit sexual desire." Of course, Wolf is rightly cautious about just what that "aspect" is, and to this we shall return in due course.

Let us end our examples where we started, in the kibbutzim of Israel. Before her tragic death, Yonina Talmon was one of Israel's most talented sociologists. She, like Spiro, had been struck by the lack of inclination to mate among sabras, and after my 1962 paper appeared, she wrote kindly and excitedly about it, realizing that we were on the track of something special. But what she was doing was extending the study from the individual kibbutz and comparing three well-established kibbutzim.[21] She looked at all the marriages of the second generation, 125 of them, to see if any of the sabras had married. She found not a single case where two people reared in the same peer group had married. What is more, she could find no record of love affairs between members of the same peer group. The seeming exception involved an outsider who came to the kibbutz after he was fifteen. Talmon, being a good sociologist, looked for an explanation in "sociological" terms.

Following up on Talmon's work, another Israeli sociologist, himself a kibbutznik, gathered even more impressive—virtually complete—statistics. One could always have argued that Spiro and Talmon had, for some reason, picked on some exceptional cases, but Joseph Shepher set out to get the records of all known kibbutz marriages ever.[22] He ended by obtaining the records of 2,769 of them. Now, bearing in mind that the elders of these kibbutzim *wanted* their children to marry, his findings are staggering. At first he found only sixteen exceptions to the Talmon rule. Then, like her, he looked at the ages involved and found that his exceptions had not been together between birth and six years old: They had been introduced after this initial period of contact. He therefore formulated the proposition as follows: There are no known instances of marriages or publicly known love affairs between sabras who were socialized together between the ages of zero and six years. The data on love affairs are, of course, more impressionistic and come from Shepher's own ethnographic and survey research. But his result concurs with that of Spiro and Talmon, and like them, he stresses the very "public" nature of the kibbutz, where these things tend to be hard to hide. If there are a few exceptions anyway, we must remember that Westermarck himself pointed out that the aversion could in some instances be overcome. What is staggering about the Shepher evidence, then, is the seeming lack of exceptions—of any. The kibbutz becomes established as a test case in this as in so many other things.

Shepher, while also a sociologist, had been bitten by the ethological bug to the point of coming to America to complete his thesis with me. What he reckoned he had found was a classic example of a "critical" or "sensitive" learning period: a period in an animal's life when it is "programmed" to receive certain information and store it for future use. (Of course, if it does not receive the information or receives misinformation, then nature's purposes are not served, and one can always expect some such cases. Thus, ethologists write of "malimprinting"—the most famous example being Lorenz's goose, which, as an infant, imprinted on his boot rather than another goose and was sexually misled for life.) The period for learning incest avoidance, claims Shepher, seems to be fixed from zero to six. It may be that the suckling experience, which universally involves the mother and in many primitive societies lasts for three years, might have something to do with the seemingly universal avoidance of the mother. This would leave the period from three to six an essential for learning sibling incest avoidance. Because experience here would be very variable, we would expect some variability in later life, and we have examined some in the foregoing examples. The role of the father being even more variable here, we can expect not only the greatest variety but the least avoidance, as seems to be the case.

We shall return to these considerations later. For now, let us simply record Shepher's contention that what we have here is a "negative imprinting" period: As long as the "siblings" are closely and intimately associated during the critical period, they will "learn" aversion and avoid postpubescent sexual relationships with each other if they can. Thus, it may be that intensity of interaction is involved but not on a simple stimulus-response basis: The "message" is being given to a programmed "learner," one who is primed to receive it, much as, at much the same period, it is primed to receive language.

The aim of this excursion into comparative ethnography was

to illustrate the range of variability in the response to adult sexuality between siblings that followed on various childhood experiences. In particular we wanted to see what indeed were the results of our rewritten Westermarckian category on propinquity: intensive tactile interaction, as I somewhat pompously put it. From the impressions of the classic ethnographers to the Chinese and Israeli statistics, there has been a constant theme: that childhood propinquity, understood as physical interaction, does seem to lead to positive aversion. The test cases here were the two instances where the averse couples were forced to marry—Chinese and Arapesh, and the one where they were enjoined to marry but chose not to—the kibbutzim. These, along with the cases where aversion seems to have been inculcated and where the result is indifference to the sibling and little interest even when incest occurs (Tallensi, Pondo, Tikopia), all point to variations along the continuum of propinquity that involve physical interaction. The Apache show us the other end of the continuum, where there is propinquity but harsh separation combined with maximum anxiety and vicious punishment—the true grisly horror. The Trobrianders give us a beautiful example of a similar childhood situation and a similar horror of incest, set not in a sexually repressive regime like the Apache but in a permissive environment which leads to self-punishment, if any, and much evidence of guilt and anxiety. Quite a lot of similar cases could have been given, and a number of other grisly horror stories could have been told. But these have held the stage for too long, and here I wanted particularly to lay out some of the evidence for Westermarck's position, since it has been so abused and declared so decidedly wrong.

We can see that it is not wrong: It supplies one set of alternatives. But then neither is Freud wrong: He merely supplies another. The Viennese Jewish family with which he was familiar and from which so many of his patients came was probably a typical example of "propinquity plus separation" coupled with the lack of sex objects that seems to provoke the Apache-like horror. The sibling is close and tempting yet forbidden. That so many of Freud's patients should have confessed to incestuous guilts and fantasies is perhaps not surprising. His scheme is only wrong, then, like Westermarck's, if it is taken to apply universally. Can we generate, as the jargon has it today, a more general proposition that will embrace both camps? Not one, perhaps, that will take in sanctions, but we can try this as far as motives are concerned:

> The intensity of heterosexual attraction between co-socialized children after puberty is inversely proportionate to the intensity of heterosexual activity between them before puberty.

That is how I formulated it in 1962, and although the language may seem a little quaint and old-fashioned now, that is how we thought we had to do it then, and it does have the merit of being unambiguous and concise. If Shepher is right, then it should read "between them before the age of six." I am quite prepared to accept this if further evidence bears it out for other cultural groups, as I am prepared to accept that there is a sensitive period during which the aversion learning can take place most readily.

The latter concession, in fact, brings us back to the point made at the start of this chapter: If nature is working toward the avoidance of incest, then one economical way is to program the creature with a readiness to learn incest avoidance. The learning situation had to be, I argued, one that was common to most members of the species early in the life cycle in order to work. It would not work 100 percent necessarily, but nature is not interested in 100 percent: It suffices that among those for whom the aversion is learned there will be quite a high number of real siblings. An unintended consequence of this mechanism, however, is what we have seen in the Freud effect: that if you do not let nature take her course, then you must not be surprised if you distort her aims, and in this deliciously human case, your own into the bargain.

You will rightly complain that this may well account for siblings—for their aversion to each other under the appropriate circumstances and even for mild sanctions (given that they don't like other people doing what they feel uneasy about themselves), but you have not explained either how this mechanism came to be there in the first place, nor have you explained how this applies to incest between adults and offspring. True. At this point, I can only plead that without getting the Freud-Westermarck thing out of the way, it was hard to proceed at all, and that keeping our gaze on the red lamp for a while, we shall now hesitantly follow Freud a little further into the tropical heat of the incestuous family, in search of answers to both these queries; a search that may take us into some unexpected open country beyond the jungle of family sexuality. We shall have to hold more than two ideas in our minds at the same time, but in so doing, and in fulfilling Fitzgerald's requirement that we continue to function, we may discover the origin and nature of that "first-rate intelligence," which enables us to do this and everything else that is distinctly human.

THREE

The Primal Horde

Malinowski, Rivers,
Benedict and others
Show how common culture
    Shapes the separate lives:
Matrilineal races
Kill their mothers' brothers
In their dreams and turn their
    Sisters into wives.
                W. H. Auden
                Heavy Date

Of the twelve companions of Thorin, ten remained. Fili and Kili had
fallen defending him with shield and body, for he was their mother's
elder brother.
                J. R. R. Tolkien
                The Hobbit

While Freud may have had the behavioral scientists of the world
singing his Mass against Westermarck with enthusiasm, the same
chorus was pronouncing his own attempts to solve the problem—
in *Totem and Taboo*—to be anathema. Remember his remark that
the roots of opposition to incestuous love choices "are not to be
sought in the psychology of the individual." They are, he went on
to argue, to be found in the evolutionary history of what he would
have called the "race" but what we would call the species. Only by
examining this could we discover the reason for the "opposition"
to incest between parents and children. But his own analysis has

52

caught him more abuse than ever Westermarck's mild comment on childhood familiarity.

If we have at all solved the problem with the latter and seen how Freud was right about incest wishes only when nurture was thwarting the designs of nature (although it must be admitted, with the same end result—little sibling incest), we are still left with the famous oedipal problem—parents and children. We could again invoke familiarity, and it may be a component: No one is more familiar with a son than a mother who suckles him, and some anthropologists have seen in the suckling experience precisely one of those universal, early imprinting traits that might account for mother-son incest aversion. This would not apply to fathers and daughters, but incest opposition is at least as strong here, which makes sense, since there is usually less familiarity. But this is all a little too cozy for Freud. For a start, we are dealing here with the case of sexual attraction or lack of it between already mature and quickly maturing organisms. It is not at all like the case of prepubertal siblings. If mothers or fathers wished to have sex with their immature children, there would be little physiological to stop them, and the parent at least knows what it is all about. Again, we are up against the fact that there is, proportionately, very little of it, and this lack cannot be explained solely by sanctions, since these are often nonexistent or inoperative. But Freud will not let us have a simple mechanism here, and he is again probably partly right. Because what he noticed in the parent-child case—and he dealt exclusively with parent-child cases in his practice—was evidence of intense *jealousy* and *hostility:* possessiveness and hate. And all this was accompanied by crippling guilt. Something other than mild aversion seemed to be going on here.

But was this just the behavior of a few Viennese neurotics again? Freud thought it was obvious that it was not. For a start, he could point to numerous examples in history, literature, and legend, where the theme of incest ran like a sinister thread through the warp and woof of the plot. Also, Freud was a great reader of the anthropology of his day. He had read Darwin and Westermarck (of course), and also Frazer's *Totemism and Exogamy*, McLennan on totemism and primitive marriage, and Robertson Smith on *The Religion of the Semites,* and those great, early ethnographic accounts of the Australian Aborigines to which everyone was turning for evidence on the life of our paleolithic ancestors. Freud recognized, with more sophistication than many anthropologists of the time, that all contemporary races have been evolving as long as all others; nevertheless, the best estimate we had of our ancestral patterns, he reckoned, was the life of the most technologically primitive and geographically isolated—the Australians.

And what did he find there—or what did he think he found there? Exactly what he found in history and legend, in his patients, and even in children—incestuous wishes coupled with "an unusual horror of incest." All these—Aborigines, neurotics, children—represented for Freud a kind of "primal man": man stripped of the cultural trappings of civilization and, therefore, in different but complementary ways, exhibiting primal traits free from civilized inhibitions. Neither children nor savages have been civilized out of their primal traits, while with neurotics, the usual controls have broken down, and the primal traits have broken through in various distorted ways. How Freud puts all these facts together is the story of *Totem and Taboo,* first published as a book in 1913.[1] Freud complained that A. L. Kroeber, the dean of American anthropology, dismissed it (in his first thoughts on the subject) as a Just-So story. (In fact, it was R. R. Marrett who made the remark.)[2] Lévi-Strauss has kindly suggested that the whole thing be added to the stock of oedipal myths and treated as such,[3] and Freud himself did not help when, at the crucial moment of his theorizing, he lapsed into the language of myth: "One day, the brothers who had been driven out . . ." Solid social scientists and their puritanical brethren in the laboratories—so concerned in the twenties to establish themselves as real scientists rather than renegade philosophers—could only curl their toes in horror at such language. Lévi-Strauss is nice about Freud's myth. He thinks that as myths go it's not half bad and represents an interesting "transformation" on the earlier versions. Well, one learns in this business not to be too condescending too soon. And when virtually to a man the whole tribe of social and behavioral scientists—and even the Freud-worshipping psychoanalysts—pronounce the theory to be mere fantasy, I can't help nursing a stubborn suspicion that it has more than a 50 percent chance of being right.

Let's look at the package Freud puts together, for one quickly notes that some of the most vociferous critics show the least familiarity with what Freud actually said. As a student, I was told not to read the book at all—a waste of time. It was "known error"—and one "reader on comparative religion" even printed Kroeber's two criticisms without printing a word of *Totem and Taboo!* Well, it is a bit embarrassing nowadays to have a book around that speaks freely of savages, children, and neurotics in the same breath, and this as much as anything has put people off. But we have to see it in the context of its time and try to extract the essential message, for this is the bridge to the next step of our argument.

He starts with the savages: the Australian Aboriginals. Several things stand out:

1. They seem to guard strongly against the possibility of incestuous relationships.
2. Totemism—the identification of social groups with natural phenomena—is prevalent among them.
3. Totemism, incest taboos, and exogamy often coexist.
4. The totem relation is substituted for real blood relationship.

Whence, he asks, the relationships between totems, incest taboos, and exogamy? Totems, as we know, are features of the natural world that are used to identify social groups—particularly groups of people who claim to be related by common descent such as clans, phratries, moieties, etc. Very often these are animals, birds or other natural creatures with whom the clan is supposed to have a special relationship: Typically the clan members cannot kill or eat the totem except on special, communal, ritual occasions. Typically, also, the members of the same totem clan are not allowed to marry each other and, often, to have sex with each other.

We saw in the first chapter how this set of relationships was not universal, and as early as 1910, Goldenweiser pointed out that all these features of the "totem complex" were not universally found together.[4] But Freud was interested in the Australians—they were, to him and many others, the true primal man. And in any case, once he had built up the logic of his argument, he felt that he had strong evidence that "in the beginning . . ." these things must have been associated, thus strengthening his belief about the Australians. He firmly links incest taboos with exogamy, although he does make the point that blood relationship is often simply assumed between members of the totem clan and is sometimes quite remote. This only goes to show, he says, how far the savages will go to make sure incest does not occur.

It is not only the totemism-exogamy-incest taboo complex that guards against incest, but other customs, like mother-in-law avoidance: the mother-in-law being too much like the mother for comfort. These things come out more clearly in savages, as they do in neurotics and children, since in modern man they are mostly unconscious, appearing only in disguised form in dreams.

So much for totemism and exogamy. But why totems and why are they taboo? What is taboo? It is like conscience in some ways—the inner voice that tells us not to do something. On the other hand, it is also communal rather than individual. Since incest—breach of the exogamic restrictions through marriage or sex—is "taboo" (derived from a Polynesian word *tapu*, meaning "forbidden"), then if we could understand the nature of taboo, we might better understand its application to incest.

Neurotics have taboos. These are maintained by an inner anxiety and fear, not by fear of punishment. If the tabooed thing is done, then punishment follows automatically—exactly what the savage fears. Almost anything can become the object of taboo— "Why animals?" will have to wait for a discussion of children. But for the neurotic—our other primal man—there are a number of correspondences between his taboos and those of savages:

1. The origin of the prohibition is unmotivated and enigmatic.
2. The nucleus of the prohibition is often an act of touching.
3. The prohibition shows a capacity for displacement—there is a risk of "infection" from the prohibited object.
4. Violators of taboo become taboo themselves.
5. The situation is usually handled by inventing elaborate ceremonials to expiate the taboo.

The common theme that Freud sees running through both the ritual acts and attitudes of the neurotic and the savage is *ambivalence*. Both desire what is forbidden yet are terrified of breaking the taboo. This ambivalence is not confined to totem objects—animals or other members of the totem clan—but he thinks this must be the oldest source of ambivalence: "Don't kill the totem animal or have sex with totem members even if you want to." And as he argued against Westermarck, you must want to or why forbid it, be ambivalent about it, feel guilty about it, and surround it with taboos and ceremonies?

Killing of the totem animal—whatever it represents—and in-

cest with totem companions must be two of the oldest desires of
mankind, is his conclusion. But he still has to establish why this
should be. It is, after all, on the surface a bit bizarre, this relationship between desire for incest and the killing of an emu or a kangaroo. Ambivalence is again the clue. What else do savages taboo:
that is, what else are they ambivalent about? Many things, but two
stand out: the slaying of enemies and the power of rulers. Toward
both, one is hostile and afraid. Rulers may, on the one hand, break
taboos (like the incest taboo), but on the other hand they are
blamed when things go wrong and often put to death. Freud had
read his Frazer, and the scapegoat king who is put to death by the
people who have worshipped him haunts Freud's pages much as
those of *The Golden Bough.* Neurotics, too, display the same para-
noid and hostile wishes toward those in power over them—in particular their fathers. The plot thickens again.

Freud brilliantly probes on. What is the other great realm of
taboo? The dead: especially the newly dead who are regarded
often like enemies. The Aborigines taboo the names of the dead for
fear of reprisals—children show the same fears, as well as the idea
of the mystical bond between the name and the person; this also
pervades folklore. Why do loved ones change into enemies after
death? asks Freud. Ambivalence again. The survivors feel guilty
about the dead, because they harbored secret wishes of hostility toward the deceased. Death, for them, is always a result of evil
wishes. The hostility is projected onto the dead, who are then expected to seek revenge. Children, dreamers, and savages are all
alike on this point: They have ambivalent emotions toward dead
loved ones. This fear can change to reverence over time as the fear
recedes; the ambivalence is always there.

Freud is preparing to tie all this together—the totemism with
its associated taboos, the murderous wishes, the ambivalence, fear
turning to reverence. It will all explain the origins of conscience, he
says, but unfortunately, modern neurotics are the best evidence we
have for this. Murderous wishes, incest phobias, contamination
taboos (touching phobias), fear of attack, are all the neurotic's private attempts to deal with what savages handle publicly and cere-
monially.

Now we come to his crucial chapter four. The threads start to
come together. He returns to the totem and the associated feature
of exogamy. He sees that exogamy and incest are technically differ-

ent, but he wants to argue that the two "arose" together, since for him, exogamy is simply a way of expanding incest taboos. This raises complications that we must deal with later, but for the moment, we shall accept his premise for the sake of argument and follow the reasoning. We also have to accept that totemism arose with exogamy, and these, too, for Freud, are the same thing: The forbidding of the killing of the totem and the prohibition on sex/marriage among the totem-clan members are part and parcel of the same process for him. So, how did the totems originate and get linked to exogamy/incest dread?

Here Freud makes his momentous turn to Darwin and the notorious primal horde. He describes Darwin's attempt to explain the origins of exogamy as "historical" as opposed to other attempts that are merely rational. Darwin, in other words, tries to point to something in human history that happened to cause exogamy, rather than simply suggesting reasons why we "must" have it. This is very important, because Freud obviously shares this view: We must locate an event or events in time that gave rise to the phenomenon. Darwin, taking such scant evidence as there was from the great apes (and it was largely hearsay) concluded that:

> Primaeval man aboriginally lived in small communities, each with as many wives as he could support and obtain, whom he would have jealously guarded against all other men. Or he may have lived with several wives by himself, like the Gorilla; for all the natives "agree that but one adult male is seen in a band; when the young male grows up, a contest takes place for mastery, and the strongest, by killing and driving out the others, establishes himself as the head of the community" (Dr. Savage, in *Boston Journal of Nat. Hist.* vol. v, 1845-7 p. 423). The younger males, being thus expelled and wandering about, would, when at last successful in finding a partner, prevent too close interbreeding within the limits of the same family (p. 125).

Dr. Savage (of the strangely appropriate name) was not quite right about the gorillas, but note that Darwin's conclusion was that this threat, killing, and/or expulsion acted to limit the possibilities of incest in the ways we have already canvassed in chapter one. For Freud, however, it goes deeper. He accepts the conclusions of Atkinson and Lang, that primeval man must have lived this horde life, gradually transforming the brute rule of "win or get out" to the gentler prohibition of "do not mate with those females controlled by the most successful male," which in turn became "do not mate with those of the same totem"—thus putting the onus of the prohibition onto a supernatural source rather than a living tyrant.

The gentlemen quibbled genteelly about which came first, the totem or the taboo, with Freud going for the latter. So how did the taboo become attached to animals and women? He starts with his other primeval man, the modern child. Modern children have animal phobias. This, in his experience was always a projection of fear of the father: So, for totem read father. In each case, there is both ambivalence toward the "totem" and complete identification with it. In the "male's formula of totemism," then, the father is both loved and hated, murderous wishes are directed toward him, these concern possession of his females, this is projected onto animals, and identification with the loved/hated father becomes identification with the animal. Here are contained the child's primal oedipal wishes whose insufficient repression and reawakening form the basis of perhaps all neurosis. The totemic system, then, arose out of the conditions that underlie the oedipus complex.

There is one stop on the way before we get to the central myth. Freud, in his voluminous reading, had not failed to study carefully Robertson Smith's *Religion of the Semites.* The origin of this religion, Smith argued (almost at the cost of his academic career) had been the totem sacrifice. Found again among the Aborigines, this consisted of the whole totem clan getting together and ritually, often cruelly, killing the totem animal and eating it. They then imitated the animal in dance and ceremony while bewailing its death, after which they all celebrated with feasting and orgiastic behavior in which normal rules of clan incest and the like were for a heady moment ignored.

It was all too remarkably coincident for Freud. Nothing better than the totem meal and festival could have expressed everything he had been putting together. But back to the key question: How come? What had happened in "history" to provoke such a far-reaching result, not only in the collective lives of savages, but in the deepest fears of children and the obsessive-compulsive reactions of neurotics? And even, if he is right, into the highest reaches of religion, where God is simply the super totem animal who has to die for us—to be killed for us—and whose body we ritually consume.

Turn again the pages of Frazer to find those gruesome details of
king after king killed, resurrected, worshipped, consumed. What
could it have been that left such an indelible, sinister, and gothic-
ally fascinating legacy? Freud goes back to the primal horde. The
sons/brothers—that is, the young males of the horde—would have
stood the situation just so far, he says, and then:

> One day the brothers who had been driven out came together,
> killed and devoured their father and so made an end of the patriar-
> chal horde. United, they had the courage to do and succeed in
> doing what would have been impossible for them individually.
> (Some cultural advance, perhaps, command over some new
> weapon, had given them a sense of superior strength.) Cannibal
> savages as they were, it goes without saying that they devoured
> their victim as well as killing him. The violent primal father had
> doubtless been the feared and envied model of each one of the com-
> pany of brothers: and in the act of devouring him they accom-
> plished their act of identification with him, and each of them ac-
> quired a portion of his strength. The totem meal, which is perhaps
> mankind's earliest festival, would thus be a repetition and a com-
> memoration of this memorable and criminal deed, which was the
> beginning of so many things—of social organization, of moral re-
> strictions and of religion (pp. 141–142).

But "the brothers" had to go further, it was no use going to all
this trouble to eliminate the tyrant and then have to resort to civil
strife amongst themselves over the object of their revolt—the
women. Paradoxically, therefore, the first social contract was one
of agreed renunciation.

> The tumultuous mob of brothers were filled with the same contra-
> dictory feelings which we can see at work in the ambivalent father-
> complexes of our children and of our neurotic patients. They hated
> their father, who presented such a formidable obstacle to their
> craving for power and their sexual desires; but they loved and ad-
> mired him too. After they had got rid of him, had satisfied their ha-
> tred and had put into effect their wish to identify themselves with
> him, the affection which had all this time been pushed under was
> bound to make itself felt. It did so in the form of remorse. A sense of
> guilt made its appearance, which in this instance coincided with
> the remorse felt by the whole group. The dead father became
> stronger than the living one had been—for events took the course
> we so often see them follow in human affairs to this day. What had

up to then been prevented by his actual existence was thenceforward prohibited by the sons themselves, in accordance with the psychological procedure so familiar to us in psychoanalyses under the name of "deferred obedience." They revoked their deed by forbidding the killing of the totem, the substitute for their father; and they renounced its fruits by resigning their claim to the women who had now been set free (p. 143).

Lévi-Strauss is right; it is the very stuff of myth itself, and even if that is all it turns out to be, together with its brilliant supporting argument, it surely ranks as one of the greatest literary episodes in modern science. Even Kroeber, when criticizing it, declared that Sapir, for example, had been too harsh.[5] He "first spread out its gossamer texture and then laboriously tore it to shreds. It is a process too suggestive of breaking a butterfly on the wheel. An iridescent fantasy deserves a more delicate touch even in the act of demonstration of its unreality." But both Kroeber and Sapir were laboring under a gossamer-fine delusion themselves: that man has no inherited tendencies to social behavior. We know better now, and so we can look with even more sympathy at Freud's myth. For what he was doing was saying: All the force of the logic of our observations of neurotics, children, and savages, to say nothing of human guilt and the paraphernalia of religion and politics, force us to conclude that something pretty drastic happened in the evolution of man to produce such a creature that would be so obsessed by, and so compulsive in, its acting out of these bizarre fantasies.

Is what happened in history in fact what Freud describes in the Myth of the Primal Horde? In some sense we can never know for certain, since no one remains who witnessed it. But without treading lightly on the gossamer cloths of Freud's argument—rather, instead, treating it with fairly rough scientific cross-examination—I am going to argue that indeed *something like it must have taken place.* And the marks left by this process are what contribute to the incest avoidance mechanisms between parents and children.

The Unilineal Objection

Let us take one of our by now familiar brief pauses to look at some of the anthropological criticisms of *Totem and Taboo,* explicit and implicit. What we shall see is that, as in the case of the Freud-Wes-

termarck argument, a more than satisfactory reconciliation is possible and helps to shed light on some seemingly odd beliefs and
practices that are part and parcel of the incest problem and the related question of exogamy.

We shall plunge in with one of the most telling pieces written
on the subject, not only for its intrinsic interest, but because it will
help fix in our minds some facts about kinship systems that will be
useful later on. Jack Goody, in writing a comparative study of incest and adultery, accuses behavioral scientists generally of a "bilateral bias" in their theories of incest—including Freud, and for
the record, Malinowski, Radcliffe-Brown, Seligman, Murdock,
and Talcott Parsons.[6] Their notions of what is or is not incestuous
are governed, he says, by our own notions of kinship, notions which
are not necessarily shared by all cultures, even by a majority of
cultures. Since kinship is, with us, reckoned bilaterally, we regard,
for example, both father and mother as in some way equally related to their child and to see sisters' children as exactly the same
as brothers' children and so on. Such symmetry, says Goody, comes
from having the nuclear family as the basic kinship unit, and we
tend to weave theories of incest prohibition out of the necessities of
the nuclear family. These are "internal relations of the family"
theories, says Goody, and they tend to stress, as we say in chapter
one, the terrible things that might happen to the family if we did
not have the taboos.

Over against this, Goody develops another position. These
theories, he says, ignore that the majority of the world's societies do
not reckon descent bilaterally—equally on both sides of the family—but unilaterally; that is, descent is reckoned in the male or the
female line. Where it is reckoned in the male line, it is called, in the
jargon, "patrilineal" and in the female, "matrilineal." Much argument went on in early anthropology about the priority in time of
the two methods of reckoning descent, with McLennan and Morgan opting for matrilineal and Maine and Westermarck for patrilineal. The argument of the "matriarchalists" stressed the "sexual
ignorance of savages"—if they did not know who their fathers were
(through ignorance or promiscuity), how could kinship be reckoned through males? Anyway, we shall return to this issue. For the
moment, let us look at how Goody uses this fact of kinship reckoning in his criticism. In such "unilineal" societies, he argues, members of the nuclear family are not thought of as being equally re-

lated to each other as they are in ours. If descent is through males, then a father is "more" related to his children than their mother will be; if it is through females, the opposite is true, and the mother is reckoned to be more related. What is more, groups (lineages, clans, etc.) are often formed on the basis of these descent principles, and this strongly affects an individual's life—far more than the "nuclear family" does. We have come across these "descent groups" in our discussion of Freud on totemism. And this is a key point—the totem groups are usually unilineal.

Anthropologists have argued that this has to be so, since a "bilateral" system of reckoning cannot assign an individual to one exclusive group on the basis of kinship; a unilineal system can. This can be seen more easily from figure 1.

The figure shows a nuclear family of father, mother, brother, and sister, and various secondary relatives. Under our bilateral system, all these relatives are equally related to the nuclear core, but under a unilineal system there are certain crucial differences. If the system is patrilineal (those within the solid line), then the brother and sister are members of their father's group, but not their mother's, nor are the sister's children members of the group. In the opposite case, the matrilineal (those inside the dotted line), the children are members of the mother's group but not the father's, and the brother's children will not be members of this group—lineages, clan, moiety, or whatever it is. Note, also, that under the matrilineal system, the "nearest" male relative of the children will not be their father, but their mother's brother. The brother, likewise, will be the closest male relative of his sisters' children (his own children will belong to his wife's group).

Armed with this information, let us look at Goody's argument. It all depends on who the reproducers of the group are, he says. In a matrilineal society, it is a man's sister who continues his lineage, not his wife. His mother will, also, by producing more siblings, continue it, as will his mother's sisters, his sisters' daughters, and so on. In a patrilineal society, on the other hand, it is not one's sister, but one's wife who does the reproducing. By extension, so does one's brother's wife, one's father's brother's wife, and one's father's wife. The latter is, of course, one's mother, but to put it in this other formula—the strict patrilineal formula—is more correct, says Goody. In the matrilineal case, she is a "woman of the lineage" helping to reproduce it; in the patrilineal case, she is a "wife

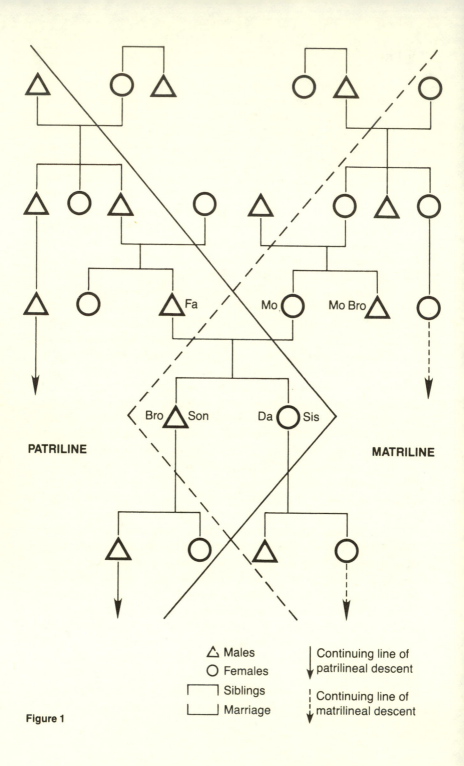

PATRILINE

MATRILINE

Fa Mo Mo Bro

Bro Son Da Sis

△ Males
○ Females
� Siblings
⎣_⎦ Marriage

↓ Continuing line of
  patrilineal descent

⇣ Continuing line of
  matrilineal descent

Figure 1

of a lineage male" helping to reproduce it. In the first case, she is directly related to her son by descent; in the second case, she has simply reproduced her son "on behalf of" the lineage of which she is not a member. It is more striking with the sister who in the matrilineal case produces a man's direct heirs, while in the patrilineal case she produces him nothing at all—except insofar as she may be "swapped" for a wife, or her bride price used to obtain one—but that again is to jump ahead.

The outcome of this, as far as incest and adultery rules are concerned, says Goody, is quite profound. Matrilineal societies, he maintains, seem very concerned to stop incest with the sister, while patrilineal societies seem much more concerned about adultery with wives of other members of the lineage. The general rule, he says, is not "do not sleep with related women," but "do not sleep with those women who are reproducing the lineage for you." It is not that matrilineal societies do not have adultery laws—although they are often notoriously lax—or that patrilineal societies do not have incest taboos—although they are often again remarkably indifferent about it. It is rather the intensity with which they pursue one or the other category of offenders: "incestuous people" or "group-wife adulterers." Goody is not all that clear what the motivation for all this is, but it is something to do with the solidarity of the males of the lineage. If they are competing for the women who reproduce the lineage, he seems to be saying, then there will be trouble within what should be a "solidary" group. This is another of the wouldn't-it-be-terrible-if arguments, of course, but it is not directed at the nuclear family, and so, according to some anthropologists, takes more notice of ethnographic reality.

One can, of course, find exceptions—the patrilineal Hottentots abhorred incest with the sister as the worst of all crimes, and the patrilineal Nuer don't mind at all it seems if one sleeps with a brother's wife. Goody rather eats his cake and has it here since he claims that the Nuer lineage is *so* "solidary" that it can ignore the general principle. Also, his argument may be correct as concerns the mother, but it can never be proved that the almost universal avoidance of incest with her and prohibition of marriage with her has not got something to do with her being the mother *per se* and not just her being a "group wife of a senior male" in the patrilineal system and a "senior reproducer of the lineage" under the matrilineal. However, Goody has raised an interesting issue, and while

several of the ingredients are still very Freudian—generation, se-
niority, renunciation of women, and the solidarity of the males of
the "totem group"—we have to take seriously the implications of
unilineal descent.

Edmund Leach followed up this point in a dispute with
Meyer Fortes.[7] The latter still holds an internal-relations-of-
the-family view of incest taboos, while Leach wants to make the
same essential point as Goody—that things are different in unilin-
eally organized societies. Leach is anxious to point out that anthropologists have been emphasizing descent at the expense of affinity—the marriage bond. In patrilineal societies, he says, a man's
mother is in some sense an affine (a relative by marriage), rather
than a consanguine (a relative by blood). Some patrilineal tribes
even go so far as to treat intercourse with her as adultery rather
than incest: It is a sexual offense against the father—interference
with his rights over his wife. This is the extreme logic of the patrilineal situation: If kinship is through males, then the mother is not
kin but, as Goody insisted, the wife of a senior patrilineal kinsman.
Equally, Leach argues, in a matrilineal society, if the interpretation of kinship is strict, a man's daughter is not kin to him. From
the point of view of the daughter, at least, her father is an affine—a
relative by marriage to her mother. Leach concludes that whatever
the nature of taboos or laws against sexual relations in these cases,
they cannot be held to be breaches of exogamy or the crime of sexual relations with kin. So when we define incest blithely as "the
crime of sexual relations with near kin," we have to ask, "How are
kin defined?" And we must remember that other societies define
them differently. No students of classics or the drama need to be
reminded of the case of Orestes who killed his mother and was
pursued by the Furies—avengers of murdered kin. At the pleading
of Apollo, he was acquitted by a jury of Athenians and the casting
vote of Athena on the grounds that a man is *not* kin to his mother,
only his father. Athena should have known, for as she pointed out,
she sprang from the head of Zeus with no maternal intervention.
Not the most impartial judge. But then many observers have seen
the play as a fine social comment by Aeschylus on the changing
mores of Greece from matrilineal to the more fashionable patrilineal. But Greece was not alone, and we shall return to this question
of the ideology of procreation.

However, where does Freud stand in all this? If he indeed rep-

resents an internal-relations-of-the-family position, and if this position does indeed miss the point that sexual prohibitions are different in unilineal societies, then Freud has made an important
mistake, since his prototypes—the Australian Aborigines—are indeed unilineal. Their totem clans recruit either in the male or the
female line. But this is precisely what puzzled Freud. When speaking of the "remarkable" prohibition—that people of the same
totem may not have sex with each other—he says:

> Since totems are hereditary and not changed by marriage, it is easy
> to follow the consequences of this prohibition. Where, for instance,
> descent is through the female line, if a man of the Kangaroo totem
> marries a woman of the Emu totem, all the children, both boys and
> girls, belong to the Emu clan. The totem regulation will therefore
> make it impossible for a son of this marriage to have incestuous in-
> tercourse with his mother and sisters who are Emus like himself
> (p. 5).

He then adds this footnote:

> On the other hand, at all events, so far as this prohibition is con-
> cerned, the father, who is a Kangaroo, is free to commit incest with
> his daughters, who are Emus. If the totem descended through the
> male line, however, the Kangaroo father would be prohibited from
> intercourse with his daughers (since all his children would be Kan-
> garoos) whereas the son would be free to commit incest with his
> mother (p. 5).

This is, of course, the Goody-Leach position (although Goody
would save the mother as a group wife). Also, Goody regarded the
main thrust of prohibitions as being against the junior males and
Freud couldn't agree more. He concludes his footnote:

> These implications of the totem prohibitions suggest that descent
> through the female line is older than through the male, since there
> are grounds for thinking that the totem prohibitions were princi-
> pally directed against the incestuous desires of the son (p. 5).

Which, of course, they were in the primal horde, where the jealous
father kept the sons from the females until the fateful day and
where "deferred obedience" and their own sense of collective guilt
and the need for solidarity kept the brothers from the women even
after the murder.

Freud, then, would not have any problem with the different incidence of prohibitions in different unilineal societies. But, following the evolutionary thinking of the anthropologists of his day, he would put this down to different stages of development. Thus, the logical outcome of the primal situation, after the rebellion, would be matrilineal kinship with its taboos on mother and sister; patrilineal kinship came later and added the prohibition against the daughter. In those societies, like our own, where unilineal descent does not operate, we can assume that it "fell away" but left the core prohibitions intact, with the emergence of the nuclear family.

Freud concludes:

> We can see then, that these savages have an unusually great horror of incest, or are sensitive on the subject to an unusual degree, and that they combine this with a peculiarity which remains obscure to us of replacing real blood-relationships by totem-kinship. This latter contrast must not, however, be too much exaggerated, and we must remember that the totem prohibitions include those against real incest as a special case (p. 6).

Freud then is in no doubt that the prohibitions arose to prevent incest among matrilineal relatives in the first case and then added the patrilineal—but that the nuclear family prohibitions were thus a "special case" of the unilineal prohibitions. We know his later reasoning on the "obscure peculiarity" of the ban on sex with the members of the totem clan—all the women of the totem were literally the father's women and the brothers (the clan) had renounced these. The primitive Australians are simply closer to their origins than we are, he argued. We have forgotten what the totem clan was about. They still remember. We cling to our "nuclear family" incest taboos. They still respect the prohibition on the totem clan women—a unilineal prohibition. If Freud does not adequately explain why, then, sexual prohibitions apply to non-clan members even in unilineal societies, neither do Goody nor Leach. Despite her status as a non-clan member in patrilineal societies, the mother remains a forbidden sexual object. And many matrilineal societies frown on intercourse with the daughter, while some patrilineal societies actually allow it. So it is not all that clear cut when it comes to prohibitions.

Ideologies of Procreation

We saw in the first chapter that concentration on prohibitions can lead us astray because we are not always sure why things are being prohibited. What has come out very clearly from this discussion, however, is that different kinship systems seem to provoke very different ideologies of procreation, and it may be that these can tell us more than prohibitions about the residual motives left over from the primal rebellion. Why, after all, should some people want to insist, almost vehemently, that the mother has no role—or a very secondary one—in the procreation of her child? It seems on the surface of it absurd, since she clearly does give birth to it—the father's role in this is always, as Roman law recognized, inferential. But, on the other hand, even though the mother does carry and deliver the babe, why should other people want to deny that the father has his share in creating it?

Much was made in past anthropology of the sexual "ignorance" of savages. When they denied the father's role, it was simply because they were ignorant of the facts of procreation. But as Leach beautifully pointed out, we do the same thing with the birth of Jesus. When we deny the procreative role of the father here, we are pious; when savages do it, they are ignorant.[8] Enough evidence now exists that what is involved is an ideological denial for us to forget the ignorance and look at the denial itself. This, rather than the prohibitions, may give us the insight we are searching for.

We have said that the logical outcome of the horde would be a matrilineal band of some kind. This was Freud's reasoning, and we should follow it out. The sexual desires of the sons in the horde (and, don't forget, also their desire for *power*) were directed toward their mothers and sisters, who were controlled (the power) by the horde father. Having rebelled, killed, and eaten him, they were smitten with remorse and guilt and deferred obedience and so renounced the women of the horde that they had killed the father to obtain. The logic of this is that they would have to hand these women over to men of other hordes and take women from other hordes, thus creating exogamous matrilineal groups: brothers, sisters, mothers and the children of sisters as shown in figure 1 (those within the broken line again). In the full version of the myth, they would, of course, institute totem rituals by projecting

their guilt feelings onto the totem animal, which would, paradoxically, be the symbol of their guilty solidarity, only to be eaten on
the special totem-feast occasion when they could suspend their
guilt for a brief moment.

Let us look at a prototypical matrilineal situation where we
have a thorough discussion of the ideology: Malinowski's famous
Trobriand Islanders. They provide us with a good case because
they became a *cause celèbre* in the dispute between Malinowski
himself and Freud's valiant but sometimes overzealous champion
Ernest Jones, on the whole issue of the universality of the oedipus
complex.[9] Point one: In the Trobriand Islands, these matrilineal
"sons" direct their oedipal hostility to their mother's brother, not
their father. Malinowski was, in fact, making an earlier version of
the Goody-Leach argument in saying that unilineal descent "cut
across" the family differently in different societies. The Trobrianders vested authority in the mother's brother, and it was he
who punished the boy—his sister's son—and controlled his marital
destiny, not the father. This is more or less true in all matrilineal
societies, although they, of course, vary in the nature of their insti-
tutionalization of the maternal uncle's authority.

But the Trobrianders accompany this with a most extreme
version of the father-denial ideology. It is not too much to call this,
in a structural sense, the "elimination" of the father. He is not
killed, he is simply defined out of existence as far as his children are
concerned. His role, as the sociologists would say, is reduced to the
companion of the mother and children. They accept that intercourse is necessary to procreation, but only in that the father has to
"open the way" for the child to emerge; he does not contribute,
however, to the physiological constitution of the baby. The mother
is impregnated by a spirit of the totem-clan. Once her son is old
enough to prepare for marriage and adulthood, he leaves her and
goes to the village of his mother's brother, under whose authority
he remains until, in turn, he becomes the guardian of his own sister's children. The "brother" symbolizes his continuing control of
his sister by making annually a payment to her husband in
yams—the famous *urigubu*. This is for the support of the sister and
her children.

Consider this in terms of the myth. The "father" is here eliminated, the women are renounced. But while the women as such are

renounced, their children are not. These do not belong to the mother's (sister's) husband because he has not created them; they are a creation of the clan. The "brothers" then claim them back. If the brothers cannot have intercourse with their sisters, they can at least claim the fruits of their sisters' intercourse. It is, in a sense, the ultimate realization of the incestuous fantasies of the brothers, which as we saw in chapter two, are extreme and compelling.

What is ingenious about this situation from Freud's point of view is the clever way this cultural ideology deals with the father. He is not hated, and there is no hostility directed toward him— that is saved for the maternal uncle. In fact, he becomes a friendly fellow and companion to his sons. But he is socially castrated, rendered ineffective, defined away. Actually, in this carefully constructed social and emotional choreography, no one really wins, since the maternal uncle takes over the father role, and as Auden so wittily expressed it, becomes the object of hostility in turn. There is always an older generation of males whose business it seems to be to interfere with the sexuality and particularly the marriages of the young males. And thereby hangs another tale.

The Trobrianders lack two things essential to the Freudian myth: elaborate totem rituals and remorse and guilt with respect to a symbolic father. Freud would simply say that these had been lost with the passage of time, but in fact he leaves us a way out. One thing we did not discuss in outlining *Totem and Taboo* was Freud's own digression on the child's "omnipotence of thought"— the idea that thought actually has effects on the world, which is the basis of magical thinking everywhere. Seeing much of this in the thought again of neurotics, children, and savages, Freud at the very end of the book offers us a way round the unpleasantness of the bloody rebellion. There may not have been a bloody rebellion at all. What is true of neurotics—that they overvalue the effects of their psychical acts to an extraordinary degree—may have been true of the primal sons.

> Accordingly, the mere hostile *impulse* against the father, the mere existence of a wishful fantasy of killing and devouring him, would have been enough to produce the moral reaction that created totemism and taboo. In this way we should avoid the necessity for deriving the origin of our cultural legacy, of which we justly feel so proud, from a hideous crime, revolting to all our feelings. No dam-

age would thus be done to the causal chain stretching from the beginning to the present day, for psychical reality would be strong enough to bear the weight of the consequences (pp. 159–160).

Freud was not alone in wishing to spare us from the embarrassment of such bloody origins. He also notes that Atkinson, who also derived the primal horde idea from Darwin, supplemented by his own observations of animals, was inclined to favor a less violent transition.[10] The sink-or-swim competition of the animal stage gave way to the fraternal horde as a result of maternal affection. To begin with, the youngest sons, but gradually all of them, remained with their mothers and were tolerated by the "father." In return for this toleration, they acknowledged the father's sexual privilege and renounced all claim to the sisters and their mother. Thus, we have two other hypotheses here, giving us three altogether.

1. The violent transition via the killng-eating-renunciation complex.
2. The peaceful transition via the effects of hostile fantasies being internalized.
3. Another peaceful transition via maternal intervention, which leads again to renunciation and obedience.

Freud was sorry that Atkinson did not have the benefits of psychoanalytic observations to correct him. But let us keep Atkinson's suggestion firmly in mind. It may well be one of the more acute of the many Just-So tales that were circulating at the turn of the century along with Freud's.[11]

One way or another, the outcome of either the violent or peaceful transitions was the matrilineal organization. We have seen how such an organization carries the Freudian elements, and if we accept the "fantasy" hypothesis, then we are on the way to covering those societies where there is no elaborate totem ritual. They have peacefully dispossessed the father, thus not requiring the totem complex. I suggest the following version of the myth for these:

In the beginning the sons were kept from the women of the horde by the fathers, and much as they would have liked to, the sons did not kill the fathers but simply withdrew from sexual competition with them. The frustration of their sexual drives was so intense it was frightening to them, so that when the fathers died (or were driven out) the sons could not face sexuality with the women. Their sexual interest in them was so intense, however, that while they took other people's sisters to bed, they acted out the fantasy of having children by their own sisters. They claimed the sisters' children as their own and denied the genitor any part in the process. Thus at one stroke they eliminated the fathers both as authorities and as sexual rivals.

Here we still have incest wishes and matrilineal exogamic institutions, but because no one killed and ate anyone, we have no need for totemic rituals. It is fear of their own motives that leads the brothers to renounce the women, not fear of the dead fathers. And note how I have allowed myself to lapse into the plural here, writing fathers where Freud would have written father. I have to anticipate, along with Atkinson, what is to come, and this is an important qualification that again we must bracket off and return to in the next chapter.

In the meantime, what of the patrilineal case? We have already seen what the Athenians thought of the role of the mother, and in many patrilineal societies it is equally derogated—although in others it is accepted. In the extreme case, the mother can best be described as being regarded as a kind of incubator. This "incubator-wife" receives the sperm, which develops into the child, without contributing more than a temporary home for the fetus. The Tikopia, for example, say that the mother does not create the child but is merely the "shelter house" for it. Albanian hill tribes and West Indians, among many others, subscribe to a similar philosophy. Typically, given our bilateral organization of kinship, we accept that both parents contribute—and this is not a result of enlightened genetic knowledge; most bilateral peoples think likewise, and we thought this even before we were enlightened. There are many variations, of course, and most allow some dual contribution with the mother contributing the flesh and the father the bone, or the mother the body and father the soul, or whatever. We are concerned with the extreme, but quite common, version, which denies the mother more than the incubator role.

It is, in fact, nothing but a logical expression of the nature of patrilineal descent. Descent is through the males, but this has to come up against the awkward fact that the women have the chil-

dren. Thus a male of the patrilineal clan has to acquire an incubator so that he can continue his line. His denial of the mother's role
in creating the child is simply the logical opposite of the matrilineal male's denial of the father's role. But why is it so fierce in some
cases?

That extraordinary, and underestimated, intellectual mis-
chief-maker of the anthropological world, John Whiting, has come
up with an explanation that matches Freud's in its ingenuity while
totally turning it on its head—a veritable Marx to Freud's Hegel.[12]
Denial of the mother's role, he says, could be an outcome of repressed resentment against the mother. But why would the "son"
resent the mother? Whiting links mother resentment with sex and
weaning. The father of the primal horde (we shall go back to assuming there was only one) was a notorious old polygynist, and
Whiting links polygyny with the *postpartum sex taboo.* This is the
taboo on intercourse between a man and his wife after the birth of
a child, which can last up to three years in extreme instances. Prohibited from intercourse with one wife, the father has recourse to
another—indeed this may be the basis of polygyny as Whiting
suggests. In the meantime, the son is in exclusive possession of his
mother, and he is receiving from her food, love, and stimulation,
and above all security. Sooner or later, though, he has to give up
this privileged place as his father comes round again. This return
of the father may or may not coincide with the weaning of the son.
If it does, he loses both the exclusive possession of his mother and
the maternal milk with all that this means. If at this point—the
ending of the postpartum sex taboo—the mother turns him out
and ceases to stimulate, feed, and sleep with him, his resentment
will know no bounds. The frustration of his oral drives will lead to
cannibalistic and aggressive wishes directed at his mother. (Why
not his father? you might ask. Whiting answers that the child per-
ceives the mother as rejecting him, not the father as displacing
him.)

Following out the logic of this, Whiting makes the marvelous
suggestion that turns Freud on his head: that the totem animal
which is killed and eaten is the mother, not the father! (In looking
through *Totem and Taboo,* in fact, I find only one actual example of
a cannibalistic wish: It is little Arpad who wants a "fricassee of
mother," on the analogy, Freud ponderously explains, of a fricassee of chicken.)[13]

Whiting does a cross-cultural survey and finds that when you
get totemism and eating taboos, it is highly associated with a coincidence of weaning and the end of the postpartum sex taboo. Totemism *not* linked with eating taboos occurs where exclusive possession ceases but suckling carries on and where the resentment is
presumably less. In passing, we should note that Whiting and his
associates also found that polygyny, patrilineality, long postpartum sex taboo, and late weaning were also strongly associated with
fierce initiation ceremonies—where the young men, having been
almost totally identified with the women until their adolescence,
are then taken away to be "made men," often with prolonged humiliation and severe genital mutilations.[14]

To go too far into this would take us too far afield, but again,
we should note the correlation with fierce initiation ceremonies for
future reference. It may be the price the sons have to pay for being
kept close to their mothers—the price for Atkinson's solution in
fact. But for present purposes, we should note that we seem here to
have a strong suggestion about the origins of the patrilineal ideology that ties it up with totemism, initiation, and the general ongoing battle of the generations that we have seen running through all
these systems.

It only covers the mother in patrilineal societies. What of the
sisters and daughters? I think Goody is right here. It is not so much
a matter of renunciation as of indifference. Since the sons have not
repudiated fatherhood, they do not need the sister to reproduce for
them; they can do it for themselves—with the minimal assistance
of the incubator-wife. Since the sisters have not been denied to
him—in this myth at least—the brother has no frustrated desires
toward them, to both attract and repel him. We have seen in
chapter two how easy it is for indifference to sex with the sister to
be generated, and our more recent information would suggest that
patrilineal societies should leave well enough alone and let brothers and sisters rough and tumble up to age six. The father's control
over the females is asserted in some patrilineal societies, however,
by allowing intercourse with the daughter—or at least not punish-
ing it. But as Goody points out, sisters and daughters are not that
much a concern to the dedicated patrilinealist: He is more concerned with the monopoly of the use of the incubator, hence adultery is the chief problem; and purdah, seclusion of women, insistence on virginity at marriage, chastity belts, and ferocious

punishments for female adultery (rarely male) are all common enough to require no elaboration.

Psychology or History?

Again I must ask the readers' indulgence to pause and take stock. It has been another heady flight through some unfamiliar territory, and in the glee of intellectual pursuit we are apt to forget what it is we are after. Our question started with a certain smugness at having reconciled Freud and Westermarck on siblings and nailed the reasons for the variation found in reactions to sibling incest. Nature takes care of it, we decided, if you let her. If not, you get the phobias and the repressed desires and all that. But this did not explain the other two forms of incest which involved the two generations. Our question then was, can Freud's much abused theory in *Totem and Taboo* shed any light on this, for he was concerned primarily with the hostility between the generations over sex, power, and the disposition of reproductive potential.

There is no question that on these issues all human societies have come to some arrangement. It is rarely left to random choice. In fact, it is often the most highly structured of the institutional complexes of any society: It is the system of kinship and marriage laws. Ignoring the "fact" of the primal deed, what are its basic ingredients?

1. A power struggle between older males and younger males
2. Over the control of women for sexual purposes
3. Leading, by one route or another, to the invention of exogamic restrictions
4. Through the intermediary process of the development of conscience and guilt.

The struggle, which was once out and out—the war of all against all—was transmuted into a game with rules, the basic rule of which was that a body of males "renounced" a body of related females. Since this renunciation was a result of guilt, we got also the institution of totemism—but as we saw, this need only have happened if the killing took place, not if it didn't.

Human societies, as our second section showed, illustrate the highly variable ways in which these basics can be patterned. Totemism either follows the whole course Freud suggested or exists but lacks the killing-eating taboos or doesn't exist at all. It either is or is not associated with exogamic groups. Unilineal systems lead to a very different incidence of concern about and interdiction of sex within the nuclear family. Hostility can be displaced from the "father" to the mother's brother, and either the father or the mother can be denied a role in procreative activity.

We tried to show how some of these things hang together in an intelligible way—in a series of "totem complexes," where various of the elements made sense in conjunction with various others. In this we used the myth, not so much as an origin myth as a myth of timeless validity, which spoke to us of those basic ingredients we have listed. The myth said, "Here are the underlying elements of all human breeding systems—now see what humans have done with them, given the diabolical cunning of the unconscious."

Thus, we can turn Goody and Leach on *their* heads. They argued that unilineal systems "cut across" the family differently, thus "causing" different kinds of emotions, prohibitions, etc. We could argue that as a result of the development of different emotions (father denial, sister obsession, etc.) unilineal systems themselves came into being. If you deny the mother's role in procreation as a result of infantile, cannibalistic, aggressive wishes, then you can hardly avoid totemic patrilineality!

I don't think we need to play the chicken-and-egg game, however, only to accept that there must be a constant feedback between institutions and deep motivations such that they voraciously feed upon each other. Here the myth is useful, because it provides us with the constants around which the institutional-motivational systems must organize themselves. We have the three possibilities of incest, and each one can be highlighted, played down, ignored, enjoined, prohibited. Yet behind all the variation is, for example, *the constant of the power struggle between the older males and the younger for control over the sexuality of the young women.* Who controls that, controls the society. In this eternal struggle, the myth says, there will be a compound of hostility between the two generations of males and also a need by the junior generation to identify, ultimately, with the older generation. They have both to defy the "fathers" and yet to step into their shoes. Why do they not simply passively obey? Well, sometimes they even appear to do that, but, Freud would say, only when their natural hostility has been sublimated.

Now, this basic hostility can be stretched and changed in various ways. We can borrow the image Leach took from topology of a diagram drawn on rubber sheeting.[15] You can stretch, twist, or even tie in knots the rubber sheet, and while the diagram will consequently *look* very different, it is the *same* diagram—the *relation* between the points stays constant, only their appearance changes. So with the mythical ingredients, the hostility can, under the right circumstances, be directed against the mother—but it will surface then in initiation rites, for the boys must identify with their fathers. After initiation they can marry. The hostility, in matrilineal societies, can be transferred to the mother's brother who becomes "older male who has power to order my mating behavior." In patrilineal societies, on the other hand, and many bilateral ones also, the mother's brother becomes an object of almost sacred affection—to be defended to the death as was Thorin by his very Anglo-Saxon maternal nephews. Sometimes the totem animal can have all the projected ambivalence directed to it as in the full "totem complex"—in other places it is little more than a name. Sometimes the exogamic prohibitions in marriage can include ferocious rules about sex, sometimes not, sometimes the opposite.

But what I have tried to show in this chapter is that these are not simply random conglomerations of customs, but topological variations in the underlying themes. It is to these we must constantly return—and they are indeed the themes of the myth. They can be slanted or inverted, but they are always there, and even in the case of an inversion, the two points remain the same.

Here, though, we might be falling into the trap that Kroeber fell into—we are deliberately refusing to treat this as a myth of "origins" and treating it as a statement of "timeless reality"—or as Kroeber would have put it, what Freud is *really* talking about is "recurrent psychic events" rather than a single "historical" one. Well, it is useful as a first approximation to treat it this way, in order to see how well it holds up as a "timeless" reality. If it does, then it is telling us *something*. But Freud was quite definite about this: He was talking about origins—about history, about actual events in the hominid past that actually happened. This has been the primary embarrassment from which Kroeber and Lévi-Strauss tried to rescue him. Convert the supposed historical happening (which can't have happened) into a timeless "psychic reality" or "mythical transformation" and you preserve its importance while avoiding the foolishness of claiming it occurred, sometime, some-where, somehow. Again, let's do some headstands, but this time, let's stand Freud back on his feet and examine his stubborn claim that what he described *must have* happened, not forgetting that he gave us two alternatives: the killing or the fantasy of killing.[16]

People should read his footnotes—although I sympathize with those who avoid footnotes. They are important here. No sooner has he written the momentous "One day . . ." than he adds this quick reminder

> To avoid possible misunderstanding, I must ask the reader to take into account the final sentences of the following footnote as a cor-rective to this description (p. 141).

Need we add that "possible misunderstanding" has hardly been avoided! But what do these "final sentences" say?

> The lack of precision in what I have written in the text above, its abbreviation of the time factor and its compression of the whole subject-matter, may be attributed to the reserve necessitated by the nature of the topic. It would be foolish to aim at exactitude in such questions as it would be unfair to insist upon certainty (pp. 142-143).

What could be more disarming and more intellectually hon-est? We don't *know* what happened, says Freud, but putting all this together with Darwin-Atkinson, here's a damn good guess! Of course, he implies, I am not going to spell it out in proper Darwin-ian evolutionary form—this would give it an exactitude it would be dishonest to pretend to; I shall present it just as a brief story summarizing the main ingredients that must have been involved.

Note how he insists on the "abbreviation of the time factor." The time factor is important. Freud clearly did not mean that there was *one* horde, and *one* rebellion at *one* time. He meant that *at the horde stage* of human evolution the structure of relations in the hominid band must have been as described by Darwin, and that after the advent of weapons (probably) the possibilities of rebellion must have occurred over and over again in horde after horde. To put it into the jargon, there must have been both natural and sexual selections pressures for the development of conscience and guilt and their manifestations, and given the horde structure, they must have been as follows.

Note also the "compression of subject matter." Darwin was unsure whether the horde would have had several jealous older males or, as was supposed to be the case with the gorilla, only one. Freud compresses this to "the father" and "the sons"—but it is open whether this should be "the older, mature, dominant males" and "the younger, maturing, peripheral males." Atkinson realized that the one-male-to-a-troop system didn't always operate in animals.

But we must reinforce that for Freud this was crucial. He may well have been talking about "recurrent psychic realities," but they recurred because *at a crucial period of human evolution natural selection had programmed them into the creature.* To be correct, sexual selection had helped and we shall tediously spell that one out—but that is the guts of it. We go on producing the weird combinations of kinship, sex, mating, power, initiation, ritual, and other games that we do, because these have been programmed into us by evolution—like the ankle bone, or the opposable thumb. The mediating mechanism is conscience—without its categorical imperative, the systems would not work. But it, too, got there by natural selection.

Freud, unfortunately, like Darwin himself, was an inveterate Lamarckian in this respect. The characteristics acquired in the horde stage were subsequently inherited. It doesn't work like that, we know now, but it is easy to retranslate the whole thing into correct selection terms. Freud saw that "direct communication and tradition" were not enough to explain this persistence over the generations and went on to make a remark so perceptive that it is amazing that it has been overlooked by the modern theorists of instinct:

> Social psychology shows very little interest, on the whole, in the manner in which the required continuity in the mental life of successive generations is established. A part of the problem seems to be met by the inheritance of psychical dispositions which, however, need to be given some sort of impetus in the life of the individual before they can be roused into actual operation (p. 158).

And, we can add, depending on the nature of the impetus, they will take on various of the protean forms we have already discussed. Inherited psychical dispositions, then, but only brought into play by environmental factors. Every instinct, the modern theory holds, needs "experience" for its final realization, and the variation in the experience can lead to much variation in the expression of the instinct. We have seen this with brothers and sisters, with fathers and sons, with sons and mothers: The inherited psychic dispositions are there—the "impetus in the life of the individual," that is, his socialization patterns and the culture in which they are embedded, can turn and twist the inherent diagram on the rubber sheet and rouse them into actual operation in a series of variations on the primal themes.

The horde stage existed then. In it, the older males of the hordes struggled with the younger for sheer possession of the females of the horde. By some transformation, through selection over time, this became a fraternal clan organization, with rules and taboos concerning the women and an exogamic means of controlling the access to mates. The old still ruled, and the young still resented, but rules and the capacity to obey them—mediated by conscience and taboo—replaced the straight power struggle. The psychic dispositions, then, that this selection process left behind, are those we have already listed, and their outcome will always be a struggle in which *the older males control the younger by controlling their access to the females.* Exactly how this will happen can vary a lot, depending on the "impetus" from the culture, but systems of exogamy—kinship systems generally—are always responses to this problem.

We have lost totemism somewhere. It is indeed related, but perhaps not in the way Freud thought. Also, we are back to emphasizing exogamy and have let our gaze wander from the flickering red lamp. The two are related, but not in the way Freud thought—simply because exogamy prevents incest. It doesn't—but neither do incest taboos for that matter. Something does, however, and that something may be part of the inherited psychic disposition that produced rules, conscience, exogamy, kinship, initiation, totemism, ritual, and indeed, all of culture. We shall now try to follow out how all these became connected in evolution, following Freud's lead, but rewriting the script with the benefit of hindsight.

The lamp still glimmers at the center of this maelstrom of events, but its glow is becoming diffused through many prisms, and we need to gather the refracted colors back into one master beam of light if we can, with both Freud's example and his argument as our inspiration.

FOUR

The Monkey Puzzle

There are apes in Troglodytae *which are maned about the neck like lions, as big as great Belweathers. So are some called* Cercopitheci, Munkies, Choeropitheci, Hog Apes, Cepi, Callitriches, Marmosits, Cynocephali, *of a Dog and an Ape,* Satyres, *and* Sphynges, *of which we will speak in order, for they are not all alike, but some resemble men in one way, and some another.*

Konrad von Gesner
Historiae Animalium 1551–1587

So we must stretch our imagination and our knowledge back into the past. Like Freud. This is the most lasting message of *Totem and Taboo:* Look to what happened in our evolutionary history and note the marks it left; for the marks will be the stigmata of the species, those things that distinguish it from all others in its anatomy and its behavior. This is easy to see for anatomy and has been accepted for a long time now, but it is harder when it comes to that soft correlate of the physical substrate—our behavior. Again, this is more or less accepted for animals: their behavior evolves as their bodies evolve. Indeed, natural selection works on behavior to change the bodies, and then in turn on the changed body/behavior, and so on to mold species in their particular paths of evolution. And the behavior of animals is not all that simple either, as we shall see. But how do we study this evolutionary process? To what

83

evidence should we turn since we were not there to witness the millions of years the process took?

Freud had only the slenderest threads on which to hang his theory: savages, neurotics, children, and the hearsay evidence on the gorilla. He lacked what Darwin lacked: a genetic theory to account for the workings of natural selection; a realistic time-scale for human evolution; fossil evidence of the actual passage from ape-ancestor through ape-man to true man; adequate evidence on the behavior of our closest relatives, the other primates; and even, for that matter, accurate data on the nature of human kinship systems. That he managed at all, given this absence of information, is truly remarkable. And he was right, in a way, in his use of children, neurotics, and savages, if only for this reason: that the best evidence we have for the evolution of the behavior of any species is the contemporary behavior of the species itself. Which behavior you pick is important, and we can perhaps rightly quarrel with his notion that these three sources were the prime ones, but he was not wrong to use the present to reconstruct the past—nor was he wrong to look at our cousins. Again, granted, a few stray facts about one species are not much, but ethologists, in reconstructing the history of behavioral evolution, have taught us that we should look closely at the behavior of closely related species to see how it varies, since this will tell us a lot about how and why the divergences came about. If we can first establish the baseline similarities, then we can ask, how come these differences?—or if you prefer the jargon, what were the selection pressures that caused these divergences to occur and be maintained?

We then should look to the other primates—our cousins the monkeys and apes—for clues to our own evolution. But which primates, and for what clues? Note that Darwin-Atkinson looked to the gorilla to give us clues about the state of society before the advent of culture, reason, consciousness or whatever we want to call what it is that makes us man and makes us different. This is not because man is descended from the gorilla—we are both descended from some remote common ancestor—but because man has clearly made more drastic changes from his ancestral state than the gorilla has from his, and therefore, the gorilla gives us some idea of how a less complexly evolved anthropoid organizes its life. We can, the reasoning goes, project ourselves back into the past with the help of this more primitive cousin and find the point of divergence.

We are interested in this point of divergence and in whether or not Freud was right about the nature of it and, in consequence, what role the fear of incest, renunciation of women, development of guilt, etc., played. We can look to our primate cousins then to tell us what it was like to be a primate *without* all these things, which our ancestors must have been without themselves before whatever it was that happened to change them. Man clearly emerged from a largely vegetarian, forest-adapted animal, into the omnivorous, culture-bearing, open country creature that he is. By looking at our cousins, we can glean a picture of that cultureless, speechless, vegetarian past. We have several choices as to exactly how.

We can lean heavily on blood relationship. What Huxley established so firmly for anatomy is now more firmly established for both blood and behavior: We are very closely related to the great apes, especially the chimpanzee and the gorilla—more remotely to the orang and gibbon.[1] Indeed, for most characteristics, we are closer to the chimpanzee than the chimpanzee is to other primates. The classification is more realistically: man-chimp versus apes versus monkeys. Ever since chimpanzees have been taught, by using signs, to use rudimentary human language, the barrier has become even fuzzier. Whatever happens, we must look to the chimpanzee, and what we know of the gorilla (which is not much) as clues to our own past, because even though these are highly evolved animals, they have diverged less drastically from their ancestral forms than we have and are therefore closer to whatever the creature was that is our common forefather.

But they present us with an embarrassing problem. Despite their obvious abilities, they never left the forest. At least we suppose they didn't. They have made it their home, and many of their adaptations are still of the semi-brachiating type that marks them as creatures of the trees where they play and where they always sleep in roughly constructed nests. Our problem is that the great divergence for man started with his ancestor *abandoning* the forest and striking out for the savannas—almost certainly in east Africa. Our permanent bipedal, upright gait—a strange and startling divergence from the primate norm—is the clearest evidence for this.

At first we probably waddled a bit, but later we strode purpose-
fully into a different future, far, far different from that of the
chimp. He got the forests, perhaps even in successful competition
with our little ancestor, his even closer cousin, but in so doing he
sealed his fate and arrested his development. It was the less promising and less successful little primate that went on to conquer the
open spaces.

But not all that quickly and not alone. We shall look at the
dates and details later, for now you must take for granted that this
is the general picture that fossil evidence presents. As the forests
shrank, those creatures that were specially adapted for them—for
the branches and the trunks and the fruit and leaves—either had
to cling to their ancestral habitat or get out onto the expanding
plains and savannas of the African continent. It was not always a
matter of choice, but for whatever reason, some struck out, like our
own ancestors. Among these were the ground-dwelling monkeys.
(The gibbon had clung to the treetops; the orang to the deepest
jungle; the gorilla to the mountain forest.) They began to exploit
the forest fringe, moving back and forth cautiously, and some
stayed there. Others moved right out, using their binocular vision,
fast quadrupedal gait, and their equally effective canine teeth to
adapt to life in grassland, savanna, and even desert and snow.
They were the ancestors of the old-world monkeys, the baboons,
macaques, langurs, vervets, etc., which are to be found today in almost all known ecological niches from the Himalayas to the Ethiopian desert, from northernmost Japan to the Cape of Good Hope,
from the temples and forests of India to the West Indies, where
they were taken on the longest and oddest voyage of all by the intervention of their adventurous cousin, who had long since sur-
passed them. But at first, at that testing time when the scramble
for the forest and its fringe was on, they would probably not have
predicted it—no one would. Indeed, our adventurous ancestor
may have looked a very poor thing at the side of the ancestral baboon—bigger even than his descendant—with his massive canines,
his speed and his strength.

But these more remote cousins have this over our chimpanzee
brothers: They got out, they left the forest, they left their options
open, they moved into the dry, unfriendly world where they had to
readapt or perish. Like our ancestor. Like us. If we are, then, to
look to a primate example for light on our evolutionary past,

which should we pick? The almost miraculously similar chimpanzee (and his cousin the gorilla), who despite his closeness did not
follow our path of evolutionary adventure, or the humbler monkeys who did? It is a vexing question: Should we go for commonal-
ity of genes or for common experience? Both are important. Selection ultimately works on the genes—they are the raw material. But
selection works through perturbations of the environment over
time, and the ground-dwelling monkeys have shared our own evolutionary experience while the apes have not. The pressures that
acted on them acted on us also, so their adaptations could tell us a
lot about the history of our own, since, again, they have diverged
less widely from their ancestors than we have. In looking at them
now we are almost looking at their ancestral past laid out for us. So
should we not pay attention to them, rather than the timid chimp
who stayed home and lost out?

  Surely the answer is we must do both. If the closeness of relationship is there, we cannot ignore it. Our ancestor was even more
closely related all those millions of years ago. But neither can we
ignore the common experiences, which molded us as it molded the
monkeys. We are a kind of chimplike creature by genetic composition, but one which made the break onto the savanna, like the
monkeys. In a sense, then, we should perhaps take a chimplike ancestor and project his passage through space and time after the expulsion from Eden. But we must keep it in mind that our ancestor
was *not* a modern chimp—again, just a close relative. It matters
what came out of that forest—or perhaps more nearly what was
left stranded as the forest receded—and this is still shrouded in ar-
boreal gloom. But unlike Darwin and Freud, we know quite a bit
about what happened afterward, so we can make better conjectures. They are, of course, always conjectures, but so is any scientific hypothesis until it is proved or disproved. What matters is the
nature of the proof, and while agreeing with Freud that we "cannot aim at certainty" in this area, we can reduce the area of uncertainty, which isn't at all bad.

The Great Apes[2]

So, realizing that we are not necessarily drawing analogies from
the other primates but simply using them as clues to the primate
past and our own adaptations, let us proceed to the simian world.

We should bear in mind while en route the questions raised in the first chapter—the nature of the state of nature before culture, the mechanisms of incest avoidance in animals, etc. We have seen how central these were to Freud"s argument, and we must push on from that.

But should we start with the gorilla? In one of his more pointed criticisms, Kroeber said:

> First, the Darwin-Atkinson supposition is of course only hypothetical. It is a mere guess that the earliest organization of man resembled that of the gorilla rather than that of the trooping monkeys.[3]

Precisely the point we have been making above. What is more, the gorilla does not really provide the evidence Freud wanted from it. Derek Freeman[4] was the first to point out, basing his criticism on the work of Schaller, that the mountain gorilla is far from having a cyclopean family.[5] He stresses particularly that:

1. There is usually more than one adult male in a group.
2. While there are relations of dominance among the males, there seems to be little aggressiveness and competition.
3. The dominant male is not "jealous" and allows females to copulate with younger males (but this may be outside their period of ovulation—a point to be discussed later).
4. There is no evidence for young males being actively driven out, but they may leave and wander for a time and then join other bands.

The problem with the gorilla generally is that it seems to be a species bent on its own extinction anyway. Schaller witnessed only a few copulations during his whole stay, so the "jealousy" angle could scarcely be explored. The gorilla has capitalized on its size, but needs to spend all its time grinding up vegetable material with its massive teeth to support its huge bulk. It hides up in the mountain rain forest and chews its cud—the cow of the primate world. Whatever there is here cannot give us much of a clue to our ancestor—except for the baseline things: There are more females than males in the troop; there is a dominant male with subordinate followers; the young males do leave, and since they obviously do not all end up in other troops (or the sex ratios would be equal), then one can presume there is greater attrition here than among females. More recent evidence shows the older "silver-backed" males copulating more frequently than their "black-backed" juniors with the more mature females who have borne children.[6] Black-backed males start new bands by "kidnapping" young females—a process startlingly like that of the Hamadryas baboons to be discussed later. We have then the elements, but they are toned down in the gorilla. But if this is not the primal horde that Freud thought he would find, then neither is it the nuclear monogamous family that Westermarck looked for—to counter arguments about "primitive promiscuity."

The nuclear family *is* found among the gibbon. But the gibbon is an even bigger problem. If the gorilla took command of the forest floor, then the gibbon decided to monopolize the other extreme—the terminal branches. It fed on the small leaves, of which it required a large number to support its weight. The only organization, ecologists would argue, that it could "afford" to survive, would be a monogamous family guarding a large treetop territory—like many species of big birds. This is precisely what we get. The gibbon with its extra-long arms and permanently hooked fingers is perfectly adapted for these treetops—too perfectly, for he is stuck there like the gorilla is stuck with his bulk and the eternal food quest. The gibbon cannot afford to keep his young around, and at a year old they are dispersed and must set up their own territories. A classical case of dispersion, but not a primal horde.

What then of our great hope the chimpanzee? First reports on the chimp—those of Jane Goodall—tended to stress its fairly amiable characteristics—*My Friends the Wild Chimpanzees*—and rightly so.[7] The beautiful creature being introduced to the world by its charming hostess and the whole thing, with commentary by Orson Welles, was captivating beyond belief. It was also a stunning piece of zoological fieldwork, make no mistake about that. But in the process of following the antics of Flint and Flo, Leakey and David Greybeard, the Disneyesque aspects threatened to overpower the more sinister undertones. Jane reported one episode of hunting in which berserk chimpanzee males killed and ate a young baboon, but this was dismissed as aberrant by all those commentators who needed the chimp to prove that our ancestors were promiscuous, egalitarian, happy-go-lucky hippies with not a grain of Freudian malice in them. This suited the mood of the late sixties and early seventies. Unfortunately, the wealth of later fieldwork has given us a different picture that we must face, however offensive it may be to liberal or radical notions of the perfectible universe.

We find the chimps, living on the forest floor and occasionally moving out to the forest fringe and crossing open areas, arranged in seemingly loosely structured groups. The total group may be up to eighty animals, with more females than males again, but not substantially more. The core of the group can be viewed in either of two ways: as the stable female-based families, which have definite home ranges where they wander for food, or the roving all-male bands, which go much farther afield. Let us look in turn at these two wings of the chimpanzee social system. The female groups constitute large or small maternal families. Typically, there will be an old female (Flo is a good example) with her female offspring and even their female offspring, as well as her dependent male young and those of her daughters. The grown sons/brothers of the family leave it for periods to go off in all-male bands, but when they return they know their female relatives and greet them and stay around them. Older sisters will often "adopt" younger brothers if a mother dies—and certainly younger sisters. There tends to be virtually no mating in these groups—certainly not with the matriarch, and although the brothers may make advances, the sisters reject them. This is perhaps strange, because like all other primates, chimpanzee females come into heat once a month (not just in a breeding season either), their genital areas swell and turn bright red, and they actively solicit males. They may be mounted by a number of males at this point, but they resist their brothers. Some females also do a thing unique in the primate world (outside human society that is): They leave their own band and visit another to get pregnant, then return with the infant. Touching readmission ceremonies have been filmed in which the old, silver-haired males accept the begging advance of the returning female and gently touch her neck, after which she joins her female relatives again. At least a proportion of the females get pregnant elsewhere, then, and quite a few seem to change bands permanently. Meanwhile, the maternal families continue to play, sleep, move, and feed together.

What of the males? A young male stays quite a long time with his family—longer than in most monkeys—but at five or six, he tends to move away more and more and join the bigger males.

These have previously been quite indifferent and even hostile to him. Chimpanzee males don't seem to like their females and young very much—except their matrilineal relatives. They beat up their females in aggressive displays, and the mother has often to rescue an infant from the temper tantrum of an adult male. But the growing male will eventually be accepted, although probably at a low spot on the hierarchy. For despite early disclaimers, the chimpanzees have a pronounced dominance hierarchy, and upper-rank males will make no bones about asserting themselves over their juniors. Rank is volatile, however, and an enterprising chimp can rise through aggression, attacks, and displays to the point where the others defer to him, and he gets, for example, first choice of food, sleeping places, etc.

The all-male groups go off on sorties around the forest. They beat the bounds of their territory and repel rival bands, attacking, killing, and even eating defeated enemies. They look for good sources of food—mostly fruit—and when they find it, they drum on trees to attract the females who come to feed. They occasionally go on hunts, chasing young gazelles and small baboons. In this they cooperate, surrounding the animal in silence—most unusual for so noisy a fellow as the chimp. One animal usually makes the kill and takes the meat, but he will succumb to begging from the others and share with them. The males also visit female groups, where if they find a female in heat they may all mate with her, but not without some consideration of status: The old and established take precedence over the young. There seem to be even some individual preferences between males and females who often mate together on successive occasions. A higher-ranking male can sustain his personal choice, while a low ranker will often lose out to his senior. If a lone female from another troop comes on one of her mating visits, a kind of gang rape ensues, and she is often lucky to make it back alive. (It has been speculated that the monthly bright-red genital swellings of the female chimp might have evolved to "announce" that she is receptive, thus lessening the chance of an attack.)

Since it is the females who move about to mate (if they do) while the males stay put, the likelihood is that most of the males of any band will be related—and what is unusual in the simian world, through their fathers. Some will have been fathered in other bands, but the majority will be paternal kinsmen. This is a sharp contrast to the baboons and like animals that we shall soon be discussing.

To the reader seeing this for the first time, it will be intrinsically fascinating, but he must remember that it is the most recent word. This is important, because much has been made in the literature of the great differences between the society and behavior of the chimp and that of the baboon—our other favorite animal for comparative purposes.[8] Well, differences there undoubtedly are but not on the scale that these critics had supposed, and most can be attributed to the forest environment and lack of predators. The chimps do have a rather easygoing existence—less than the gorilla perhaps, but then they don't have the gorilla's problems. This, however, is the thing that we have seen renders them embarrassing, because our ancestors *didn't* have an easy time; they were expelled from Eden—or at least they left—and what they went out to was scarcely the Club Med of the tropical forest. What is remarkable, though, is that all the same elements persist. The chimps and baboons, for example, do not differ fundamentally, only in details of their organization and the intensity of various behaviors.

We shall summarize the elements of chimp society and then move quickly on, brief as we have had to be.

1. The fundamental division is between the (related) males of the all-male group and the females and their families.
2. The young males have gradually to work their way into the male hierarchy, which is organized on a dominance basis.
3. The females are organized in maternal families and the bonds endure over time (this may be less pronounced than we thought).
4. The all-male band is territorial, aggressive to other bands, hostile to females and young as a group, and indulges in occasional hunting and cannibalism.
5. Mating, while promiscuous, is governed by considerations of status, and there is evidence of some "consortship"—consistent mating between individual pairs.
6. Females in heat will often go to other bands to get impregnated; some females move permanently to other bands; maternally related males and females do not seem to mate.

Pause to consider the enigmatic orangutan—the original "wild man of the woods" from Southeast Asia. Again, until recently, not much has been known of this relatively large, probably quite intelligent, but seemingly solitary animal. Currently, the outlines of a social system are emerging.[9] As with the chimp, the females have home ranges, but they do not seem to collect in families. So, they are spread out evenly over the forest. Males, as they mature, try to take over areas of forest, thus gaining both food and females. Males compete for these areas and these privileges. Thus, the situation is somewhere between the gibbon and the chimp. The females disperse into territories, but a male does not stay with one female, nor do groups of males form. Male-male competition, however, may explain the relatively large size of the orang. One current theory is that chimps may have started this way themselves but then evolved the "male band," because groups of bonded males (probably related) could do better than single animals under certain conditions.[10]

This could be elaborated, but it will do for now. Let us keep it in mind when we come to look at the other primates. The differences are important, but it is important to nail down just what they are. Readers who have half an ear still cocked to Freud will have been wiggling it a lot during this discussion, as will those who are harking mentally back to the discussions in chapters one and two about mechanisms of outbreeding, avoidance, etc. We shall have to resist a gleeful rush into that debate again and be patient with a little more of the simian world for a while. But once again, we have to keep reminding ourselves that sympathetic as the chimp is to a lot that we want to examine in our past, he is a contemporary animal, and he does not necessarily represent an accurate image of our ancestor. Indeed, it may well have been that because our ancestor was very *different* from the chimp, he lost the forest to him. But we must try to winkle out those differences. Later.

The Munkies[11]

For now, let us make the move our ancestor made: out of the forest to the forest fringe and the tree savanna.[12] For our ancestor, it was the African savanna, and we should perhaps start there, but the trooping monkeys have taken the adaptations forged there into many different habitats, where they have readapted in ingenious ways. For the moment, let us stay with the prototype of the com-

mon baboon (yellow baboon, chacma baboon, olive baboon, cynocephalus baboon, etc.) and his little cousin the macaque, found
now distributed from Gibraltar and Morocco (the so-called Bar-
bary apes) to northernmost Japan—the amazing Japanese snow
monkey. Baboons you have seen in zoos—almost doglike in their
gait, but with those amazing front "legs" that have the very
adaptable hands; the macaque—mostly the rhesus—is well known
as "The Monkey" in most medical research. (Researchers are notoriously indifferent to such matters as species differences. Napier
invented a catchall species for them to take care of The Monkey
wherever it appears: *Pithecus incarceratus*.)

Despite local variations, what we find among most species is a
kind of social structure that has been described as the "concentric
circle" system. Common to them all, also, is that at the center of
this circle there will be a group of mature males—as few as one in
extreme circumstances and six or more in large groups—and
groups can range from nine to several hundred. This has led primatologists to introduce a taxonomy here, a type. They call this
the multi-male group, to distinguish it from its opposite, the one-
male group. It may seem excessively chauvinistic to make the criterion the number of males, but this does turn out to be decisive for
many reasons. However many males there are, there are always
more females in proportion. The ratio is roughly, on average, four
to one, and this raises its own problems. Where are the other
males? The answer is: on the peripheries of the group, in an all-
male band, moving between groups, or out on their own—god
knows where. And in the intermediate circle? The females in their
families with their dependent young.[13]

We can already see the same elements emerging here as in the
chimp multi-male structure, but arranged somewhat differently—
more rigidly, with more clear-cut definition. The chimps do not
have the definite peripheral-male phenomenon, but a young male
has to make his way into the hierarchy. And when chimps move
out into the open savanna themselves, they tend to form up like
baboons with the big males in the center, the females and young
around them, and the young males at the extremes.[14] And that
may be the clue. Once you are out on the savanna, things are different. You lack the protection of the trees—on the one hand, to
shield you from predators, and on the other to disperse and infor-
malize mating behavior. After all, even the most dominant and

jealous chimp can't see what's going on behind the trees, while out in the savanna everyone can see everything. The baboons have tightened up. Their dominance hierarchy is harsher (although when they visit the forest it becomes noticeably more lax); their consort behavior has become formalized, with one male taking a female in heat to the edge of the troop and staying with her through her period of estrus (although afterward and before he may let the young males have a go); the expulsion of the young males has become more organized—they go literally to the fringes of the society once they show signs of sexual maturity, where they form the analogue of the chimps' all-male group in which they stay for a while. But unlike the chimp group, this is a group of outcasts, not a group of dominants. These youngsters must either get back into the center of their own troop or leave it and try their luck elsewhere. The baboon dominant males don't rove about; they stay put with the females, juveniles, and infants. But they do perform some of the same functions as the chimp dominants: They police the group, they protect it from predators, they determine its movement in search of food, they display against rival troops, and they, too, occasionally hunt small animals and eat a little meat. Like the chimp males, they do not share this with the females and young. Primate societies are all alike in this: Once weaned, the animals get their own food.

In stark contrast with the chimps, however, it is not the females of these troops who move off to mate. They never seem to leave; they are born, mate, give birth, and die all in the same group. The males, on the other hand, are restless and often move off, even if they have achieved dominance status. Sometimes, they spend time as solitaries; sometimes, they quickly find another troop where their novelty value or the fact that they have male kin there (often the case) gets them in. This whole business of males changing troops is more evident in some species and circumstances than others. The forest-dwelling macaques of Japan, for example, show it markedly, as do forest-using baboons. Open-country animals, on the other hand, show it less. This again may be due to predation, and we should bear it in mind. But, nevertheless, a considerable number of males must breed in troops other than their own if they breed at all. This is the reverse of the chimp situation, but it has the same effect, as Darwin saw clearly for the gorilla, of reducing the possibilities of inbreeding. Also, the attrition rate among the peripheral males must be quite high. Such figures as we have run as high as 80 percent.[15] During the breeding season—among those species that have a definite season, and this varies—the older males will savagely attack the younger who die of tetanus from infected wounds, or of malnutrition from being too anxiety-ridden to eat, or from sheer stress, or from predators who can pick them off more easily in their disheveled state. This is one of the reasons that there are more females than males, plus the fact that the females mature more quickly.

At the center, then, are the big dominant males—themselves arranged in a hierarchy—and the female families. The males maintain their dominance relationships by threat and ritualization rather than too much overt fighting, but they have, of course, established who can lick whom anyway. A show of red gums and canines and an erection of body hair serves to remind the subordinate animal of its place. This hierarchical relationship can endure even after the top male has become toothless and lame, such is the habit of deference. But the top-ranking males do better if they can cooperate as well as bully. Coalitions of lower-ranking animals can overthrow a tyrant, and a straight aggressor will not last, since the female groups will not accept him. There is more to dominance than just size and strength and age, although these are important. Much hangs on this point.

The female families—as I have been loosely calling them—are much more clear cut than their chimp counterparts. The baboons and macaques have a matriarchate with an old grandmother and her female offspring and their dependent young. The young males leave earlier than the chimp juveniles but with this important proviso: A high-ranking female and her lineage can keep a young male around longer than those of lower rank. The mechanics of this are not clear, but it seems that the high-status female gets deferred to, and this rubs off on her sons, who also are deferred to by the lower-ranking animals of either sex. (It is interesting that the deference is shown in all these species by the subordinate animal turning and "presenting" its rump to the superior. The superior mounts briefly and then gets off. The presenting is very effective in turning off an aggressive attack. It says, in effect, "Don't attack me, mate with me.") These favored sons, then, may never need to go to the peripheries, and even if they do, their way back is smoothed, because the big males know them and have already learned to tol-

erate and accept them at the center—a privilege their lower-rank
cousins have never enjoyed. The best way to get to the top, as
someone said of the Kennedys, is to start there.

This points up the importance of the other hierarchy in these
groups, that between the female lineages. In early work, this was
missed and some wrong deductions made in consequence. It was
thought that a female's status rose and fell with that of the male
she consorted with. If she was favored by a top male then she
would temporarily rise in status, falling again after the period of
consortship—the four or five days at the peak of the menstrual
cycle—was over. Something of this kind may happen, since a low-
status female will be under the protection of a top male for a while
and will share in the deference due to him. But what was not properly understood was that any female had a status that was independent of the one she derived from the consorting male: She had
a status derived from her place in her own female lineage. What
is more, at least initially, so did the young males. That is why
they could be kept around the center of the troop if the status of
their lineage was high enough. The other ear—the one cocked
for Atkinson's hypothesis—should be wiggling like mad at this
point.

How do these "lineages," as we are boldly calling them, function? Here are some of the things primatologists have found out
about relationships between the members of such a group—and remember its "matrilineal" structure. The membership persists at
least during the lifetime of the old matriarch and may stretch to
four generations—it may persist after that but only long-term observation will tell. The studies of the Japanese macaques, which
have been in progress since the late forties, suggest this longer persistence. Many females whose relationship we do not know but
who associate closely with each other may well be maternal cousins. And this is the first point noted: that members of these lineages
simply stay closer to each other than to members of other lineages.
While close, they feed together more than with others, groom each
other more, play together more, touch each other more, and sleep
together more—and this is much more, not a small difference.
Very importantly, acts of aggression are much lower among lineage members than in the group at large. Even when groups are
experimentally crowded—a sure way to produce aggression—the
general rate of nastiness rises, but that among lineage members

stays steady or rises only slightly. Lineage members combine to
defend each other or attack other lineages.[16]

The most important thing, however, is that these lineages are
themselves ranked. We used to think that rank was an individual
thing, but it turns out to be heavily dependent on lineage—lifelong
for females and initially for males. Study after study has shown
this. It is not simply that one individual of lineage A ranks higher
than one of lineage B, but that all of lineage A ranks higher than B,
and hence, the individual will rank higher. A male initially, then,
takes his status from his mother. If she is from a top lineage, he is
deferred to by members of lower lineages. He is even, as we have
seen, tolerated by the high-ranking males, who usually have little
time for pushy juveniles. This tolerance begins to lessen as he
passes puberty and begins his bid for the hierarchy—but by that
time he is halfway there. Ultimately, size and strength and all the
other factors will count in deciding whether or not he holds his position, but the initial shove comes from his family connections. It is
all too depressingly familiar a picture and the bane of egalitarian
dreamers.

One other thing. Uncannily, we find that among the things
members of a lineage do *not* do with each other with a very high
frequency is copulate.[17] Different observers have found different
rates, but none are very high, and the mother seems to be more or
less verboten. Young males, when they begin to try out their
breeding skills, may mount their mothers, but they do not set up
consort relations with them or go through the process of courtship.
It is like a brief trial run. The net effect is certainly virtually no offspring between mothers and sons. Brothers and sisters do not rate
much higher, it seems, but once a male becomes dominant, he may
mate with his sisters. On the other hand, the majority of males
seem to move between groups so he may not. Since he doesn't
know who his daughters are, it is up for grabs how many he mates
with. There must be some, but again movement may cut down this
rate. But his daughters are not members of his lineage anyway—
ears awiggle for Freud again.

It is tempting to stop immediately and discuss all the obvious
implications of this astounding, complex primate social system.
But we have to look a little further, since this one can only be
judged when compared with its counterpart the one-male group
system. We have been stressing that we should treat the baboon-

macaque system with respect, since it represents an adaptation to the savanna where our ancestor moved in that crucial stage of his evolutionary trajectory. But he moved further, for as the forests receded and the climate became drier still, he moved into the even more inhospitable sparse grasslands and even the desert fringes. The common baboons and macaques themselves did not do this— they stuck to the forest edge as closely as they could and were always near some trees or other where, like the chimps, they slept at night for safety. But the animals that move into the arid savanna have to cope with more severe problems. What kind of social organization, then, do we find among the baboons and others who inhabit the open, dry savanna and even the Ethiopian desert? At first glance, it is very different.[18]

Why a one-male group at all? At least one reason seems to be ecological. One male can impregnate several females—there is no need of more; what is more, more males mean more mouths to fill. Big males take a lot of food. At the extremes of their ranges, for example, where the environment is not so lush, macaques have been found in groups containing only one big male. It is as though the other males have had to be "shed" to provide more resources for the mothers and young. The multi-male system is then a kind of luxury that can be afforded when the environment permits it. It is also a good defense against predators: Several big baboons are a match for any leopard or lion. There is a trade off here, obviously: One must sacrifice something, and under harsh conditions one cuts down on the number of males. At least that is the theory. It doesn't quite hold up, since some forest-dwelling animals have one-male organization too—but the same organization can arise in two different environments for different reasons, so the dry-environment theory is not necessarily wrong.[19] Before we explore this further, let us look at the structure of the one-male group systems.

I put it in the plural because there are more than one. In a sense, the monogamous gibbon is a one-male groupie, and the "nuclear family" may simply be a limiting case of the one-male group, where ecology demands the shedding of females also. But let us look at the desert and dry savanna "baboons." (Some of them are not baboons—like the patas monkey and the gelada, but as one wag has put it, "baboon" is not so much a species, more a way of life.) The prototype here is the hamadryas baboon—the sacred baboon of Egypt, with his doglike muzzle and, in the male, his lion-like mane. Along with the gelada, he inhabits the harsh, arid grasslands of East Africa, extending into the deserts and mountains of Ethiopia. The troop organization is very different at first glance from that of the common baboon, since the constituent units are not maternal families or a male hierarchy: The constituent units are polygamous families—one male and several females (average about four) with their young. The sex ratio of baboons, we saw, was about four to one, and it is as if the males had parceled the females out among them rather than leaving them in a "pool" of potential consorts. The consorts of the desert baboon are permanent. The overlord "herds" them, keeps them close to him, and if they stray too far or show interest in other males, he chases them and bites them in the neck. This specialized neck bite is calculated to hurt a bit, but in common with many such ritualized gestures in animals, its ferocity is mitigated by being directed to a well-padded part of the anatomy. It is more of a nip. But it is enough to keep the errant mate in line. Several of such families make up a troop, which is, however, a much more loosely organized entity than the concentric circle system. It moves about together and finds the same cliff areas for sleeping (there are no trees), but the males do not associate much with each other. Each is too busy keeping his harem together, and they are definitely suspicious of one another. There is no hierarchy among them—how could there be?—and they tend to space out from each other and keep their distance. There seems to be a sort of compromise going on here. It is as though the one-male harem system evolved, perhaps for the reasons we have explored, but that pressures of predation in particular pushed the groups together for defense, even if they didn't want to be. Their worst enemies seem to be village dogs—and there is evidence that hunting-dog ancestors came into Africa at a relatively late stage in evolution for the baboons, perhaps forcing them to form herds and incidentally providing unwelcome competition for our own ancestors.[20]

(Among the hamadryas, some observers have noted what they choose to call clans. It seems that there are subgroups of the herd, which are probably related males who have been successful in gathering harems. They tend to stay closer to each other than to unrelated males and to come to each other's defense, etc. The details are not clear, but this may be an attenuated form of the male group as found among the chimps, much modified because of the herding/harem pattern forced on them by the desert ecology.)

Whatever the reason, the large herd is common to the hamadryas and the gelada. It tends to hug the edges of cliffs, where the females and young can hide if attacked, while the big males rush out to fend off the dogs. But between this cliff-edge group of males and females lies the buffer zone occupied by—but you have already guessed—the peripheral males in their all-male group. Like their cousins on the woodland savannas, these unfortunates are the early-warning system of the troop defense. When predators approach, they set up a howl, which alerts the senior males. Sometimes, these males rush out to do their bit, but sometimes, also, they take off with the females, and this leaves the peripherals open to attack. It must be at least one of the reasons why there is a considerable attrition of the young males. With the desert baboons the same thing happens. These are the young males who, reaching puberty, or even before, leave their mothers, sisters, and cousins to go to the periphery. There seems to be no rank or privilege here—they all go. The question is, how do they get back to the safety and power at the center? How do they get harems of their own? For a while, we were in the dark about this, but we know now that they have two methods.

The first is to "apprentice" themselves to an established male with a harem. They follow discreetly and ingratiate themselves, not challenging, but helping to herd, ward off other males, etc. After a while, the older male tolerates them. Once he becomes too old and feeble to herd anymore, they take over. The apprentice takes over the mating entirely, but allows the old man to look after his own offspring already born. The literature doesn't show it, but one wonders if the apprentices too are favorite sons of some kind? The other method of getting one's own harem is the kidnap method, which we have already encountered among the gorilla. This is truly strange. A peripheral male will kidnap an immature female from a harem and "mother" her. He rides her on his back, nurses her, cradles her, grooms her, and generally looks after her until she is mature when he starts to mate with her and turn on the neck-bite treatment. If he is successful, he will attract other females in the same way and build up a harem. Other young males simply try to challenge their elders, almost always unsuccessfully unless the elder is senile, or to make daring forays into the herd to try stray copulations with an errant wife. These animals—like many desert dwellers—have a pronounced breeding season, so the frustration must be pretty acute. But this very fact gives the lie to the theory that it is sex that holds primate groups together. For most of the year there is none, but the harem stays intact. Meanwhile, the peripheral all-male group has to be satisfied with playing dominance games among itself, and some homoerotic behavior.

This herding of females under the exclusive possession of one male is found in many mammals of course, particularly ungulates and sea mammals. But there is a crucial difference. With the other mammals, the harem is a seasonal affair. The baboons cannot afford that. They must stay together all year, for in those dangerous circumstances, the females and young cannot wander about alone for ten months.

In the case of the little patas monkey, also a dry savanna dweller, we get the classic one-male group, which is not aggregated into larger herds. The harem owner expels the maturing males, who have to fend for themselves and try to find stray females to make up a harem. The attrition rate must be particularly high here. The overlord, however, is more of a gentle watchdog with his harem than his baboon counterpart. His primary display—and in this he resembles some ground-dwelling birds—is to offer himself as a decoy to a predator by pretending to be lame, thus allowing his harem to escape.

Another interesting variant of the one-male system is found among Indian langurs.[21] Here, the one-male groups are attacked by peripheral males, and the established males are driven off or killed. The attacking males then often fight among themselves until one is left in charge. In the process (or after it), the children of the group females are killed. The new master then proceeds to mate immediately with his new conquests, who seem to be provoked into coming into heat by the whole gory business. This may only happen in extreme cases when population density is high,[22] but that it happens at all is remarkable and as near as we are going to get in the primate world to the bloodier version of the primal horde. The primates run the gamut from blood and mayhem in the breeding process to gentle exclusion and even male-male cooperation.

The Baseline

On the surface of it, then, these systems appear different, and indeed the differences count.[23] But can we formulate for all types a set of propositions that will outline the basic commonalities? Let us try the following:

1. There is a fundamental division between the males of the hierarchy and the males of the periphery.
2. There are groups of females who are variously under the control of the hierarchical males (but who are also pursuing their own strategies of reproduction).
3. The peripheral males have to work their way back into the center by one means or another; many fail.
4. The big males are responsible for the defense of the group and for its movement patterns.

There are others, but we are concerned here with the structural features. What is common is the division into three groups: the established males; the females with young; the peripheral males. What is different is the way the periphery is related to the center and hence the way in which the young males can get back in.[24] In the multi-male system, family influence counts for a lot, because the subgroups are maternal families, which are themselves ranked. In the one-male system this does not work, since the subgroups are the polygamous (strictly speaking, polygynous) families. These do not endure over time in quite the same way as the female lineages of the multi-male system. They last only as long as the overlord lasts, and they may well consist of unrelated females anyway. I have not seen this reported, but if an apprentice takes over a harem, it may be that he keeps the females intact and inherits daughters as well as mothers, thus preserving something of a lineage. But even so, this is clearly a more chancy affair than with the multi-male system, where the female-based lineages can even be seen as the enduring core of the troop, or with the chimpanzees and their almost patrilineal male groups. We can refer back to the ungulates. What the stags, for example, compete for during rut are these female lineages to which they attach themselves if successful. With the multi-male primates, it is as if the ungulate system had evolved to the point where the females decided to keep several

males permanently around rather than having them there only
seasonally. The same is not quite true in the one-male system,
where the females are more subject to male whim and are not
groups of related animals anyway most of the time.

Each system has something that the other does not. The
multi-male system has the enduring kinship groups, while the one-
male system has the permanent polygamous families. If you like,
one has kinship, but no marriage; the other has marriage but no
kinship. This is just an analogy, but it may be an important one.
(Of course, neither has either in a human sense, but there is the
basis there.) And what intrigues me is this: Both these things—enduring ties based on relatedness and enduring mating relationships—exist in primates, but *not together in the same system.* Only in
the human primate have they been put together. We invented neither, and they were there in our primate repertoire. But our combination is unique, particularly when one considers that the basis of
exogamy is the use of kinship to define the boundaries of marriage:
One defines certain kin as unmarriageable. The monkeys already
seem to define certain kin as unmatable, so they are on the way
there too.

This point is going to become crucial in what follows. Remember that we decided the real question was probably that of the
origins of exogamy rather than of the incest taboo? We haven't
forgotten incest and it figures in here somewhere, but we have seen
that the primates have quite effective mechanisms for avoiding too
much inbreeding already. What they do not have is the exchange
of mates implied in exogamy. But we shall come back to that in
due course after noting one more feature of the social structure of
multi-male groups. This concerns group fission.[25] When the groups
get too large—how large this is depends on circumstances—they
split up. How this happens, at least with the Japanese macaques, is
interesting. We have an excellent account of this from Japan.
There were sixteen lineages in the troop, ranked one through sixteen. When the group split, lineages one through seven remained,
while eight through sixteen left to form another group. Let us call
them A and B. The males began moving around, and after two
years, all the males of A had moved to B and all those of B to A.
This may or may not be unusual—similar movement has been recorded among African baboons in the shelter of the forest edge,
but it is remarkable. For what we have here is only a step away

from a human kinship system consisting of two matrilineal moieties with ranked matrilineages and a rule of moiety exogamy. The step is, of course, precisely the exogamy. Before they moved, the males of A mated with the females of A. We would have to institute a rule forbidding this to get exogamy. But would we have to have a taboo on sex altogether with females of A? Not necessarily. Exogamy concerns marriage, not sex. Even if we had, in our human circumstance, no ban on sex with women of A, we would likely have one on sex with women of a man's own lineage. But again, as has been demonstrated, the monkeys have an avoidance pattern here also—so a ban on such sex could simply be an expression of something that was already there in the primate pattern. We are jumping ahead. But the pieces are beginning to fall into place.

Even the Freudian pieces are starting to look more like a complete picture. Consider our three basic examples here: the gorillas, orangs and chimps; the common baboons and macaques; the dry country baboons and geladas. Whatever the differences, they have this one thing in common: The established males try to monopolize the females, and the young and unsuccessful males are excluded. The attrition rate among the latter is high, and they have to work their way back into the center by a series of means differing according to the species. There is not a single horde father here (except with the patas and some extreme groups) but there are the horde *fathers:* the established, dominant, hierarchical, senior, or whatever you wish to call them, males. They stand implacably opposed to the young when it comes to their mating privileges, and there is the rub. They are, true to Freud's model, keeping the young from the females for mating purposes. Even when they let them in, it is to mate with the females when it doesn't matter. This is the crux: The females come into heat at the peak of their estrous cycle. They begin, in the chimpanzees, to swell and redden around the genital area, they give off pungent odors, and they solicit males by presenting. At this point, the consortship of the male begins (in the common baboons and macaques), and the big male takes over the female for precisely the *period of time that she is ovulating.* Thus only he gets to impregnate her, however many times she may be mounted outside this period by juniors. This is the payoff then. This is what dominance, getting back into the hierarchy, forming a harem, and all that are in aid of: breeding. It is a breeding privilege—those genes and only those that are crucially passed on at peak of estrus will be represented in the next generation. The chimps have a toned-down version of this, but the elements are there. More dominant animals fare better in the mating game. The one-male groupers have made it permanent and keep their mates around all the time.

The evolutionary significance of this has not been lost. It is a marvelous sexual selection system. The females keep themselves intact, as it were, while the males waste themselves on competition. Those that make it get the privilege of breeding, and the females thus procure the best genes for themselves ("best" in terms of survival and reproductive success, not in terms of any abstract values). If, as in the multi-male system, the females can boost the chances of their own male candidates, then they win both ways, since they ensure that their male relative gets to breed and thus that the genes he shares with them are perpetuated. They don't know this, of course, but they don't have to. If it works, selection will declare them winners and the pattern will persist anyway.[26]

We are still quite a way from incest and exogamy and human kinship systems. But not nearly as far as the orthodoxy would have us believe. This state of nature is certainly different from the unordered, incestuous chaos of Lévi-Strauss. If we are going to ask what tipped the balance over onto a truly human state of affairs, then we have to start from here, from what Linton[27] called the "raw materials of society" and what we have dubbed the "primate baseline." And it is a very rich and dense baseline containing many of the elements of human kinship systems and systems of mating— but not in human combinations, and lacking human motivations.

So what of Freud? We have seen that the primal horde exists in various forms among our cousins and so presumably did among our ancestors. Quite *which* form we must explore later, but common to all of them is the primal situation in which the "fathers" stand between the "women" and the sex and power that goes with possession of them. Or rather, with the breeding and power: One may get a little sex, but to no avail unless one *controls* the situation. Being a dominant means more than just sex: It means space, food, grooming, deference, life. But these are all means to nature's end, which is to get the successful genes into the next generation. The old males, then, try to control the breeding situation and exclude the young. This, with all its hostilities, subterfuges, maternal interferences, and the like, is the baseline for the primate male. What was the event that transformed it into an exogamous, kinship based, rule ordered, language speaking, ritualized human society? We have seen that the structure is basically Freudian, but what of the dynamics—killing or fantasy—that produced the human structure? What of guilt and conscience, what of initiation, what of incest taboos? With the help of our cousins once more, we shall take up the scent by plugging all this into the course of evolution.

FIVE

Sex in the Head

It isn't the names of things that bother me; nor even ideas about them.
I don't keep my passions, or reactions, or even sensations IN MY
HEAD. They stay down where they belong.

D. H. Lawrence

What we call impulses of the heart, is but the unreasonable jostling of
our thoughts; it is still in the head that the drama is enacted, and it is
again the brain that man needs in order to love.

André Gide

To use our knowledge of our primate cousins in order to interpret
our own past we need two things: as much information on this past
as archaeology can give us and a theory to help us make the link. A
great many things were happening in concert during the course of
human evolution: improving bipedalism, prolonged infant dependency, hunting and gathering, language and symbols, social complexity. But the coordination of these was dependent on the evolution of the brain, on the development in particular of those large
frontal lobes—the neocortex—which are chiefly responsible for the
unique human abilities that mark us off as a species. We specialized in the brain rather than in speed, size, strength, coloration, or
any other physical capabilities (except perhaps the striding walk,
which is our very own form of locomotion—a not unconnected development).[1]

In doing this, we were capitalizing on the already well-devel-
oped brain of the primates, our ancestors. And this, in turn, was

forged during our time in the trees. The tremendous emphasis on both binocular vision and the grasping hand and the subsequent downplaying of, for example, the smell centers had already led to an enlargement of the frontal lobes on which selection could then build. Nature has no purposes. The enlarged frontal lobes evolved to help us stay in the trees not to help us develop into men. But once evolved, they had the human potential.

It is often this way in evolution. It has been dubbed "preadaptation."[2] Something that originally arose to help an animal adapt to one environment becomes the basis of adaptation to a completely new one—by accident. Our ancestor took those frontal lobes out onto the savanna where they could serve different purposes than they had in the forest. But then so did the ancestral baboons, etc., and up to a point, the purposes were the same. The point where they become different is crucial, of course, and it must be related to systematic hunting, since that is the crucial difference. But that is to leap ahead again. For the moment, let us look at a theory that will suggest how we might make a link between archaeological evidence of our evolution and the primate breeding system we have just examined. And it is a theory about the evolution of the brain.

Look back to the breeding system again. What we have described is a system of sexual selection in which the "best" genes get sorted out for transmission to the next generation.[3] This, of course, happens in all systems where the males compete with each other and only some succeed. But in the primate systems, we have the startling feature of the year-round relationship between the males and the females. The males do not just go away after breeding, they stay around. In consequence, therefore, a different kind of male "best genes" must be the object of selection, if only because the males have an unprecedented task: dealing with the females and other males on a permanent basis. A great many qualities other than just size, strength, and fighting ability are called for. And this goes for the female too. She cannot just use the male for mating purposes and then retire into the female club for most of the year. She, too, must come to terms with the permanent residence of the males. A generally more complex social system is called into play, and there is a lot more to take account of, to learn, than in those sexually selective systems where the only association is during the mating season. (The same holds true for the social carnivores—wolves, hunting dogs, etc.—and thereby may hang another tale.)

The objectives of the females are similar: to get themselves impregnated by the "best" males and to try to rear the maximum number of offspring to maturity. But the female's tactics have to be different, especially in the multi-male group system. She has to take account of the dominance order among the males and work that against the dominance order among the female lineages. We know that high-ranking females tend to mate more with high-ranking males[4] and, also, that they have greater reproductive success—more of their children live to breed than with lower-ranking females.[5] Also, as we saw, their sons will be more likely in their turn to become high ranking and so continue the process. The high-ranking female is also surrounded by her female relatives who are similarly successful and from whom she receives support and whom she supports in turn. Seen in terms of the "success of the genes" of the top female lineage, we can see how these females (a) attract the best genes, (b) send out the best genes (male) to repeat the success, and (c) have more female offspring to go on attracting good genes, and so on. Success breeds success, literally.

The male also has a lot to take account of. He needs to get himself into the breeding hierarchy and, once in, to try to get an advantageous breeding position, if he is going to get a chance at the best female genes—those represented by the females of the high-ranking lineages. His position is more precarious and his chances chancier. Females only have to stick around and come into estrus to get impregnated by *some* male. But to get to breed at all, the young male has to tread a delicate and difficult path, and he may never make it. Even if he does, he may be so low ranking for so long that he doesn't score highly in the genetic competition. Selection is thus more fierce for the male qualities, as is usually the case in nature, but the successful genes that spread in the population at the expense of the less successful will be a combination of the genetic qualities of the successful males and the higher-ranking females. For while the females are not so severely selected as the males, they do have considerable differential reproductive success, and the coalitions of female relatives can ensure, by the mechanisms we have discussed, that their "pool" of related genes gets a better chance of being reproduced than that of less fortunate rivals.

Equilibration, Breeding, and the Brain

But what are these qualities that we are discussing? The first person to propose this theory in detail was Michael Chance, a born-again pharmacologist who, after twenty years of studying the effects of drugs on the "normal" behavior of animals, realized that no pharmacologist knew what the normal behavior was and so started observing monkeys.[6] Chance concentrated on the males, since at that time most was known about them. The ranking of female lineages, for example, was not well understood, and in any case, as in all these systems, the burden of selection seems to be on the males. After all, every fecund female gets to reproduce, and if one does not know about the differential success of the lineages, then it appears that every female has as good a chance as any other of contributing to the gene pool. We can fill out the picture now with the female contribution, but let us take this last and look at what Chance proposed for the males, then bring it up to date.

What the males had to do to be successful in such a system, said Chance, was to "equilibrate." Equilibration was literally the balancing of alternatives. The animal is driven by certain emotions—literally the things that move it, such as fear, hunger, sex, aggression, etc. Many basic instincts are more complex than these, but they have in common, in most of the lower animals, that the creature simply acts them out when prompted by them. This does not mean that it does not monitor the environment and adapt to it in many ways, but its capacity for this is limited the more we go down the phyletic scale. Roughly speaking, the larger the brain of the creature, and particularly the frontal lobes, the more it is able to monitor the environment—including other animals—and act in accordance with decisions rather than just emotions. It is all a matter of degree, but there is no question that the larger-brained mammals, and in particular the higher primates, have this capacity to a larger degree than lower animals. (Strictly speaking, one must take the ratio of brain weight to body weight to compare. An elephant has a larger brain than man, but in relation to the body, the brain is quite small.)

The larger brain gives more ability to equilibrate, but what Chance proposes is a causal relationship: The more the species has had to equilibrate, the greater will have been the selection pressures favoring the larger brain. This is the essence of the theory, and we must spell it out a little more. What equilibration consists of is the growing ability to time responses: to make the response more appropriate to the external conditions. This may mean, for example, and typically does, that the animal has to delay a response that it might be moved to make. It might have to inhibit the impulse to feed, fight, or copulate in the light of information it has perceived about the situation—particularly the information that if it does indulge its impulse it is likely to get beaten up or killed or otherwise prevented from achieving its goals there and then. What Chance is saying is that the more complex and crucial the information the animal has to deal with—that is, the more complex and dangerous the social situation it finds itself in—the more it will have to develop the capacity to equilibrate in order to survive. And the capacity to equilibrate lies in the complex relationship between the newer and older parts of the brain—between the limbic system, which is the source of emotions and which we share with all mammals, and the new parts of the cortex, which are so greatly expanded in the primates.[7] Mediating these is an area known as the amygdala, which is concerned with the control of emotion and has connections with the cortex, and the hippocampus, which itself controls memory.

We don't have to go deeply into brain anatomy. All we have to see is that equilibration demands the growth of these controlling and inhibiting areas, so that the impulses from the brain stem and the limbic system do not just erupt into behavior but (a) become subject to information from the environment in the form of (b) control and inhibition, which enable the animal to delay and time the emotional responses. This requires an improvement of what Eugene Marais called the "causal memory" over the "phyletic memory."[8] The latter is the store of "species memories"—essential responses that are deep in the species' survival repertoire: sex, flight, self-defense, fear, rage, territory, predation, or whatever. The causal memory, on the other hand, is the memory of contemporary and recent events that affect the creature's survival. These enter the new cortex and are transmitted to the hippocampus, where they touch base with the older memories inherited from the species' past. By the intervention of the amygdala, the newer memories control the older, and the animal acts in accordance with the mixture of basic emotions and newer experience.[9]

This is as technical as we dare get. An example of the kind Chance uses will help. The young male monkey is moved by several desires: He wants food, he wants to get into the mating game, he is roused to aggression fairly easily. He could simply act these out. He could stalk about in the group and take what food he wanted when he wanted, he could try to copulate with whatever female was in heat, and he could fly into rages and attack the other males who tried to interfere. Anyone who has spent any time with any group of monkeys or apes knows the end result of such a strategy. It is one very unhappy young monkey at best and one dead or expelled young monkey at worst. The older male or males will simply not tolerate him, and he will be attacked and beaten up. The females will reject him, since they are not interested in a potential loser, nor does he fit their notions of a bundle of good genes. His obviously antisocial behavior in such intensely social species will bring him nothing but disaster. Sheer strength and aggression will get him so far, but it has often been observed that the male that is individually the most dominant in this sense rarely ends up as top male in the end. He is more likely to end up as a solitary, unable to make a place for himself in the social/breeding system, thus defeating his own ends.

What is the opposite of this? In a nutshell, it is the more intelligent monkey (ape). Or if we do not want to go that far, the more controlled will do. It is the monkey who is able to assess the situation and to learn by experience what he can do effectively and what he had better leave until later. He has a well-enough developed causal memory to know that some things will not pay off, and enough foresight to see that by delaying immediate gratification he may get a payoff in the future. Clearly, the better the neocortex/hippocampus/amygdala connections are working, the better able he will be to do this. But conversely, selection will favor those monkeys having any genetic mutations that tend to increase the size and efficiency of newer organs at the expense of the emotional parts of the old brain. The development of the frontal lobes in the trees gave natural selection something to work on: a head start. Increasing social complexity gave this a push by demanding more and more by way of equilibration—of memory, control, and inhibition—from its creatures and by selecting out those that showed such improvements. The method was twofold: Sheer natural selection in the face of environmental pressures would favor those animals that performed better generally, and since the group-living primates needed each other in the struggle for survival, sexual selection would prefer those males in particular that showed greater powers to equilibrate, since they would have a greater than average reproductive success. Not only would they be more likely to survive against the "hostile forces of nature," as Darwin phrased it, but they would also reproduce more than their fellows who survived, since they would do better in the breeding system.

In all this, as we have said, the females are not inert partners. In Chance's original model they were, and it has been argued that this does not much matter, since any genetic improvements in the male brain would be passed on to female offspring anyway. But it is obvious that females, if they are to get into a favorable position in the breeding system themselves, have their own equilibrating to do, although it is not so spectacular as the male's. But the female, too, was working toward a growing control of cortical over hormonal behavior.[10] She was still subject to the estrous cycle, and she could not avoid coming into heat, but she could influence selection through her behavior toward her female relatives, on the one hand, and her selectivity toward males, on the other. For we know that an important part of the dominant male's dominance lies in his acceptability to the females. And above all, the female can influence the selective process by the start in life she gives her sons. This will differ in degree, according to the kind of system, with females in the one-male group system seeming to have less say in what happens in the selective process than their cousins in the multi-male groups. But even here the last word is not yet in. It does seem, however, that the one-male groupers are off on a more divergent path of evolution. The difference in size between males and females, for example, is huge, and their breeding is vigorously seasonal. This is off the trajectory that led to man where sexual dimorphism is not so large (although it is there), where seasonal breeding is lacking, and where females are certainly less overtly under cycling hormonal control than their primate relatives.

We have to go back repeatedly to our point that we cannot necessarily pin our ancestors down to any *one* form of breeding system in detail. All we need to know is that whatever the details—

and they may have differed from group to group, population to population—there were the three subunits of the group: the successful males, the females with young, and the excluded males. As long as the latter had to make their way back into the hierarchy with all the selective consequences we have discussed, then the stage is set for the growing importance of equilibration and, hence, for the evolution of the brain to the point where we know it now: capable of language, rules, deferred gratification, conscience, guilt, and imagination, and foresight on a scale not envisaged by the struggling ancestral primate whose only aim was to stay in the system or see his genes lose out.

This caveat is necessary, because a large body of work in primatology has been devoted to showing that dominance is not important in some groups that lack firm hierarchies, and that even where they exist, the male hierarchies do not always have a linear fit with breeding success. Opinion seems about equally divided, and the contrasting positions are detailed in the notes to this chapter.[11] But the whole debate is really beside the point as far as our hypothesis here is concerned. Of course, primate groups differ a lot in how serious the dominance hierarchy is to the group and how much it does or does not correlate with breeding success. While it is my opinion that the lack of correlation has been exaggerated, it is not unthinkable that there may be groups in which lower-ranking males do better than higher ranking for various reasons. But—and this is the point—*to do anything at all about breeding they have to get into the hierarchy in the first place.* Many of the groups studied by primatologists are in enclosures, or are provisioned, or in some way in unnatural conditions. In the wild, there is no question of the importance of the hierarchy and of the strong imbalance in the sex ratio. This will, again, vary, but it is always there. As long as we keep at the forefront of our minds the fact that a goodly proportion of the young males will not make it at all into the breeding system, then the point is made. If there is differential success among those that do, then this fits the theory. The most dominant male in terms of who can beat whom among the males need not be the best equilibrator, and so not necessarily the best breeder. By definition, in the system we are talking about, the best breeder *is* the top male, even if, in the pecking order, he ranks lower than some other bully boys. The whole thing is, if anything, more clear-cut in the one-male group system. There, it is obvious that some males get harems and

others don't. It is a kind of all or none affair rather than the more
or less of the multi-male type. But in each case, some will make it
and some not, and that is what counts for the purposes of equilibration.

It has this corollary, however. The more relaxed the system—
the more young males are allowed access, the less stringent are the
conditions for entry to the breeding area, and the less steep the hierarchy—the less intense will the pressures be for equilibration and
the slower the process of selection. Ideally, if there is a mutation
favoring equilibration (increase in the size of the amygdala, for example) then only the male showing it gets to breed, thus "fixing"
that mutation in the population very rapidly.[12] If he gets to breed
much more than others, but not exclusively, it will have a similar
but slower effect. If he must take his chance with all the others in
an equal breeding situation, then the mutation will spread much
more slowly.[13]

In the evolution of the primates and then of the hominid line,
however, there have been millions of years and generations. There
has been plenty of time for selection to proceed at an almost zero
pace for millennia, then speed up, then slow down again. We do
not have to assume then that only one form of breeding system has
characterized our ancestors all the time. Indeed, the record of evolution shows just such spurts and slowdowns, and we must examine
it. But for one period at least—that leading up to the appearance
of the genus *Homo,* there was one thing that stands out: a relatively
rapid increase in the size of the brain; rapid, that is, in evolutionary terms, where half-a-million years is a short time.

Chance—working like Freud with some inadequate data but
seeing through it to the main issue—saw this increase as being
somehow linked to the process of equilibration. "Equilibration demands of the animal," he said, "an intensification of the control
over its emotional responses, both facilitatory and inhibitory."[14]
The enlargement of the neocortex in the primates generally was
"an anatomical adaptation to the circumstances requiring an
equilibrational response."[15] This would have required "some special form of breeding system"—one based on "rank ordered social
relationships." Chance puts all this together thus. "We therefore
conclude that the ascent of man has been due in part to a competition for a social position . . . in which success was rewarded by a
breeding premium, and that at some time in the past, a group of

primates, by virtue of their preeminent adaptation to this element and consequent cortical enlargement, became preadapted for the full exploitation of the mammalian cortex."[16] If only we knew, he laments, whether or not man's first distinctively hominid ancestors, the Australopithecines of South and East Africa, had a large amygdala or not, it would help.[17] We do not know that. But we know other things about our ancestors, and it is to these we must now turn.

Ecology, Evolution, and Breeding

The details and controversies about human ancestry would fill a book—would fill volumes. We only have time to take up a rough outline of the most agreed-upon features that are relevant to the question we have set ourselves on the basis of Chance's hypothesis and the monkey puzzle: What is the relation between the evolution of the brain, the equilibration process, and the breeding system? Is it too early to suggest, however cautiously, the route we are following? That if these are all related, then the form of the primal horde and its social dynamics may be the very factors that have molded the most characteristic features of human emotion and mentality through the selective forces that caused the brain itself to take on its human form and functions. Freud's great event—or series of events, the conflict between the old males and the young over breeding access to the females—may indeed lie at the root of what makes us human. But there must be something more, for all the primates have this in various degrees, which is why they are primates—the first among the mammals, the brainiest. What did the ancestral hominid add? Chance's "group of primates" in the past had a "preeminent adaptation to this element" and so went on to the "full exploitation" of the cortex and humanity. But was it by the killing and cannibalism or the fantasy or something else or both or what combination of what? And where does the incest taboo come in? Well, it is a rule among other things, and rules demand a creature that can (a) make them and (b) abide by them by deferring immediate gratification in favor of rule-obedience. All part of the Freudian formula after all. We are on the way. But there is some tough thinking ahead before the pieces of the jigsaw puzzle even fall roughly into place.

We must first get the whole thing—primates and hominids

and the brain and all—into a time perspective. And time in evolution means geological time and ecological change. As the millennia went by, the natural conditions changed drastically and the various lines of primates had to adapt or move on or die out. Leaving the forest, as we saw, was not voluntary. Those that did leave had to make some drastic adaptational changes. In the previous chapter, we saw how the chimpanzee ancestors kept the forest and how other primate ancestors moved to the fringe, the woodland, the savanna, and beyond. Our relationship to the chimp suggests that our ancestor at this point was chimplike although probably more generalized in his anatomy and perhaps, therefore, his behavior. When was this?

The answer must be imprecise, but we do know that the forests began to recede in the late Miocene epoch, and the beginning of the Pliocene, which itself became progressively drier as it went along. This in turn gave way to the Pleistocene epoch, which culminated in the great Ice Ages, and the appearance of modern man. Geologists, dealing as they are with millions of years, do not always agree exactly on dates, but we can say roughly that the Miocene started some twenty-five million years ago and ended about twelve to thirteen million years ago. The Pliocene then began and ended in its turn about three million years ago, ushering in the Pleisto-cene. These, then, are our rough anchorage dates. The excursion onto the savanna began about twelve million years before the present day, when the great drying out took place. The crucial era then was the Pliocene, when the savanna animals were making their basic adaptations to life beyond the forest. The problem was until recently that we had no fossil record of the Pliocene to guide us about the hominid road of adaptation. Now the record is a little better. For the more recent era—the Pleistocene—we have many fossils, still few in absolute numbers, but for archaeology almost an embarrassment of wealth. We shall get to the fossils, but first let us look at an interesting fact of primate ecology that may help us.

A number of observers have pointed out that the multi-male system characterizes the primates of the forest, the woodland, and the tree savanna, while in the desert, the one-male system prevails. This has led to the hypothesis that hominid groups, having passed in time through the same progression of environments as the forests receded, must have made the same social adaptation.[18] The idea is appealing and has appealed strongly to those looking for an origin for the human "pair bond," as they like to call human marriage on a bad analogy with the mating process of some animals. The bond in this case would be polygynous on the analogy with the hamadryas and gelada baboons. We have already canvassed this idea and found it wanting, but we must look at it carefully.

If indeed the process of adaptation through time has its analogue in the present distribution of primates in space, then we cannot dismiss the ecological argument. We have already, to some extent, accepted it in taking seriously the mating systems of the baboons anyway. Common ecological experience, we decided, was important in giving us clues. But only that—clues. We have resisted pinning our ancestors down to any one *detailed* form of mating system on the analogy of any of the living primates. We have agreed that they must conform to the baseline, but beyond that it would be dangerous to pin them down exactly, for the very simple reason that it was a different creature that came out of the forests, and if it had not done something different from the other primates, it would still be like them and not the unique animal it is. This is terribly important, since we must avoid the charge that we are reading primate behavior directly into human social structure. We are not. We are looking at the primate behavior only to see what we have in common at base: The crucial things, then, to tease out are the differences. I repeat: We must have been doing something very different from the desert baboons, or there is no reason to suppose that we should not have remained exactly as they are.

Take the ecological argument. The one-male group style of social organization (the harem) is a known adaptational response to dry and desert climates. The transition from the Miocene to the Pliocene was a change from forest to desert, eventually. Our hominid ancestors went through this transition. Therefore, they would have made a one-male group adaptation on the lines of the hamadryas, etc., in order to survive. Here, then, is the origin of the human tendency to form polygynous families.

This may well be, but the important thing is this: Even if our ancestors did make such a response, it was with very different equipment from the baboons, so we cannot simply read off our ancestral experience from the present-day organization of the desert primates.

For a start, it is not all that clear that our ancestors were wholly confined to the desert in the way the one-male group spe-

cies are today. (In any case, one-male groups appear in some forest-dwelling lower primates as well, so their preeminently desert
adaptation is not so certain.) They may well, with their developing
bipedalism, have ranged through whole series of environments,
adapting primarily to none in particular but developing a generalized ability to adapt to a wide range of niches. This fits with their
present abilities rather than a rigid desert style of adaptedness.
Also, other primates have ranged very widely and varied their social structures accordingly, like the versatile langurs, which range
from arid plain to the snowy Himalayas, or the even more versatile
macaques, which seem able to live anywhere. Man is not the only
primate, then, to have moved through a number of ecological
zones without primary adaptation to any particular one.

Also, look at the highly specialized adaptations of the desert
baboons. They have strongly seasonal breeding periods—indeed
their survival seems to depend on this. They are sexually dimor-
phous—the males are much bigger than the females. They have
seemingly fixed their herding of harems as an inbuilt behavioral
feature—they will reproduce it in captivity, for example, never
having known it in the wild. Females mature at roughly twice the
rate of males—thus ensuring a supply for the successful polygynist.
There is a marked lack of cooperation between the males and
marked sexual antagonism.

In all these features—some shared with other baboons, of
course—they are off on a different tangent to the course of hominid
evolution, judging by the end product. A lack of seasonal breeding,
modest sexual dimorphism, variable mating behavior, roughly
equal maturity rates, cooperation and sharing within and between
sexes (with naturally some antagonism, but cooperation as well)—
all these characterize the hominid baseline toward which our ancestral behavior was moving, and all are the opposite of the developments that seem essential to behavior fixed genetically in the
desert adaptation of the one-male groupers.

This is not to say that the formation of polygynous families
does not enter the hominid picture at some point. It most surely
does. It is to say that it probably did not enter in the early Pliocene
and certainly not for the reasons that make it a physiological feature of the desert baboons. We must have been doing something
different or we too would have stuck at that phase. And this is

clinched for me by the versatility of our later behavior. Our ancestors at this point must have been hanging loose, genetically, and not putting all their eggs into one adaptational basket. Consider only the anatomy. The baboons came out of the forest as quadrupeds—descendants of the quadramanous branch runners. They had large size, high speed, massive canines, fur capes—as well as binocular vision, good brains (as mammals go), and handlike front paws. They put these to good use, *but they didn't change much* except to get a bit smaller. As we have already seen, our little ancestor had none of these more obvious advantages and so was forced to be more versatile, to change more, to adapt more flexibly—possibly even in competition with the baboons. He could not afford to be too like them; he had to be different. He had to take the baseline and weave it into a different pattern—or rather several different patterns. And the clue lay both in his incipient bipedalism and the fact that he probably had a better brain than the baboon to start with—one at least as good as the chimpanzee's.

I have dwelt on this theory, since its proponents have made a strong case for it and it deserves examination. Also, if it is true, it makes the history of human evolution very difficult to understand as far as the end product is concerned. Some of its more cautious proponents have realized this for some of the same reasons I have advanced and have argued for a "chimpanzee type of social structure later modified in a one-male group direction" or something such, which is more like my own position.[19] But I would not even want to be so definite as that. We do not need, as I keep stressing, to pin it down that precisely. And indeed, there is good reason to believe that if it had been so pinned down, genetically, that such creatures as ourselves would never have emerged. All we need to posit for our ancestor of the late Miocene and early Pliocene is a breeding system with the three elements—old males, young males, females with young—and the competition for breeding success. Given the outcome, it would appear more plausible that our ancestors had a looser structure of mating on the multi-male model. This not only demands less of the genes by way of specialization, thus leaving open the possibility for rapid changes, but gives a role to the female more consistent with her final outcome and a greater role to kinship, which, we have reason to believe, is more basic than permanent mating. Overall, it allows for flexibility in response, for changes in the rates at which sexual selection could work, and these seem to have been necessary, again, to provide the end result—ourselves.

Brains and Ancestors

Instead of trying to read the desert baboons into our Pliocene ancestry, let us try the tougher approach of asking what that ancestry was and how it developed insofar as we can tell from the fossil bones. And we must remember that the hunt is for information on the growth of the brain, since that is the clue here. When did the brain make its evolutionary move and why? When did we start to leave the rest behind? What else were we doing when it happened?

This is, unfortunately, a murky area, and the nonspecialist is likely to be dismayed by the thundering disagreements about bits of fractured bone that divide scientists into warring camps for reasons that might appear almost too minute to a disinterested observer. Again, I do not intend to get bogged down in the details, since most of them are irrelevant to the hypothesis we are pursuing. A general outline—with a few awkward kinks—is emerging from the fossil record, particularly as regards the growth of the brain, and that is all we need: the general trend.[20] Where shall we start?

The earliest candidate for hominid ancestry is a Miocene animal found in East Africa and North India and known at first as either *Kenyapithecus* or *Ramapithecus* (the latter name has stuck). He was small, and we know not too much about his anatomy, but his teeth were remarkably human in their shape and disposition. He lacked large canines. As to his brain, it was not impressive, and while we cannot be precise, it was certainly no larger than a chimp's. Anthropologists argue about whether he was the first hominid or a freak—with the hominids starting up in earnest much later. But at least at this stage—fourteen million years ago—we have no better candidate. At the very least, then, we can say negatively that at this point our ancestor has a brain no bigger than a chimpanzee, and this figures, since he was, however different in his dentition (bespeaking a more omnivorous diet?), adapting to the same niche: the forest floor.

It also figures, because the next candidate for hominid status had a brain that was, on average, slightly bigger than a chimpanzee's—not much bigger, but somewhat ahead. This candidate is the famous *Australopithecus*, of which a number of subspecies have been named, some large and chimpanzeelike, some smaller and more "gracile," as they like to say, but all under five feet, bipedal although not perhaps very efficiently so, having a pelvis remarkable for its likeness to our own and very different from the chimp's (indicating the move to permanent uprightness), and with that telltale humanlike dentition—the small canines and the rounded dental arch.

For a long time, *Australopithecus* was thought to have originated in the Pleistocene—quite recently by evolutionary standards, a mere two million years ago (1.8 million to be exact). This left a big gap—the Pliocene. Nine or ten million years were unaccounted for, and the distance between *Australopithecus* and *Ramapithecus* uncomfortably large. Now, however, startling finds in East Africa have begun to reveal a Pliocene full of fossils. Small brained but bipedal and definitely hominid *Australopithecus* appears earlier and earlier. Three and a half million was extended to more than four and probably now more than five. Assuming that he did not appear suddenly, one can always assume him to have been around for a while before the earliest date he is discovered. So perhaps five or six million years ago at least, a definite hominid, anatomically quite different from the chimp although not a great deal smarter if the brain is anything to go by, was walking the earth in East Africa, unsteadily upright, carving out his own place in the primate scheme of things. What is more, they were still walking about there, and in southern Africa, as late as 1.05 million years ago—after true men with larger brains had appeared.

This tells us something very important: all Australopithecine species were not ancestral to true men, only perhaps one of them was. This went on to produce a new species while its cousins lumbered around finally becoming extinct. The same was probably true of *Ramapithecus:* There were a lot of species around, one of which went on to produce the ancestors of the Australopithecines. Finally there was only one species left—*Homo sapiens sapiens,* ourselves.

But we are getting ahead. Let's fix some facts about brain size first. We shall leave until later the question of whether or not size is really the answer to anything. For the moment, it is all we have. And while there is here again much dispute and disagreement that is downright disagreeable, one thing no one disputes is that in the long run, over the evolution of successive species the one from the other, a larger brain means a smarter creature. And yet again, that is all we need for the moment; nothing finer, and no quibbles.

Brain size is measured in terms of cranial capacity—the size of the inside of the skull, and this is measured in cubic centimeters. Measuring the cranial capacity of fossils is technically very difficult as is the dating of them, but we can arrive at some decent *averages* that most experts would agree to, give or take some cubic centimeters. Having got, then, an average brain size for our fossil populations, we have to ask the question we have raised earlier: Is this just a function of the size of the animal? In the mammals, for example, the brain tends to be larger as the animals are larger: It is proportional to body size. If we are looking for some significant change, then, we have to look for a brain that is larger in relation to the body size than we would expect from the trends. This is indeed what we get for man, but more of that later. Let us follow the story through its chronological sequence.[21]

The primate baseline we can work from here is the brain of the chimp—our nearest relative and a smart enough fellow as it is. He averages 394 cubic centimeters. What about the first definite hominid, *Australopithecus?* Our best estimate is an average of 486 cubic centimeters, with a range extending upward to 540 cubic centimeters. Since he was—again, on average—a smallish creature, this represents a bit of a jump on the chimp, but not a large one. An important fact to store away, then, is that this little hominid wandered around East and South Africa for as much as four million years or even more without a significant change in brain size.[22] The next leap came with a successor hominid species that has been named *Homo habilis*—handy man—and for the very good reason that he seems to have made tools and crude shelters and to have hunted for at least part of his living. More of that later. For the moment, let us fix his brain size if we can. Many experts would not want to give him special status, and consider him a large Australopithecine or a smaller version of the next grade up, *Homo erectus.* But he seems distinct enough to merit a rung on the ladder. His brain averaged 666 cubic centimeters (probably an underestimate), which is 180 cubic centimeters larger than *Australopithecus* and, what is more, the ranges do not overlap. In time, *Homo habilis* appears, about 1.75 million years ago. Shortly after this, about 1.5

million years ago, *Homo erectus* appeared in Java, China, and East
Africa. Man was spreading out over the globe—striding out, we
might say. His new name indicates his unquestionable status as a
representative of the genus *Homo*—our own genus. Our relation to
habilis might be disputed, but the upright man of the middle Pleistocene was unquestionably one of us. He was named for his clearly
upright posture—he was as tall as modern man—and his brain
shows the progressive increase we have already noted: he averaged
about 873 cubic centimeters, which is larger than *habilis* by 207
cubic centimeters. *Homo habilis* is clearly closer to *erectus* than the
Australopithecines, and the two species overlap in time considerably. But there are no Habiline finds after one million years, while
erectus lasts until half-a-million years ago at least. What is more, the
upper limits of his brain-size range reach 1,030 cubic centimeters,
which brings him into our own range. He was clearly on the
march. We can see this in the difference between the earlier *erectus*
skulls from Java and the later ones from China and Africa.
The latter averaged over 1,000 cubic centimeters, a big improvement on their earlier colleagues, over a period of a hundred thousand years.

Following on *Homo erectus* came what were once thought to be
two distinct subspecies (or even species): our own direct ancestors
Homo sapiens sapiens and their ancestors/cousins *Homo sapiens nean-
derthalensis*—the famous Neanderthal men. Whether they were ancestors of true *sapiens* or a cousin branch that was either absorbed
or wiped out is still disputed. But no one now disputes their *sapiens*
status. In fact, the Neanderthals had an average cranial capacity
slightly larger than ours: 1,398 cubic centimeters. (The later and
larger ones averaged 1,470 cubic centimeters.) Their average is
greater than even the largest (Chinese) Erectines by 355 cubic centimeters. We must take them as our zenith. The species *sapiens* appeared about 275,000 years ago; modern man as we know him,
about 35–50,000. And one thing that happened in the course of
this evolution, is that the general *range* of brain sizes had greatly
increased with each step.[23] There is reason to believe that this
would happen in a creature as widely dispersed as man is today,
but it can be misleading because the modern *range* (1,000–2,000)
overlaps with the ranges of even *Homo erectus*. But it is the mean,
the average, that counts in looking at the progress onward and upward, and that is undoubtedly what it is.

Whatever the minor disputes and quarrels, it is clear that the brain got larger and over a relatively short evolutionary period. And it was not just change in body size that did it. Our brain is *six times* as large as is typical for a mammal of our size. This, in the jargon, is known as marked positive allometry—a disproportionate increase in the size of one organ relative to others. In the human case, the disproportion is with the brain.[24]

Where and when did the significant changes occur? We must caution that we are dealing with only a few fossils in fact, and that we must therefore think of them as representative of *grades* of evolution. There are millions of fossils that we shall never find and millions more that have disappeared forever. The most we can establish with the ones we have is rough trends at rough times— nothing more precise. Even so, some things stand out as obvious and are illustrated in Figure 2.

There is a big jump from *Australopithecus* to *habilis*, another from *habilis* to *erectus*, and yet another from *erectus* to *sapiens*. Taken together, the three jumps represent an upward trend that involved a trebling of brain size within two million years.[25] It was not necessarily a smooth upward curve, but it was steep and in evolutionary terms rapid. It started just short of two million years ago and coincided with the first evidence of true tool making and the hunting of large mammals. It cannot have been coincidence.

Over the last two million years, the brain increased from less than 500 cubic centimeters to almost 1,400 cubic centimeters, on average, and in absolute size has topped 2,000 cubic centimeters. On average, we have a threefold leap, while from the largest Australopithecine brains to the largest *sapiens*, we get a fourfold leap: all within two million years and following a long period of brain-size stagnation in the hominids/pongids in which no particular increase occurred. (The ancestral apes, the Dryopithecines, which are thought to have given rise to the great apes, had cranial capacities no larger than their descendants.)

Argument goes on among the scholars about just how rapid this rise was. Some put it in the A range of evolutionary advance; that is, the fastest-known rate of evolution for an organ.[26] Others do not think it was so spectacular,[27] but no one denies that it was, in evolutionary terms, a pretty dramatic takeoff and an even more dramatically sustained trajectory. Something happened between two and three million years ago: something dramatic enough to

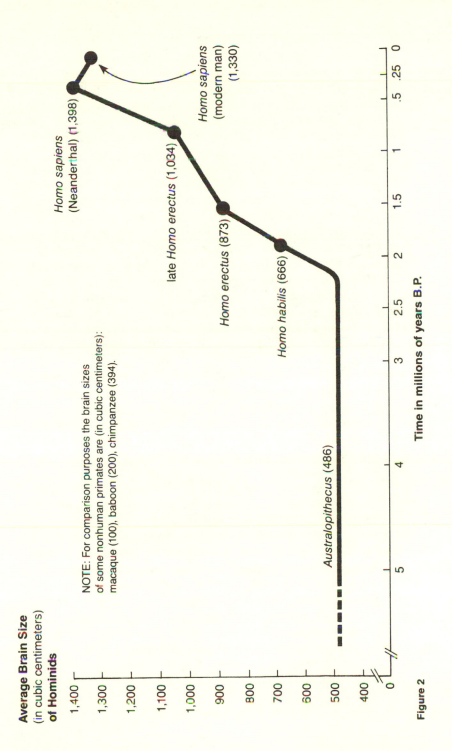

Average Brain Size
(in cubic centimeters)
of Hominids

NOTE: For comparison purposes the brain sizes
of some nonhuman primates are (in cubic centimeters):
macaque (100), baboon (200), chimpanzee (394).

Homo sapiens
(Neanderthal) (1,398)

Homo sapiens
(modern man)
(1,330)

late *Homo erectus* (1,034)

Homo erectus (873)

Homo habilis (666)

Australopithecus (486)

Time in millions of years B.P.

Figure 2

cause selection pressures for bigger and better brains in the little hominids and to sustain those pressures with increasing intensity over two million years. Whatever it was, it was not bipedalism and the human walk: These had evolved earlier in the Australopithecines. But for whatever reason they had evolved, it was not sufficient to require the huge investment in brain that *habilus* introduced and that *erectus* brought into the human range.[28]

Was it simply the introduction of meat? Not that alone. Chimps eat some meat, and the Australopithecines certainly included it in their diet. There are certain vitamin sources (B^{12} and niacin for example) that are hard to obtain from plant foods and can be gotten from meat.[29] Also, as we know, a little meat produces a great deal more protein than a lot of plants and is more easily converted into energy. The early hominids certainly had meat in their diets. But they could have scavenged it or simply hunted small and helpless prey. It has been speculated that bipedal walking and the freeing of the hands helped the hominids to carry meat and plants back to their offspring, since they could not, as carnivores do, swallow it and then regurgitate back at the den.[30] This same bipedal walking has been held by some to have caused a reduction in the intensity of the estrous cycle in the hominid female, thus taking us another small step away from the other primates.[31] Others have held that without meat the sheer physiological demands of the brain could not be met: certain "structural fats" necessary to the brain's growth are found only in meat, as are the eight essential amino acids that must be ingested together to be effective. It is particularly difficult to achieve the right balance with raw vegetables.[32] Meat undoubtedly helped the Australopithecines—their upright development, the improvement of their feet and hands, and even the extension of the period of infant dependency, since food could now be supplied to the young after weaning rather than leaving them to fend for themselves, primate fashion. But meat as such (and we are talking of wild game, not the domesticated rubbish we eat today) can only have been a necessary, not a sufficient, cause of rapid brain evolution. Meat gave the brain its chance, but something else had to happen to require the rapid increase in size.

We might interpose here the oft-heard argument that it is not just size but internal reorganization of the brain that matters.[33] Size could have stayed the same, but certain crucial linkages that did not appear before might have emerged through mutation and selection. This is true, and we can remember Chance's lament over our lack of knowledge of the nature of the amygdala relative to the rest of the Australopithecine brain (it is in fact much larger relatively in man than in other primates). The soft parts not being preserved, we have little to go on as far as understanding the internal structure is concerned; although some observers have thought they could tell from the endocasts (plaster molds of the insides of fossil skulls) that certain vital changes in areas of the brain surface known for special functions can be traced.[34] Speech areas and those governing the hand are the most popular.[35]

The only thing one can say in reply, and I doubt anyone would seriously dispute this, is that greater size allows for greater internal complexity of internal reorganization. The best evidence is simply the evolution of the brain itself. Nature is notoriously parsimonious: If there were no need for the greater size then why invest in it? Indeed there may even be a positive feedback effect: Greater size means more neurons means greater internal complexity means more effectiveness means greater pressures for more size and so on round the chain.[36] It is perfectly true that mere size does not *necessarily* tell us about internal organization, but it is the best clue we have got and not a bad one. The Australopithecines may well have had a larger amygdala with more direct connections to the hippocampus than exist in a chimp brain, for example (I think they probably did); but they could not make any spectacular leap forward without a change in the absolute size of the brain to allow room, as it were, for even greater complexities of reorganization.

So we are back to the great leap forward. It was not just bipedalism, it was not just meat. We could invoke a fluke macromutation, but that is not much better than invoking the hand of god. There are earthier possibilities, and they have been unearthed. It is almost too simple. The brain began its upward march *at about the same time as the earliest evidence of systematic large-scale hunting appears.* The rest is history. Several things developed in concert: The animals hunted grew bigger; the tools and weapons used in the hunt grew more refined; the period of infancy dependency lengthened; the brain doubled then tripled in size. (One small oddity: The body did not grow all that much larger—which is why we have the large brain-to-body ratio that we boast. Leave this one hanging and we'll return to it.)

Reader (if you will forgive the archaic address), I have sped through many things that would require volumes to do them justice. I have presented the conclusions rather than all the arguments and evidence that led up to them. That is for the specialist. And the last thing you now need are pages and pages of archaeological evidence for hominid hunting. The evidence is there, and daily it increases. All we need to establish for now is roughly when the earliest kill sites are found and what the maximum kill sizes seem to have achieved. These tell us the range over which our ancestors were operating. Let us take the earliest uncontested evidence of hominid hunting. (Primitive stone tools were found there.) It occurs at Koobi Fora, east of Lake Rudolph in Kenya.[37] The date has been set at about two-and-a-half million years ago. The animals killed include porcupine, pigs, gazelles, and waterbuck. There were hippopotamus bones too, but not the whole animal. Two-and-a-half million years ago some creature was crossing the Australopithecine/Habiline frontier and was doing it with tools for butchering and the killing of sizable prey animals.

The size increases as does the extent of the killing. At a single site, probably nothing matches Torralba in Spain, where 300,000 years ago twenty-six horses, twenty-five deer, ten aurochs, six rhinoceros, four carnivores, and thirty elephants were found.[38] Man had come a long way. The elephants were almost twice the size of their living relatives—up to 9,000 kilograms. From then on the record is clear. Man became the top Pleistocene carnivore and indulged in an orgy of overkill that eventually wiped out most species of large herbivore in Europe, Asia, Africa, and in short order once he arrived in North America.[39] (It was probably this tendency to overkill that forced him to take up agriculture and to return to the largely vegetarian ways of his remoter ancestors, but this was not until some 5–10,000 years ago.)

We need only for the moment fix this in our minds: As the brain started on its upward movement, so did the size and complexity of animal kills. As they got larger and more complex, so did the brain, so did social organization, language, and longer infant dependency. All the marks of humanity (including tools and weapons fashioned beautifully, beyond mere functional needs) grew in unison. Not all at once; not all at the same time; not necessarily in perfect harmony for long stretches. But they grew and developed as the hunt grew and developed, and they were mediated by the growing brain.

The Great Leap Forward

What gave the original Australopithecine population the initial kick? We may never be able to answer this. They had been ambling about the East African savanna for a long time after all, surviving well enough on their mixed strategy. Perhaps somewhere, east of Lake Rudolph, they ran even shorter of vegetable matter in the dry seasons and out of desperation went after larger animals. If it worked at all, then the feedback effect may have set in. Organisms don't strive to outdo themselves. Nature is utterly conservative, as we have had occasion often to observe. Animals strive to maintain the niche they have evolved for, they do not strain after some ideal future state. But a small shift in the conditions of the niche can call into play those preadaptations that have been lying dormant, and this in turn can cause a marked shift in the conditions of selection. If the shift in conditions is too great, the species, more often than not, becomes extinct: There has to be a niche for it to move into in order to change. Just such a niche existed in East Africa two-million-plus years ago. If the hominids had responded to the need for more meat by having to compete with already successful carnivores, they would undoubtedly have lost. They would not have had the millions of years of carnivore heritage on their side. They were omnivorous, made-over apes and no match for lions or packs of ferocious hunting dogs. But here is the clue: There were no diurnal carnivores of consequence in East Africa two million years ago. The "big carnivore" niche was open. Nature had a vacancy; man applied and got the job. The other diurnal carnivores moved in later, but by then, the hominids had established themselves, with their tools, weapons, and society as major competitors with all comers in the world of the top carnivores.[40]

I have borrowed the phrase top carnivores from Phillip Thompson, because he established an important set of correlations.[41] What he found was that there was a predictable ratio between the size of a carnivore's prey (its usual maximum prey size in fact), the length of its period of infant dependency, the size of its brain, and the size of its body. In short: As the prey gets bigger so

does the hunter and so does the brain, while the period of its infancy lengthens. With social carnivores, as opposed to solitary
hunters, complexity of society can compensate for smallness of
body: The pack attacks "in a body." What is intriguing is that the
correlations hold for man. His brain, in fact, is about the right size
for the size of prey he hunts, and so is the length of dependency
(which allows the carnivore to learn the tricks of its trade). The
human body is smaller, however, than would be expected, which
might help explain some of the brain-body ratio so striking in man.
This can be attributed to a combination of weapons and organization. Other carnivores have to grow bigger as their prey grows bigger, because they attack it with their bodies. Man, like other social
carnivores, can depend on numbers, but also he has weapons and
can attack from a distance in a way no other can. The made-over
ape may have turned a disadvantage (small size) into a positive
advantage through the use of weapons and the ability to kill at a
distance. Less of the brain is needed for sheer control of the body:
There is plenty left over for things other than the hunting of large
prey, even if this is what the large brain is needed for in the first
place.

The correlation, then, is there, but that does not explain why
it had to be there. Some populations of *Australopithecus* moved into
this niche and the process began. They were the primates that, in
Chance's memorable phrase were "preadapted for the full exploitation of the mammalian cortex." They were at the takeoff point,
but they needed the push over into self-sustained growth—to borrow metaphors from the economists. But why were they at the
takeoff point to start with? That brings us back full circle to
Chance's hypothesis and demands that we plug the archaeological
information into the linking theory, which was the original aim of
this chapter. We have already cheated a little, since we have introduced a helpful theory already—that brain/body/growth/society
are all correlated with prey size. But this is not enough. There have
been several such attempts to explain the rapid expansion of the
brain, the most popular being some form of the tools + hunting +
social complexity + language + whatever-you-like-to-add theory.[42] Somehow, after the initial "push" (e.g., from tools) a positive
feedback loop is set up whereby growing complexity demands an
even better brain, etc. Thompson's theory has the virtue of elegance and parsimony, since prey size is the simple constant. But

again, none of these theories address themselves to the problem: By what mechanism can the relatively rapid increase in brain size have occurred? This is where Chance's neglected theory comes in and links our primate past with our archaeological record.

Our ape-men Australopithecine ancestors must, we presume, have acquired a reasonable degree of equilibrational ability. They were probably not seasonal breeders, their females not as suscepti-ble to marked estrus symptoms as other primates. Yet they were still apelike in their brains, and we have no reason to suppose that they were not still sharing the social structure of the primate base-line: central males, females with young (in kinship groups?), and peripheral males. Indeed, if Chance is correct, it was their "preemi-nent adaptation to this element" that had got them to the takeoff position. The push comes. The hunt, as Holmes would have said to Watson, is up. But it is not just the bodies of these special primates that have to adapt to the conditions of their new niche—it is their societies. And their societies are breeding machines of a special kind as much as their bodies are, breeding machines that them-selves preadapted to speed up or slow down the rates of gene flow. The bodies were somewhat modified: They became more upright, taller, less hairy, and, of course, bigger brained. But they were not completely made over. Natural selection built on what was there and improved it for the new purpose—the big game hunt. The same must have been true of the society, which was also the breed-ing system: Natural selection works through the redistribution of genes; that is, through the breeding system. In the same way that she had been presented with a body that could be molded into a near perfect social carnivore, nature had been presented with a so-cial/breeding system that could do the molding and in the process became itself a weapon in that carnivorous adaptation.

We can easily see what happened with the body and the brain. Our bodies are still primate bodies and our brains still pri-mate brains, but they have been remarkably modified. Our socie-ties during the great push remained primate societies—and for that matter remain primate societies today—but they too had to be made over at the same time as they were the agents of the mak-ing-over process. The baseline materials, the fundamental func-tions of the primate breeding system had to continue as they had done to produce the equilibrated animal. But because of the na-ture of the leap forward, *the equilibrational functions were strained to the*

outer limits. It was, as we saw, under the *ancien régime,* the most equilibrated individual that got to do the most breeding. It was the
smartest, the most cunning, the most foresighted—not necessarily
the most sexy or aggressive, but the one that knew best how to time
and use its sexuality and aggression. These were the sum of the
"best genes." But after the great leap, what would happen when
the definition of best genes was changed by natural selection so
that it meant best hunter? And that was only the first small step for
mankind. The route from the periphery to the center of the breeding system still had to be negotiated; the females still needed the
best genes; the males still had to accommodate with each other and
both cooperate and vie for precedence. But the rules of the game
became profoundly changed, and the successful players had to go
well beyond mere equilibration to succeed. And the process
moved, in evolutionary terms, so rapidly, that they had to end up
by making their own rules to supplement nature's or the equilibrational process might have burst at the seams. They had to keep
the structure and the motivations, but change the dynamics,
change the form. And within the societies themselves, the growing
burden of change fell as always on the young male, as Freud had
seen. For somewhere on the route from the new periphery of the
hunting-primate society to the safe center of its established males,
the red lamp was lighted, and the game was played thenceforward
in its lurid glare. Sex, more than ever, became a creature of the
brain, and the most ardent games of love were played inside the
expanding skull.

SIX

Alliance and Constraint

The emergence of symbolic thought must have required that women, like words, should be things that were exchanged.

Claude Lévi-Strauss

The result (and therefore the purpose) of these arrangements cannot be doubted: they bring about a still further restriction on the choice of marriage and on sexual liberty.

Sigmund Freud

So the pieces are coming together. Our species never lost anything in evolving. It amplified, modified, controlled, reorganized. It ended up doing things in a very human fashion—which is only to say that it evolved into *Homo sapiens* and not something else. The initial question was: What is the peculiarly *human* method of cutting down the rate of inbreeding? What is the state of the argument so far?

All sexually reproducing species, we saw (with a few exceptions), manage to evolve, in the course of natural selection, mechanisms that promote outbreeding. Nature takes care of the inbreeding problem by reducing the possibilities of it happening. She will seize on whatever mechanisms happen to be handy, although some—like dispersion—are very common across species. What matters is their effect: Do they work? Species can, however, differ quite a lot in the mechanisms which evolve, and *Homo sapiens,* being the most complicated of species, manages to produce some unique mechanisms. Being human, we do it by making things difficult for ourselves. Nature, as it were, sets up the conditions that allow us to make it difficult: We usually oblige. Man could almost be defined as the animal that makes things difficult for itself. To do this needs imagination and intelligence, and this needs an advanced brain, which, as we have seen, is the clue to the flickering of the lamp: It burns fitfully and fretfully in the bony cavity under our skulls.

At the end of chapter one, I declared magisterially that one sure universal about incest—notwithstanding the welter of uncertainty—was the "ease with which we became uneasy" about it. It was always possible, therefore, to make us feel guilty about it—and about sex generally. This seemed to be taught to a ready learner. But what was being taught? Often nothing explicit. Somehow, emotions and fears just seemed to get communicated—or even indifference, as in the sibling case. Sometimes, on the other hand, quite explicit rules and taboos were involved. Thus, a mix of explicit rules, avoidances, guilty inhibitions, and no end of unconscious fantasies seemed to be easily produced. In looking at the criticisms of Freud's theory, for example, we saw some of the protean forms that mother or father denial could take and the social consequences of these. We had seen how either patterned avoidance or guilty fascination could ensue from varieties of childhood experience between siblings. Again, they were ready learners.

The question then became: What is the nature of this ready learner and how did it get that way? If it is the case, as Freud said, that we constantly repeat the dramas of our evolutionary past in our current emotional conflicts, then what were the dramas and what had they produced? It was not, as we saw, a specific anti-incest instinct. It was too flexible for that. In 1967, I tried to sum it up clumsily as follows: ". . . a syndrome of genetically determined behaviors which make the pubescent human in particular susceptible to guilt and other forms of conditioning surrounding the sexual-aggressive drives."[1] That was the language of 1967. But behind its clumsy jargon lies a latent elegance of conceptualization. What is *in* the nature of the ready learner is there genetically, but what it is is simply a state of readiness for conditioning, which, of course, can go in various directions.[2] But the conditioning itself is preconditioned by the nature of the material it has to work on. It is not just any conditioning that will produce just any results: It is a conditioning of the phyletic memories—to use the phrase we borrowed earlier from Marais. These atavistic memories are powerful and lodged in the very structure of the neural-hormonal system. Indeed, this structure *is* the memories. That has been the whole point of the argument. We have the particular relations between brain and hormones that we have because of our evolutionary experiences. We built on the primate base: The brain that left the forests. And the builders—or selection pressures if you like—while they were certainly the "hostile forces of nature," were just as much the sexual-selection processes that emphasized equilibration. It was through these processes that the demands of nature became translated into genetic realities. And the brain began its relatively rapid elevation into a truly human organ when the demand spelled "hunter."

That is where the argument is poised. We have seen how the elements of the primal horde exist among our primate relatives in various forms: the dominant males, the females with young, the peripheral males; and the struggle of the young males to gain a place at the center, and so to breed. We have seen the pressures toward equilibration that this produces and have borrowed Chance's speculations on how this must have affected the growth and internal structure of the primate brain. The story is one of "increasing cortical control."[3] The cortex gradually develops more and more control over the functions of the "emotional" areas of the brain. There is recent evidence that the hippocampus—so important to the causal memory—is very *directly* connected to the amygdala in primates and, hence, to the forebrain, and even more so in man.[4] Thus the "higher" brain, with its forethought, memory, and capacity for rational action, can control the areas of hunger, sex, rage, and fear—up to a point. We saw how this was vital to the survival of the young male in his passage back to the breeding center, however he got there—by defeating the older male, by kidnapping females, by ingratiating himself with his elders, by quitting and joining another group, by Atkinson's maternal intervention technique, but only rarely by the Freudian means of ganging up on the old man and killing him. Hardly ever in fact.

But that is perhaps precisely the point. The monkeys and apes don't do that. Advanced and impressive as their brains are, ours left them far behind in an evolutionary hurry. So, as I have kept repeating, it is because we were doing *something different*—some absolutely crucial thing—that we are human and they are simians still. Well. What we did might not have been murder, might not have been patricide. But then it might; we don't really know. What we do know is that it involved killing and the use of weapons, even if the only sure evidence is that these, in the early stages, were turned against animals rather than fathers. The point is that, as Freud observed, for the "sons" to be able to take on the "fathers," and certainly to kill and eat them, "some new weapon" had to be invented. And if the use of weapons did not lead to mass patricide among our ancestors, it surely changed the rules of the game. It strained the equilibrational functions to their utmost. A young primate male, frustrated in his attempts to do what his genes urge him to do and replicate themselves, is a formidable enough threat to an older male. One armed and skilled in hunting large prey must have been positively alarming to say the least.

Yet we must emphasize the relativity of "rapidity" here. In evolutionary terms rapid, yes, but in fact, it took many thousands of generations for the effects to establish a new kind of primate, the hominid. There was time to accommodate, but accommodation there had to be. And if there were not some palace revolutions and patricides on the way, I would be very surprised. But there is no necessity to imagine them the rule. As Freud saw, the issue might well be the *control of hostile impulses* realized only in fantasy, but provoking guilt. And surely this is it. This is what the equilibrational process is about. The hostile, and other, impulses must be controlled—turned into fantasy if necessary—and the imperative urges of the individual subjugated to the rules of the group; the needs of the moment curbed in expectation of future rewards. It is there in the primates. It is many times magnified in us, because we have language and rules, and the cognitive and emotive means of living by articulated rules. That is what human society is about, and the incest rule is but another rule among many. But the truth is that the process that brought us to this point of spontaneous inhibition of self in favor of rule-governed social behavior and so enabled us to make incest rules at all, was the process by which we strove over those thousands of generations to inhibit, and control, the "incestuous" impulses of the primal horde: the equilibrational process itself.

To try to summarize those basic impulses and the changes

that were wrought by the hunting transition, here are two formulae. The primate formula for the breeding system says, looked at
from the male angle: Get into the top ranks of your group so that
you can use the females for breeding purposes. The human formula says: Get to the top ranks of your group so that you can use
its females to exchange for other females. The change is from controlling "own" females as objects of *use* to controlling own females
as objects of *exchange*. For "top" females, the formulae are quite
similar: Improve your genetic success by getting top males as mates
and by helping your sons become top males. The human formula
is almost identical, but adds: Get males who will invest in your offspring. We shall explore the consequences of these transitions later.
What they raise is the old question of the origins of exogamy, and I
have already said that we must not suppose that exogamy is simply
incest taboos writ large. So here I will jump to the book's major
conclusion (and then come back and explain it further of course):
Exogamy may not be incest taboos writ large, but *the evolution of the
ability to control "incestuous" impulses may well be at the root of our ability
to play the exogamous game at all.* For to play it, we have to be equili-
brators par excellence, and we may have *had* to start playing it in
order to control the impulses. Thus, incest and exogamy are deeply
linked in the phyletic memory—products of the same process. But
the linkage is far from the simple one that social scientists have assumed. It is more like the linkage between the hippocampus and
the amygdala than it is like the parts of a functionalist formula for
social survival; e.g., "Incest taboos are necessary because they promote out-marriage, without which there would be no wider social
groups," etc., etc., etc.

From Breeding to Kinship Systems

All primate breeding systems have provision for the due mammalian quota of outbreeding. But a certain amount of close inbreeding will take place in most of them. The systems seem to achieve a
balance between just enough inbreeding to fix genetic traits on the
one hand and just enough outbreeding to preserve genetic variation on the other. Human breeding systems do much the same, but
they add the mechanisms of rules and exchanges. I have argued
that in the absence of these—as with the protohominids for example—human breeding systems would promote outbreeding any-

way, like their primate counterparts. The human "extras" were added during the hunting transition, because, I have suggested, the built-in primate mechanisms could not handle the conflicts engendered by the changed situation; but these same mechanisms were responsible for the evolution of the brain that made the extras possible. The "instincts" of the primal horde had to be tamed, and exogamy — the systematic, rule-governed exchange of mates — was the social expression of the taming process: the outward and visible sign of an inward and spiritual grace. We must delve deeper into this transition.

Some hard facts we know, and we have looked at the archaeological record. The fossils tell us of changes in size and shape, including brain size; the sites tell us of the increase in the use of tools and the growing success in hunting. But what of the social system during the change from Australopithecine to Habiline to Erectine to Sapiens? Ever since 1967, I have been objecting to attempts to pin the protohominids down to any one specific type of social/ breeding system. In particular, it seems to be downright unimaginative to push dreary monogamy onto these enterprising creatures as so many commentators seem to want to do — reflecting their own culture-bound obsession with the nuclear family more than anything in the record of nature.[5] It also does not help, and is positively misleading, to pose the problem as the origin of the pair bond in hominids. This is simply a bad analogy with an instinctive process in lower animals.[6] Humans do not pair bond in this sense at all. *Marriage* is a legal, rule-governed institution, not a direct expression of instinctive drives. If anything *is* instinctive, it is the trio of attributes that Lévi-Strauss sees as lying behind the incest taboo (although he really means exogamy): the exigency of the rule as rule, the notion of reciprocity, and the synthetic nature of the gift. Translated into rougher English, this means that man is a rule-obeying creature, that he exchanges things, and that between two people who exchange something a special relationship exists. Kinship systems then are not about nuclear families and pair bonds, they are about special relationships set up between people who exchange spouses according to a set of rules. The human formula for breeding success, I suggested, was: Get control of the exchange system. And it is this element of *control* that is important. The young males say, "Give us females"; the females say, "Give us males who will provision us"; the old males say, "Sorry, the rules restrict all our choices here, and we must all obey the rules." The beautiful catch is that the rules are rigged to the benefit of the older males anyway. But for the young male, who, being human, knows about the future, there is one consolation: He will be an older male in his turn, and the rules will favor him. This realization and his acting on it are the triumph of human equilibration, but the urges are still strong, and the older males don't leave things to chance. This is what initiation is all about, and we shall come to that. It is the homologue of equilibration at the human level.

In the meantime, let us hazard a guess at the nature of the breeding/social system of the protohominids at the period between two and three million years ago, when the brain began its takeoff. There must have been many populations living in relatively isolated groups engaging with different intensities in hunting, scavenging, and gathering. The detailed internal structure of these groups we cannot know, and it is highly unlikely that it was uniform from group to group, since different ecological niches were involved. It was, however, competitive and hierarchical, and at this stage, there were no mechanisms other than sheer dominance to cope with the sexuality and aggressivity of young males or to assign mates according to rules. Each group would inbreed to some extent then, thus fixing the characteristics that went with dominance in both males and females. These were characteristics that natural selection would have favored anyway, but their relatively rapid fixation would have been facilitated by the breeding system.

If young and aggressive males who were not killed or enterprising females out for adventure, however, left their bands and went off elsewhere in search of breeding success, then a "Sewall Wright effect" would have served to speed up the process even more.[7] This occurs when different populations "fix" certain characteristics by inbreeding, but the process is punctuated by "bursts" of outbreeding; this has the effect of pooling the specializations, and this hybridization makes for more rapid, indeed maximum, evolutionary change. It could, of course, also work by one group taking over another, killing the males, and then breeding with the females.[8] This perhaps happened too. This method of hybridization, however, has its obvious dangers, and some form of "local exogamy" with exchange of spouses between local groups in a more systematic way would serve to regulate the process.

This is later, however. The stage envisaged here was preinstitutional, although we can see how the foundations of certain institutions were being laid. It was the stage in which the hominids were, through their newly acquired hunting way of life, adapting to the exigencies of the environment in a new way. Their success lay in the expansion of "cultural" means of adaptation—tools, weapons, shelter, language, etc., and this, in turn, depended on the expansion of the neocortex. Since the breeding system was sorting out the most "cortical" animals anyway, the net result was a gain in equilibrational ability and a growth of intelligence and imagination, which served to improve the cultural adaptations.

Perhaps we can call this the "intensification" stage. We must try a leap of the imagination to see these small-brained, apelike, but upright creatures wandering about the East African savanna, adapting their primate patterns of behavior to the new food quest. Lorenz once said that we had to imagine animals as highly emotional humans with very low intelligence if we were to read their behavior. In the case of the protohominids, this is exactly what we had, literally. The brain was on its way, but it was still small, and the animal was much more like another primate than a modern human being. This is why too much concentration on modern hunting peoples as total analogues for the protohominids is dangerous. Modern hunters are fully formed, large-brained *Homo sapiens*. We can no more "read off" protohominid hunters directly from them than we can do the same from hunting baboons. The protohominids were in between. They were leaving the baboon stage, but they were a long way from the *sapiens* stage. The most we can get from either hunters or baboons is clues, but important clues. And one of the most important is the necessity of a sexual division of labor in an omnivorous hunter: males for the meat, females for vegetables.[9]

What the intensification stage did, if our scenario is correct, was to fix even more rigorously into the pattern of hominid behavior certain primate features like competition among males (for females), cooperation among males (for hunting), cooperation among females (for gathering), and the exclusion of sexually mature but still young males from the breeding system until they could work their way back into it. At the same time, as these processes were being intensified, they were causing the brain to change and grow and thus take care of them. By the time a cranial capacity of 900 to 1,000 cubic centimeters was reached (late Habiline,

early Erectine), there was surely enough by way of cortical control
of sex and aggression, memory storage, and at least the ability to
name and classify in a rudimentary way, for genuine institutions,
that is, rule-governed behaviors, to appear.

They appeared because of the profound transformation imposed on human (as we now call them) relationships by the transition to hunting. Male groups there had been among our primate
ancestors, and female kin-groups in all probability, but they had
not had much to do with each other, apart from sex and protection. The man-ape turned carnivore could not sustain this system.
The male-female division of labor was introduced, and the relationships between the three "blocks" of the social/breeding system
revolutionized. And if this sounds Marxist, it is. Engels, in his brilliant essay, "The Part Played by Labor in the Transition from Ape
to Man," was the first to state it clearly as early as 1876, but it is
implicit in Marx's own discussion of the peculiarly human form of
"species being."[10]

The male-female division of labor has to do with vegetable
foods, which the women gather, and animal protein obtained by
the men. The trading of these products is essential to the diet of the
omnivorous animal—the made-over ape turned part-time carnivore.[11] The trading of these products of "labor" between the males
and the females, is probably at the root of a truly human society.
The change was over thousands of generations, two-and-a-half-
million years, but it was none the less revolutionary. Men no
longer needed women for sex only, and women no longer needed
men for protection only, but each had a vested interest in the *products of each other's labor*. This was a far cry both from the free-for-all
food gathering of the prehunting stage, and from the bring-the-
meat-back-to-the-den of the social carnivores. (Female carnivores
do not gather vegetable matter, and while social carnivores give us
important clues, we cannot read off the protohominids from them
either.) The hunting way of life radically altered the *content* of social relations in the band, even if the general *structure* stayed the
same. The tension between the old structure and the new content
lies behind much of the human situation as we know it today and
is mediated by the expanded and reorganized brain that was itself
the product of the process that caused the transition to be so successful.

The crucial organizational change can perhaps best be described by saying that whereas all primates have *ecologies,* only the human primate has an *economy.* The essence of an economy is *property,* that is, *things that can be exchanged.* The most primitive of these exchanges is that of vegetables and meat between the males and females—a change that forced the males to alter their relationship with the female families into something other than a mere breeding-and-dominance encounter. The next most important exchange was probably that of specialized services among the males, for as the hunt grew more complex and the society with it, the division of skills would become more important. And the third would be the exchange of mates, because the female vegetable producers were a different kind of animal from the old primate females: They were valuable labor. The successful breeding male needed not only to inseminate females but to ensure that the females would provide him and his offspring with vegetable food. Conversely, the female—even more importantly—needed the meat for herself and her children. With the period of infantile dependency lengthening (a good carnivore trend to give longer time to learn the tricks of the trade), the whole business of child rearing became even more complicated, and the somewhat slaphappy ways of the primate band could not suffice to meet the new demands. Some regularity in the assignment of mates for breeding and provisioning purposes must have ensued, although this was probably much later than the other two.

It was later because it depended on the elaboration of the first two trends and the growth of the brain to the point where it could make the necessary rules and invent the necessary categories. In the intermediate stage, there may well have been a fierce scramble for these reciprocal services that, as I have been arguing, may have helped to intensify the process of sexual selection and, hence, brain evolution. The "best hunters" (by this time, by definition, the "best genes" among the males) took more than their fair share of the "best gatherers"—the groups of foraging females based on the old primate female kin-coalitions. As the men came to need each other more, however, this free-for-all mating had to be controlled. And the marvelous ingenuity of the exogamous solution was *to make young men dependent on the old for a chance to compete for the pool of females the old made available.*

Why, we might ask, since sex ratios are equal, did they not just share the females equally? A logical solution, but not a human one. The solution had to be worked out in terms of the material available, which was the sexually competitive protohominid. The brain, which was good enough to work out the fair shares, monogamous solution (indeed, it has often tried to pay lip service to it) was a brain created by the competitive, aggressive, but equilibrational process of sexual selection. The equilibrating brain does not go in for fair shares without much inner conflict, because its basic message is "increase your reproductive success—with due caution," however much the message may get distorted and transmuted. We are not monogamous pair-bonders by nature, we are polygynous, tending to promiscuous, even if we only realize this state in fantasy—like the patricide of the sons of the primal horde—and even if most males will indeed have to be content with one female.[12] Lévi-Strauss realizes this in his argument about why women become "scarce goods." They would not be unless some men ("chiefs," in his example) were taking more than one, thus creating a shortage. The aim of the older males, then, is to get a disproportionate number of females for themselves, and to this end they must keep the young males (armed now with weapons) out of the breeding arena as long as possible. The young males will resist this and try, often successfully, to get at the females. But at the same time, they will also go along with the system if they can see a fair chance of making it to the top themselves. But the tension will always be there: The old men are saying, "If you want alliances, you must be subject to constraint." The aggressivity of the young males—a gift from nature to help them fight their way back in[13]— must also be turned away from the older men, outward, toward prey animals or other human groups. The reward for the young? Glory and wives—if they live.

I am painting a bold picture here, but it seems to me the only one truly consistent with (a) a broad conspectus of human social, sexual, and mating behavior, (b) the primate baseline, (c) the conditions of the hunting transition, and (d) the conditions necessary for the evolution of the brain. The crux of the argument is that the very mating processes that caused the brain to evolve, if indeed they became intensified, must have tended to get out of hand, but that the brain had by then evolved enough to be able to take care of the situation by introducing rule-governed mating. The tensions of the old situation, however, were still there, to be managed, canalized, and cunningly reforged, more or less successfully, in order to retain their dynamism, but to tame their worst excesses. On the resulting uneasy balance so much of our social behavior depends, including our fluctuating attitudes to incest and its regulation.

Models of the Transition

To help visualize the "transition to humanity," we can list the following tendencies (and we must remember to translate them all into the correct "selectional" language for accuracy):

> The old primate breeding system based on combinations of dominance and dispersion.
>
> The tendency of dominant males to monopolize control of the females for mating purposes.
>
> The tendency of younger males both to desire and to avoid the females so controlled.
>
> The tendency of younger males to challenge the older for places in the hierarchy.
>
> The tendency of the old males to exercise severe control over the younger.
>
> The tendency of the younger males, in order to survive, to develop mechanisms of inhibition over feelings of sex and aggression in this context.
>
> The tendency of prey size to increase and with this the complexity of hunting.
>
> The tendency for the period of infant dependency to lengthen in response to this.[14]
>
> The tendency of the brain to increase in size as a function of the interaction between all these factors.
>
> The tendency of the brain to become internally reorganized as well as larger.
>
> The tendency for cortical control of hormonal processes to increase as a result of the dominance of the neocortex.
>
> The tendency to develop increased memory storage[15] and the ability to classify, leading to rudimentary language.
>
> The tendency to increase parental investment in infants in response to their longer growth period.
>
> The tendency to internalize group rules and feel guilt over transgressions (a product of both language and inhibition).

The tendency of males to seek cooperative relationships inside and outside group boundaries.

The tendency of females to intensify their cooperative kin behavior in foraging.

The tendency of females to seek longer-term protection and provisioning from successful males.

The tendency for males to demonstrate dominance status through the control of females.

The tendency of males and females to trade animal protein for vegetable food in a regular way (leading to domestic institutions).

The tendency for males to use the control of females as a means of forging alliances with other males.

The tendency for coalitions of females to seek to further their reproductive interests by obtaining successful males.

The tendency for the period of ovulation in females to be less externally marked—a consequence of bipedalism (?) and cortical control.

There are probably more, but that is enough to keep in our heads for now. At the end of chapter four, I said that while both regular mating and kinship groups existed in primates, no primate had seemed to put them together in the same system except *Homo sapiens.* I expect that *Homo erectus* was doing it, and for the reasons in the above list: it had to reorganize its mating game by molding the old pattern to new uses in the light of the changed relationship between males and females as *producers and consumers of two different kinds of essential food.* The impulse was more likely to have come from the female kin-coalitions. The need of the female coalitions for male provisioning—meat for the children—was undoubtedly the push. The females could easily trade on the male's tendency to want to monopolize (or at least think he was monopolizing) the females for mating purposes, and say, in effect, "Okay, you get the monopoly—or the appearance of it anyway—and we get the meat." Insofar as the male was successful in turn, he would have females to trade—with the active participation of the female kin-group—for other "successful" males as sons-in-law, brothers-in-law, or even nephews-in-law (but that is to jump ahead a bit). He is also getting male offspring to add to his hunting entourage. Thus it is that the human primate weaves together the two possibilities in its own, very human, way. Its contribution is not the invention of kinship, but the invention of in-laws, affines, "relatives by marriage."

It would have been aided in this by another deep tendency in the very evolutionary process itself. This is referred to in the jargon as "kin selection," and roughly speaking means that animals can promote the success of their genes not only by the direct production of offspring but, indirectly, by helping related animals that share genes with them.[16] Since, for example, my siblings share 50 percent of my genes and my nephews and nieces 25 percent, it may pay me to sacrifice myself to save enough of them, if the number of genes identical to mine that I save is more than I might have produced by my own reproductive efforts—and particularly if otherwise all these related genes might have been lost. At certain stages of evolution, natural selection seems to favor out-and-out competition for reproductive success and damn the relatives. But once it "pays" to form coalitions of kin, then kin selection will mean that behaviors will evolve that tend to promote the welfare of kin even at the expense of the individual.[17] There is no question that the conditions of human evolution were ripe for kin selection to operate.[18] It was already operating in the primates in some species in a fairly obvious way: The multi-male groups with subgroups of kin (matrilineal or loosely patrilineal).[19] With hunting, kin coalitions would have become even more important. With the advent of rules, the *de facto* coalitions of kin—whatever their composition— would have easily become *de jure* units, with the rules serving to emphasize the things that were already established—"we must help each other" and even "we must not breed with each other" in some cases.

There is no way of knowing exactly what was the composition of such early kin groups around which the rules crystallized. The matriarchy versus patriarchy debate cannot really be settled, and it really does not matter much. There were probably considerable differences between different groups in different circumstances. There is, of course, no gene for matrilineal kinship or anything such. Contemporary kinship strategies can be seen to be based on certain inbuilt tendencies, but these are not specific to any particular kinship system. They are, rather, strategies of a flexible nature that allow us to take advantage of inbuilt properties. Thus, in some circumstances, we choose to stress the sibling relationship and bring the sister's son into prominence as a kinsman.[20] In other circumstances, we choose to stress the father-child tie, thus making the sibling tie weak and placing great emphasis on marriage. We can juggle the various bonds. Our ancestors were no doubt doing the same thing in the face of varying circumstances. It would, for example, always pay males to "recruit" other males, but whether they opted for recruiting them by alliance (brothers-in-law) or by descent (sons or sisters' sons) or both, would depend on many factors, not the genes. What would have been in the genes—and still is—is the tendency to act with discrimination toward kin, however defined, and to favor kin in the forming of coalitions. The definition of who was or who was not kin, however, would depend on circumstances: All that concerns us here is that there exists an evolutionary mechanism that generates kin-oriented behavior of a profound kind and that we are, as a species, exemplars of this trend. We can expect ourselves to be pretty conscious of kinship and careful about it, whatever variant forms our imagination makes it take. When we first came to classify things, kin were high on the list. And if we can state with confidence one human universal, it is that there is not a single known society that does not classify kin.

One of the effects of this was to divide kin into "marriageable" and "unmarriageable." We cannot have human kinship systems without this "marriageability component." This is the essence of exogamy. It is Freud's "renunciation of women"—not as sex partners on a casual basis, necessarily (although quite often), but as *assigned mates*. What our ancestors did, at some point, was to say, "Those people we classify as 'ours' on some kinship basis we may not have as assigned mates; those we classify as 'other' we may." Or less negatively, what they said to the "others" was, "We will give you 'our' women—defined on some criterion of kinship—and you will give us 'your' women" (putting it from the male point of view).

This is what the primates were close to doing. The multi-male groupers with their female kin-groups seeking to get their male relatives into a good position to mate with other female kin-groups were onto the basics. So were the chimps with their territorial groups of male kin and wandering females. But these lacked the need to make a regulated connection between the males and females, because the males were not needed for more than sex and protection. The rapidly evolving hominid females needed them for meat. The male's equilibrational capacities enabled him, eventually, to see advantages in the arrangement, and self-interest and species survival were happily married. As Lévi-Strauss saw so correctly, then, the impulse to exogamy was a positive, not a negative, impulse. We did not just, as Freud pictured it, flee from tabooed women and so bump into others. We deliberately defined some females as "our kinswomen" and made an exchange agreement with "them" (other males) for "their kinswomen." The women aided and abetted, of course, in a program that was entirely to their selective advantage and probably their idea in the first place. The original arrangements may have involved groups of males attaching collectively to groups of females or local bands exchanging males or females or, in large groups, sub-units of close-kin exchanging spouses. It is wrong to assume any rigid "model"—this is to deny the hominids one of their great evolutionary assets—flexibility.

This all makes, however, the hominid male's tendency to accumulate females a very different matter from the hamadryas or gelada male's instinctive urge to do the same thing. We put our polygynous tendencies together out of very different material, although the basic urge—to control females for mating—is, of course, there across the board. What is not there is the tendency to exogamy, the unique human contribution.

Let us postpone further discussion of this and its relation to incest and other matters until we have looked at the models of the transition, which will, I hope, help to put some of this together more graphically. The basis for the models is the three "blocks" of the basic primate system in which we still share: the established males, the females with young, and the peripheral males. Figure 3 shows how these are related in the primates, in a very general way.

The transactions between the three blocks are very simple. The block of mother-child units gives up males to the periphery whence they return by way of equilibrational cunning to the center and the breeding hierarchy (if they do). The males primarily provide protection and sex (insemination) for the females, and females, sex for the males. They groom each other. All the animals seek their own food. The control of copulation and hence of breeding is in the hands of the dominant males, who either monopolize it totally or share it on their own terms with cadets and apprentices. Some form of kinship recognition, either matrilineal or

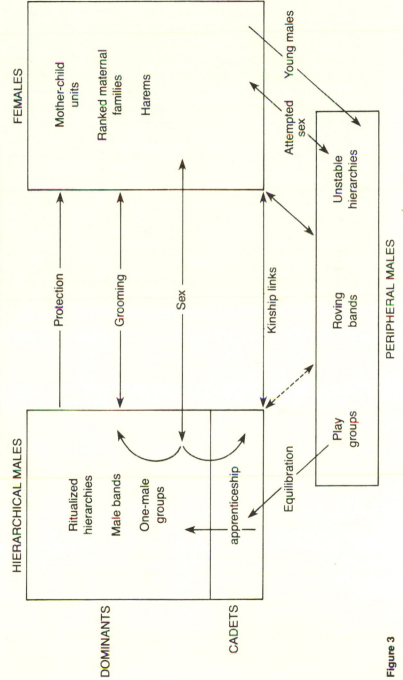

Social organization of terrestrial primates: the baseline

FEMALES

Mother-child units

Ranked maternal families

Harems

HIERARCHICAL MALES

Ritualized hierarchies

Male bands

One-male groups

apprenticeship

DOMINANTS

CADETS

Protection

Grooming

Sex

Kinship links

Equilibration

PERIPHERAL MALES

Young males

Attempted sex

Unstable hierarchies

Roving bands

Play groups

Figure 3

loosely patrilineal in nature, may link older males, females, and young males together, and may help determine dominance status.

Figure 4 shows the same basic structure but with the changes in the nature of the transactions that followed on the hunting transition and the reformed male-female division of labor. As well as protection, the males now provide animal protein to the mother-child unit (or extended maternal families). The females in turn provide vegetable food and the services of food preparation. Sons still move from the female units and become peripheralized, but this can be a symbolic peripheralization, and they enter the male hierarchy and the breeding system via the process of initiation. Some form of domestic organization links males and females because of the requirements of food gathering and preparation. Most importantly, kinship not only *links* individuals together, but its rules act as principles whereby females are *allocated* to the domestic units of various males through formalized mating. Whether this allocation corresponds to actual breeding success depends on how strictly people keep their own rules, and this varies. But it must be reasonably close. As with the control of sex among non-human primates, the control of mate allocation in *Homo* is in the hands of the dominant males (at least overtly), and again, they either monopolize or share on their own terms with initiated juniors. But the primary aim by now is not monopoly of intercourse necessarily, although this is expected to correspond roughly with power, it is *the economic and political control of women* (and for women, *the domestic exploitation of men*). In societies with established premarital intercourse, for example, many girls will be pregnant before they are assigned. This is sometimes welcomed as a sign of fertility. In many other societies, there are institutionalized forms of sex with men other than husbands. From the male point of view, it is the role of women as producers of offspring, as labor, and as objects of exchange that is now important.

The interweaving of rules of alliance with the control of allocation by the older dominant males is probably the essential clue to all kinship systems, since it is from this that they all originated. The rules of these systems do not so much restrict the sheer *sexuality* of the young males, as Freud thought; primarily *they constrain the choice of mates open to the younger males and make the choice dependent on the previous decisions of the older generations* (which was Freud's other

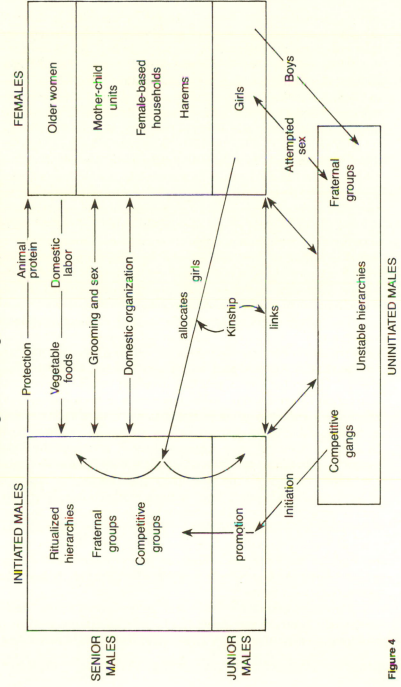

Social organization of genus Homo: after the transition

FEMALES

Older women

Mother-child units

Female-based households

Harems

Girls

Boys

INITIATED MALES

Protection — Animal protein

Vegetable foods — Domestic labor

Grooming and sex

Domestic organization

Ritualized hierarchies

Fraternal groups

Competitive groups

allocates girls

Kinship links

Attempted sex

Fraternal groups

Unstable hierarchies

Competitive gangs

UNINITIATED MALES

promotion — Initiation

SENIOR MALES

JUNIOR MALES

Figure 4

option). Sometimes, the system is blatantly weighted in favor of the older males, both in terms of gerontocratic polygyny and the rules governing the bestowal of females in marriage. Most of the Australian systems that so puzzled Freud, Frazer, Lévi-Strauss, and all other anthropologists are of this nature.[21] In others, it is not so blatant, but the sheer mechanics of the rules of the system restrict the freedom of choice of the young. In yet others, an overt freedom of choice exists in terms of the rules, but control over the actual marriage is rigidly exercised. (When the rules don't do it for them, the old men step in with transparent power plays; the subtler systems make the rules do the work in the old men's favor.) In yet others, like our own, the controls are minimal, but this is recent. The more we move away from the basic hunting pattern as in figure 4, the more likely we are to relax the rules; but the old males never give up without a struggle their right to dispose of the females according to their wishes—and for that matter, neither do the old matrons, since, in many societies, this is their most effective chance to exercise power in their own right, or through the influencing of their particular older males.

The technicalities of the various ways of exchanging spouses are beyond the scope of this book and the reader should consult Lévi-Strauss on *Elementary Systems* or myself on *Kinship and Marriage* for the details. Readers used to our own system, where the "exchange" element is muted, will have to make yet another of those leaps of the imagination to realize that this is, in historical and ethnographic terms, very unusual and that more systematic dealings in brides and grooms characterizes most kinship systems. Lévi-Strauss has called the more rigorous of these, paradoxically, "elementary." These are systems in which the spouse is a specified relative; either a category of relatives like "cross cousins," or members of a related kinship group like "father's mother's clan"—or variants thereof. Probably the easiest exchange to visualize, and one quite popular, is sister exchange—"I'll give you my sister and you give me yours." (Usually a "younger sister," since the male has to be adult to be doing this.) This can be combined with "cross-cousin marriage" in a simple way by continuing it through the generations as in figure 5.

Here each generation can be seen as "swapping sisters," or alternatively, brothers and sisters can be seen as marrying off their children to each other. On a large scale, this form of marital ex-

Sister Exchange

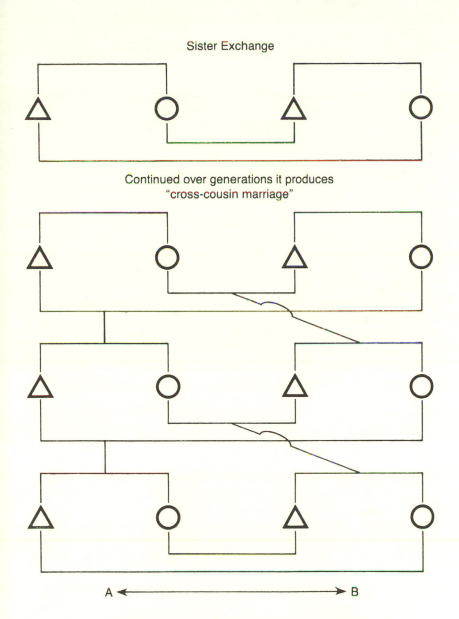

Continued over generations it produces
"cross-cousin marriage"

A ⟵――――――――――――⟶ B

If symbols are taken to represent "males of A,"
"females of B," etc., it demonstrates direct
exchange between two moieties or patrilineages;
the structure would be the same for any two
matri-units (see *Kinship and Marriage*, chapter seven).

Figure 5

change finds expression in moieties, where a tribe is divided into two groups which intermarry. The formula is always the same whatever the exchanging units are: "A gives to B and B gives back to A again" and so on down the generations. In the jargon, this is "direct exchange." It can be made indirect by having a rule of marriage with the maternal uncle's daughter and forbidding other cousins. The formula becomes "A gives to B gives to C . . . gives to A." Any number of units can join in, and spouses travel round in circles, in effect, between the units. For all the elaborations and variations, which can look quite hair-raising, the reader is referred to the detailed analyses of the experts.[22] No matter how complicated they seem to become, however, the exchanges are basically of the two types described: either straight swaps, or "circulation." Once societies get above a certain size (it is estimated that the upper limit is 5,000—about the size of the linguistic group at the "band" stage of social evolution), then these restricted exchange systems go through transitions until they become, in Lévi-Strauss's terms, "complex systems," where the spouse is not a specified relative, like our own.[23] In such systems, only a negative rule is stated; that is, we are told whom we cannot marry. The determination of the spouse, which can be quite rigid, needs some rules or influences other than those of the kinship system itself. (To keep the record absolutely straight, we should note that such "complex" systems are found also in simple, small-scale societies. But not the opposite. Large, technologically complex societies do not lend themselves— because of high mobility—to elementary exchanges.)

Most discussions of kinship systems are concerned with their mechanics: We are concerned with their origins and their effects, because their effects reflect their origins. Their mechanisms of alliance are well worked out, but their effects in terms of the way in which they constrain the young are not always so obvious. Let us take a synthetic example of an Aboriginal system from Northern Australia to demonstrate this roughly.[24]

We should imagine a tribe with the following law: A man has the right to bestow his sister's daughter on another man of an appropriate kinship category *as a mother-in-law.* This is indeed a common rule. In effect, what he is doing is saying, "I promise you the daughter of my sister's daughter as a wife." This may well be— usually is—an unborn girl. There are other variations, but the essence of this system of "bestowal" is that the recipient has to wait until his mother-in-law, who will often be younger than he is, has a daughter, before he has at least one wife. It is not uncommon for a man of forty to have two mothers-in-law, of say sixteen and fourteen, and to be just receiving his first brides. These little girls will grow up in his camp, and eventually he will cohabit with them. In the meantime, he may well have inherited, or acquired through bestowal, a couple of older women past childbearing age to start off his domestic establishment. Old men will look for promising younger men of suitable kinship categories ("different patriclan of same moiety" in fact) on whom they will bestow their great-nieces. The young men will then be bound as affines to the old men in an alliance, even before they actually have brides from them. The younger a man is when he receives his first bestowal the better, since that way he starts a household earlier and can collect more wives. Success breeds success, and if a young man is favored, then several older men may make gifts of mothers-in-law to him. The result is easy to see. Some men will monopolize the females, but all men are dependent on the favors of the old and will not have a fully functioning polygynous household until fairly old themselves. Some men will be cut out of the breeding system altogether either because they do not attract attention or because they die before they get wives. Others will contribute little to the gene pool because they only acquire one wife late in life.

Young men in systems like this have to equilibrate for a considerable time. They, of course, attempt intercourse with the young wives of the older men, and the latter attempt to keep them at bay. It is perhaps not surprising in view of our theory that Australian initiation ceremonies are among the most elaborate known to us or that they include severe genital mutilations such as circumcision, superincision, and subincision—the slitting of the urethra. In general, initiation ceremonies—which can be elaborate in the extreme and last for years on and off—seem to be ways of inflicting the message of the older males on the young aspirants to breeding and power. They vary in their intensity, from light hazing to ferocious mutilation, and seem to be fiercest in those societies where the boys have been more closely associated with the female block than in those where they have been gradually weaned into the male group.[25] In a paraphrase of the words of many native commentators, "We seize the boys from the women and carry them off to make them men." Often, further deeds are required such as bringing back a lion skin or a human head or going on a vision quest or whatever, before the boys are admitted to the company of initiated males and hence to the breeding pool. In some cases, they must wait even longer—until their service as warriors is over. Again, a number of them will not make it—lions are not too agreeable about parting with their skins, and other tribes will also have their young men out hunting heads. But those that do, on the basis perhaps of Freud's well-known principle of identification with the aggressor, will enthusiastically identify with the system that has caused them such suffering. Indeed, the identification is often directly proportional to the suffering, and the net result is that they will willingly inflict the same humiliation in their turn. New Ph.D.s are notoriously more severe with students than older hands.

That last quip has a serious point behind it. Even where there are no horrifying ceremonies, there is at least a process where the young have to prove themselves. It is rare to be let easily and without testing into the adult male world. And this is directed mainly against the boys. There are ceremonies for girls, and in some areas, nasty genital operations like clitoridectomy and infibulation. The message here is either the gentle one of celebrating the onset of puberty or the savage one of reminding the possibly errant girl that she is under the control of the older generations—of the males. Mostly, however, the girl is allowed into the female fraternity once she has menstruated, and certainly when she has borne a child. Thus she proves her womanhood. Not so for the young male. Proving manhood is a task relative to the needs of the society (i.e., the previous generations), and the requirements are often too much. Among the Plains Indians, a young man who could not meet them could, after having the appropriate vision to legitimate his choice, put on women's clothes and play for the rest of his life the woman's role as a *berdache*. Warrior or woman: These were the only two choices. It is not usually as severe a choice, but the extreme cases help us to see what the system is straining after. The reader can look again at accounts and analyses of initiation in the light of the "transition" theory and fill in many details for himself.[26]

I would like to go on and say much more about the fascinating subject of initiation, but there is already a danger of turning this chapter into an encyclopedia. Basically, the point made earlier stands: It is the human variant of equilibration. The latter alone could not cope with the aggressivity of the young males, armed and intelligent, after the transition got under way. What initiation, as a process, does, is to tap the equilibrational potentials through the very human use of symbols and ceremonies. The urge for power and sexual drive of the young males is contained by the kinship system on the one hand, which restricts their access to females but holds out the promise of success, and on the other by the many processes of initiation, which assert the power of the old males while brainwashing the young into their fantasies of power. The aggression of the young is then turned out onto prey or enemies or even spirits; tapped and then used by the older males, again with a promise of reward and glory linked to the promise of wives from the kinship system. Millions of years of equilibration have prepared both old and young males for this highly charged resolution of their conflict and for the forging of society from that struggle. But this is all part and parcel of the general struggle between older and younger males for the control of and access to the females—the elements of the primal horde—and the issue of incest avoidance. We must work our way back to that.

Let us do this by first considering the tremendous advantage that kinship and alliance (as well as initiation) would have given the hunting hominid in his race to become top carnivore. One of the essential ingredients here, which we have not considered so far (like so many other things), is the control of territory. This is basic to carnivore success.[27] Now with all other carnivores, when groups get too big, they split up and form separate territories and become rival groups. Primate groups do the same, but they are not carnivores, and control of territory is less important. Separate groups may be antagonistic, but they are not so much rivals as the carnivore groups are. The evolving hominid, however, once he hit the *Homo erectus* stage and had even a rudimentary language—and just how rudimentary it has to be we shall consider in the next chapter—has a distinct edge. He has, among other things, the precedent of the macaque groups, which split yet continue to exchange males. The hominid groups could do this, but by the method of alliance could turn this exchange into a permanent affair and make each group dependent on the other for mates, thus making them "one people" (Genesis 34:16). The net could be spread even wider by capitalizing on kinship as a linking mechanism also. As the two groups split up further, the subgroups would remember that they came from an original group (A or B), which only had to be given a name to perpetuate the link over the generations. People would know that they were "Snake" or "Eagle" people, and if they were snakes, they should marry eagles and vice versa. Thus, groups could segment and scatter yet keep their identities and their cooperation and their alliances. (These two mechanisms—the recognition of common descent and the definition of exogamy—are what kinship systems are all about, and the elaborations of them, which occupy so many pages of anthropological literature, have to do with the way the systems are geared to preserve the control of the older generations. Most anthropologists don't know that of course.) Hominids-with-words could thus extend their territories well beyond anything known to even the most sophisticated of the social carnivores. The status of top carnivore, as well as top primate, was the prize. But the price was a new set of unforeseen anxieties that came with the dawning of a truly human self-awareness and the development of mind. For at least by the Erectine stage, the animal knew what it was doing. It may not have understood it —still doesn't—but it could look at the new situation and consider it.

It could examine its own fears and work out ways to allay them; it could think of its own future and shore up fragments against its ruin; it could turn its emotions into poetry, magic, and art, as well as taboo, myth, and fantasy; it could use its intelligence for technology and science; it could make rules and either keep them or use its imagination to break them; it could ponder its own gestation and its place in nature; it knew it was going to die.

But whatever it did with this incipient "human" consciousness, this burgeoning mind, it had to come to grips with the rapidly evolved situation it found itself in as a result of the transition. Its high intelligence did not make it less emotional; the fact that it could use its imagination to create symbols did not mean that it could take off in totally arbitrary directions. The symbols and the intelligence emanating from the new brain had to deal with the problems created by the conditions that caused that new brain to exist at all. These were the conditions of the primal horde with which we should now be wearily familiar. We have seen how these gave rise to exogamy—which we have defined as the exchange of spouses on the basis of kinship rules, elementary or complex. We have argued that the conflicts of the primal horde were responsible for (a) the situation that demanded these rules and (b) the brain that was capable of making them. But we have also insisted that there is no necessary connection between them and incest rules at the level of social functions. It is still true that we could have sex within the family or lineage or clan or moiety and *still* marry out of it—and often do. Again, we often do not. Rules against marriage are often isomorphic with rules against sex, but they need not be. Freud may have been wrong, then, to think that incest prohibitions caused exogamy; but Lévi-Strauss may have been equally wrong to assume that exogamy was behind incest taboos—correct as he was to identify exogamy as an independent "operator" deriving from primitive notions of exchange.

The fact remains that we are indeed easily made uneasy about sex, and particularly sex with close kin, and I have already hinted several times at the connection. Those same brain and central nervous system functions whose evolution made exogamy both necessary and possible—the ingredients of the equilibrational process— made us *peculiarly sensitive to any and all emotions surrounding the process.* Our brain is, metaphorically, "wired" to be supersensitive to these ingredients—the power of the old males over the younger regarding access to females, the hostility of the young males to the old, the strategies of the females regarding mate selection, and so on.

The Lamp at the End of the Tunnel

To complete the picture, then, it is necessary to keep the promise to look closely at our reactions to sex with close kin in the light of this equilibrational theory. It is best to start with Freud's own insistence that incest prohibitions are directed primarily against the young male, since apart from anything else, it is absolutely true. It is a natural outcome of the young male being torn in two directions: He (or his phyletic memory) wants on the one hand to displace the old man or men and have free access to the women; on the other hand, he too is going to be an older male, and at the same time, therefore, he wants to *be* the old man. Kinship and initiation ceremonies are the social expression of the taming of these emotions and the socializing of them. But these two sets of social institutions are not free creations of the intellect. The brain is geared, wired, or what have you, to produce them in some form or other, since it is itself the product of the forces they represent. The brain faithfully reproduces a version of what produced it in the first place—or rather produced it over many millions of years of primate and hominid evolution. This is what Freud was so gallantly struggling to say, and given the hindsight we have today, I like to think this is how he would say it if he were alive now. In some sense, then, we do reproduce the evolutionary drama of the primal horde. But exogamy and initiation are truer exemplars of this than incest taboos with all their variability.

As we said, we probably would not commit much incest anyway, either for the demographic reasons we explored in chapter one or for the many reasons mammals avoid incest, as pointed out by Bischof. During the intensification stage, however, the normal mechanisms were strained. This is the context in which we must look at our current reactions to incest. The young male meets his first trial of equilibration with those older males and females that he finds himself among and who are defined as having power over him (males) or being forbidden to him (females). In the evolutionary context, such women as "mother" and "sister" would both be females controlled by older males. The effective older male might be "father" but it might just as likely be "mother's brother"— which is why there is no problem of interpretation of matrilineal societies. It is only if we are sold on the nuclear family as a biological human universal that the problem arises. If we see it as a universal problem of old males versus young males, then there is no problem. The young males will, as Auden said, "kill their mother's brothers/ In their dreams" if the maternal uncles are the present stimulus to the atavistic memories. But they will only do it in their dreams. This is what equilibration is about—the whole secret of the wiring of the brain-hormonal system. The young male goes into an inhibitory reaction against his own hostile impulses: or rather, he is easily triggered into doing so because he is easily made guilty about them. The mechanism may not be used—but it is there and ready. The relationship can, in fact, be friendly and cooperative, but the mechanism is there in case it isn't. The young male may not even know the nature of his feelings about the women. The reality may be his hostility to the elders.

As we saw in the sibling chapter, the mechanism will only be needed if natural avoidance of the sister has not been learned. Natural avoidance is there as a possibility with all its vicissitudes, but should it not be learned, should the young males indeed "turn their sisters into wives" even in their dreams, then the mechanism is there to step in—the guilt and inhibition are easily provoked. For the sister is either a "daughter" or a "niece" and thus in some older male's charge. But what of the "daughter"? By the time there is a daughter, the young male has become an older male himself with all the responsibilities of maintaining the kinship system. True, the daughter (unless this is a matrilineal society) is a "female under his control," but he has by now used his equilibrational powers to the full in learning that "own" women are means of exchange and alliance. Again, we must be consistent. There is technically no reason why he should not have sex with her and then marry her off. This is the commonest form of incest it seems on a worldwide basis, and it accords with our theory that it should be. But other inhibitions can exist, and a mature male has the fully developed equilibrational powers of an adult brain to call into play. In many cases—and we must keep in mind that our society's demography is unusual—she will already have been pledged and delivered as a wife to someone else by the time she is sexually mature. We keep young adults as children much longer than is the norm for human society, which is why societies like ours may have more problems with father-daughter incest. But not only that. It may be just as difficult to make over the protective feelings felt toward the daughter after a period of long nurture from childhood into sexual feelings. In the same way, it is difficult to make over the asexual brother-sister feelings in cases where natural avoidance has occurred. Very generalized bonds of this kind—very diffuse bonds, that is—seem hard to convert into something radically different. (Fathers and sons do not seem to work well as partners, nor old teachers and pupils as colleagues either.) But there is no question that with the father and daughter there is much more room for variability. It is here however that I would see Lévi-Strauss's argument at its strongest. The daughter has been reared for all those years as a potential wife for *another man.* This must have a powerful effect in restraining the father, and the ancient mechanisms of equilibrational inhibition will be brought into powerful play here, with the fact of exogamy itself as a stimulant to restraint.

As to "mother," we have already seen that she is ruled out, as Goody saw, because she is under the control of another man—and a man who is the focus of the whole weight of the equilibrational process at that. But she is also the mother who has nursed and suckled the boy. This is a powerful bodily relationship, and if natural avoidance can operate as a result of close body contact in siblings, why not in the case of mother and son? Suckling responses in the mother are strongly sexual as we now know and can admit.[28] (In many societies, mothers stimulate the genitals of their baby sons to calm them.) To use Earl Count's memorable phrase, the experiences of the lactation period "reverberate" throughout the males' life.[29] Add to this the age difference and that the mother is someone else's wife, and the cards are heavily stacked against the son's chances.[30]

The process weighs heavily on the young males and later becomes a problem for the old ones. What of the females? Here we are on less sure grounds, and since the males tend to make the rules, we hear less of the female case. But I suspect that the equilibrational process is not so strong in females as in males, because the conflicts are not as great and hence the reactions less charged. I doubt that unless it is severely inculcated, there is much guilt in female feelings about sex with brothers and fathers. If there has developed a natural avoidance with the brother, then there will be few sexual feelings, of course; the same may be true between mothers and sons. There is unlikely to be so strong an avoidance between fathers and daughters, and in this case where there is most incest, there is also perhaps least guilt—least inhibition—on the part of the girl. It is hard to say, but some observers believe that even where the relationship is socially tabooed, a girl can enter it without guilt or psychological damage, which often follows only on discovery when she learns of the shame attached or is treated as a "problem" by social workers, psychiatrists, and the law. Evidence is thin, but theoretically, we would not expect as much inner conflict with the young female as with the young male.[31]

If, then, we put the problem of incest motivations in the context of the equilibrational process, we can see how the various relationships and the varying motivations make more sense than if we look at them as products of the nuclear family. Even if there were no nuclear family, there would still be older males controlling the women. The nuclear family, where it exists, simply concentrates all this turmoil onto the little groups of actors who must play out the equilibrational drama amongst themselves first and in the wider

society later. Nor does it do us much good to concentrate on taboos
and injunctions and sanctions generally, for the reasons advanced
in chapter one. These, too, are highly variable. The red lamp
glimmers in our heads and hormones if anywhere, not in our laws.
We have allowed incest, even encouraged it, but this is consonant
with the theory. It will depend on how we juggle the categories of
marriageable and unmarriageable, and who we decide has power
over whom. There is no automatic universal horror. Sometimes,
groups decide to do the reverse of exogamy and *not* to exchange
women (castes, for example), and this can be carried all the way to
marriage with the sibling or the daughter. It is rare, but it happens. What the equilibrational wiring does is make it easy to prevent it happening, and most circumstances conspire to ensure that
in most cases, where natural avoidance is not working, the equilibrational process will step in and do its work. By and large, incest
will not happen, regardless of the laws of exogamy, the rules of
marriage. Exogamy is certainly not necessary to guard against incest—it might or might not have that effect. But then neither is the
incest taboo, so called. Simply to forbid it is not enough. The two
processes of natural aversion and inhibition under equilibrational
pressure will do it.

The taboos, the red lamp that has gleamed so temptingly for
all those students of human nature, are perhaps best regarded as
expressions of anxiety in circumstances when incest wishes have
been provoked in the face of either a motivation of avoidance or of
inhibition. We do make it difficult for ourselves, but that is the
human way. It is why we are more interesting than animals. It is
why we have taboos at all. It is all the work of the mind, and if the
process I am describing here has produced the brain, and if the
brain is the organ of mind (as the legs are the organ of walking or
the genitals of sex), then this process must have produced the
mind, which produces totems and taboos among other things. Is it
again producing what produced it? And is this the link between
incest, totemism, taboo, and exogamy that has eluded us so far? If
so, the fading gleams from the red lamp may illumine the darkest
corner of all: the nature of the human mind.

SEVEN

The Matter of Mind

Mastery over nature began with the development of the hand, with labor, and widened man's horizon at every new advance. He was continually discovering new, hitherto unknown properties in natural objects. On the other hand, the development of labor necessarily helped to bring the members of society closer together by increasing cases of mutual support and joint activity, and by making clear the advantage of this joint activity to each individual. In short, men in the making arrived at the point where they had something to say to each other.

Frederick Engels, 1876

Our past environment, once it is past, is no longer a sociological phenomenon. It is embedded in our brain and its use is dependent on the function or malfunction of the cerebral tissue.

Vernon Mark and Frank Ervin, 1970

In his great allegory of the human condition, *Pincher Martin,* Golding has his protagonist cast away on a remote rock in the Atlantic. Pincher is man reduced to the elemental. He is alone against implacable nature—the rock and the sea. He has no resources, he cannot survive, but he struggles nevertheless. His struggle is as much emotional as physical—knowing the hopelessness of his situation, but continuing to hope, he must stop himself from going mad. In his desperation to assert his control over the rock of nature, he resorts to the most elemental of human mechanisms: He names it.

> "I call this place the Look-out. That is the Dwarf. The rock out
> there under the sun where I came swimming is Safety Rock. The
> place where I get mussels and stuff is Food Cliff. Where I eat them
> is—The Red Lion. On the south side where the strap-weed is, I call
> Prospect Cliff. This cliff here to the left where the funnel is—Gull
> Cliff.
>
> "I wish I could remember the name of the whole rock. The
> captain said it was a near miss and he laughed. I have it on the tip
> of my tongue. And I must have a name for this habitual clamber of
> mine between the Look-out and the Red Lion. I shall call it the
> High Street.
>
> "I name you three rocks—Oxford Circus, Piccadilly and
> Leicester Square.
>
> "I am busy surviving. I am netting down this rock with names
> and taming it. Some people would be incapable of understanding
> the importance of that. What is given a name is given a seal, a
> chain. If this rock tries to adapt me to its way, I will refuse and
> adapt it to mine. I will impose my routine on it, my geography. I
> will tie it down with names. If it tries to annihilate me with blot-
> ting paper, then I will speak here where my words resound and sig-
> nificant sounds assure me of my own identity . . . I will use my
> brain as a delicate machine-tool to produce the results I want.
> Comfort. Safety. Rescue. Therefore tomorrow I declare to be a
> thinking day."

The naming of things was once more than an act of desperation. Pincher, in his extremity, recognizes this. Words had power,
they were magic. It was as though men recognized the almost magical transformation that words wrought: By their speech ye shall
know them—and know that they are men. But necessary, powerful, and magical as language is, mind is older. Consciousness is not
confined to man, and the evolving hominid was self-aware before
he spoke. He was becoming human well before the advent of language, although he could not give voice to his consciousness of his
own humanity. But we must bypass the gospel according to St.
John and disagree that "In the beginning was the word." We must
go to Goethe's Faust for "Im anfang war die Tat"—"In the beginning was the Deed." The final words of *Totem and Taboo.* The
groundwork for the word was laid by the deeds that were the stuff

of evolution as we have reconstructed it. And words, insofar as they are rules and interdictions, are themselves deeds and partake of the same history, as do the categories and the logic that lie behind them.

In this chapter, I shall take the two concerns with the mental and emotional life of man represented by the conflicting views of Freud and Lévi-Strauss on totemism and see if they cannot be reconciled within the framework of our own evolution. Mind embraces both thought (language) and emotion (behavior), and *Homo sapiens* has a unique mode of mentation. All things come together in the mind, so let us try here to reanalyze our concerns with totems and taboos, alliance and constraint, incest and inhibition, brain and behavior, from a slightly different angle. We shall ask the question: Why do we have the kind of mind we have and not something else?

Good for What?

It is often said by those who oppose an evolutionary approach to human activity that men do not operate in terms of instincts or of any messages coded in the genome, but in terms of categories and concepts that they impose on nature. They act, not as a result of nature, but in spite of nature. They act in terms of a reordered nature—reordered by the human mind. Thus, for example, social anthropologists are never tired of telling us that kinship classifications do not reflect "real" or "natural" genetic relationships.

This is all very true; I have devoted a good part of my anthropological life to sorting out the more bizarre and arbitrary seeming of such systems of terminology.[1] But it is really a half truth, for it fosters that Cartesian-like distinction between mind and nature, which, like its counterpart distinction between nature and culture, is so fatal to scientific inquiry or even imaginative good sense. It echoes Samuel Butler's complaint that Darwin "banished mind from the universe." What he did was quite the opposite: He gave us the only theory other than a supernatural one that could explain how mind got there at all. It is still true that it got there, like everything else, by natural selection: To survive, the creature needed it; it had an adaptational advantage.

After all, it could have been different. Let us take the example of language. We could design a creature with language, but one that worked entirely on dependencies between adjacent words. This "finite state grammar" is possible; it could theoretically exist; it is what a computer would undoubtedly design as the most efficient form of language from its own point of view. Chomsky laid to rest the possibilities of describing languages with finite state grammars in his brilliant *Syntactic Structures*.[2] A language *could* work that way, but "natural" languages do not. And the principles on which they do work—such as "structure dependent operations" and the "A over A rule" ("no noun phrase may be extracted from any other noun phrase," etc.)—are in a sense highly arbitrary. They have no more "reason" to be like that than the ankle bone or the thumb have to be as they are; that is, they could have been different. We know, of course, that the limbs are as they are because of natural selection. The great constructor does not always produce neat results, and this precariously balanced biped is not, for many purposes, a perfectly designed machine. But it is pretty damned efficient, given the raw material nature had to work on and the environments for which it had to be adapted.

The same must be true for mind—whatever we decide that might be. For the record, we are with Gilbert Ryle—and for that matter Leslie White—on this: "Mind" is an aspect of the body's activity, not a ghost in the machine. Mind, in White's memorable phrase, is minding.[3] As Chomsky has argued, language is a good model for mind, since thought has to be linguistically coded to be communicated. Language itself developed under certain selection pressures, and the uses to which we put language in conceptually reordering the world developed under the same pressures. The processes of mind will probably turn out to be just as arbitrary as those of the universal grammar or gross anatomy, and for the same reason: We have evolved our mental processes as we have evolved our bodily processes—through natural selection. They are rough-hewn to be sure, but they are the destiny that shapes our ends. They are not what a computer would have designed if trying to produce the perfect mind, but the computer is geared to perfection and not selection. It did not have to survive the savannas and the ice: somehow, with what was at hand. Our minds are as untidy as our bodies, but they got us here, and they deserve some respect. When James Thurber entitled one of his funnier books *Leave Your Mind Alone,* he was perhaps offering good evolutionary advice. But it is advice we can only accept as human beings, not as scientists.

We must start on our mind-probe in our own peculiar way: We must look at it ethnographically and then in terms of evolution. We must ask what mind does, and then we must ask how it got that way. In other words, we must treat it not as something that sets us off from nature but as a natural product of natural selection; as the essence to be sure of our own nature, but nonetheless natural for that.

We must start somewhere in our search for mind, so since the theories of Lévi-Strauss are important to us, it is instructive to explore further those features that he regards as basic to human mentation. In speaking of societies with dual organization, he says, "To understand their common basis, inquiry must be directed to certain fundamental structures of the human mind, rather than to some privileged region of the world or to a certain period in the history of civilization.[4] Then, in a later chapter, he asks the question, "What are the mental structures to which we have referred and the universality of which we believe can be established?" He answers himself:

> It seems there are three: the exigency of the rule as rule; the notion of reciprocity regarded as the most immediate form of integrating the opposition of self and others; and finally, the synthetic nature of the gift, i.e., that the agreed transfer of a valuable from one individual to another makes these individuals into partners, and adds a new quality to the thing transferred.[5]

Rules, reciprocity, and gifts. Universally, man makes rules and exchanges the things he makes rules about, thus setting up relationships. The "things" can vary from spouses, through goods and services, to sheer information. These objects are worked on by the mind. But before the rules comes the process of classification. The mind is a great classifier. The basic principle of classification is binary. Thus, those dual organizations (moieties) of which he was speaking reflect as much the tendency of the mind to want to arrange the world into paired objects as they do historical, economic, or other circumstances. Totemism—the naming of social units after natural objects (eaglehawk and crow; emu and kangaroo)—reflects not a lively interest in nature for its own sake or for the sake of its economic value, but simply the tendency of the mind to "order out the universe," as Tylor put it.[6] In Lévi-Strauss's own graphic words, totemic classifications are indulged in not because the natural objects are "good to eat" (the utilitarian theory), but because they are "good to think" (his intellectual theory). The natural world provides *metaphors for social classification,* which the mind seizes upon and orders in a, usually, binary fashion.

The idea is clear and striking. It does indeed, to a large extent, describe what men do when they set their minds to work. Consider the computer that has designed the perfect working model of the chicken. All you have to do is wind up the chicken and it will . . . what? Well, it will cluck, peck, brood, lay eggs, preen, etc., in certain predictable ways. Now if the computer could draw up plans for a simulated human being, what would the resultant android do when we wound it up? (There would have to be at least two of them, of course.) Answer: It would start classifying the world around it, exchanging the things so classified, and making up social relationships with the exchangers according to sets of rules (which it would then proceed to break).

All this has been familiar to us since Mauss first forced upon us the recognition of "the synthetic nature of the gift." We are a classifying, rule-making, exchanging animal. And it follows from the description of human social evolution that I have developed that this kind of mental development, this rather odd agglomeration of mental traits and processes, would have been a predictable accompaniment of the rather odd agglomeration of social and physical traits that were part of the feedback process that included the burgeoning of the neocortex. We shall explore this further later, but it is obvious that the processes of human social and physical evolution that we have been describing could not have helped but produce, at least, an exchange-crazy and rule-mad animal. As for classification, it is obvious that even the most elementary of elementary kinship systems cannot exist without some rudimentary taxonomic ability.

I believe, in fact, that the business of classification predates the shift to kinship and exogamy. It has about it what the ethologists would call an "appetitive" quality. If you leave a chicken alone in a plain white box long enough, even though there is absolutely nothing there, after a while it will start to peck. Why? Because that is what a chicken does. It will do it in the absence of any stimulus or reward and for no obvious reason, except that it is basic chicken behavior and it can't go long without doing it. In reading *The Savage Mind,* or any works on ethnobotany, or any treatise on systematic zoology, or even listening to kids discuss the kinds of football plays there are, the mind reels under the impact of vast classificatory schemes. Many of these seem to have no real purpose beyond the act of classification itself. People classify plants they never eat, fish they rarely see, and human qualities that may or may not be related to anything useful.

Again, the utilitarian approach is baffled by this phenomenon. It seems to be a free play of the ever-savage mind. It has no purpose beyond the exercise of the intellect itself. It is almost as though the mind likes to keep in good trim by the sheer act of classifying. According to Lévi-Strauss, we should indeed view, for example, totemism, entirely from this angle. It is an intellectual function, not a social or economic one, and certainly nothing to do with anything so murky as emotion. All that emotionality that Freud loaded onto totemism misses the point, says Lévi-Strauss. There are plenty of places where totems are *not* taboo. The only universality is the intellect. Indeed, in some of his more extreme statements, he seems to treat emotions as simple failures of intellect. When reason fails, we get emotion. (A very French view of things, one might think.)

The problem is, that the totem so often *is* taboo. Men do not view their classificatory schemes with detached intellectual impartiality. We can grant Lévi-Strauss his point on totemism: that the universal feature is undoubtedly the classificatory one. But so often it intersects with another interesting universal feature, one that is hard to name but can be called the "interdictory." I borrow this from Meyer Fortes, who in a fascinating but largely ignored paper argued that another reason for identifying natural objects—particularly edible ones—with social groups, was because they were "good to interdict"—they were good to forbid.[7] There is no better way of setting "us" off from "them," for example, than by food taboos—as every orthodox Jew knows. Also, if we are the only people who cannot hunt emus in a society where everyone hunts them, this is pretty distinctive. As universal as the urge to classify is the urge, identified by Freud, to interdict, to forbid, to taboo. But the point is that these interdictions so often apply to nature; they "cross" with the totemic classifications and with others (classifications of types of food, for example).

We love to classify, but we love also to put negative rules on the things so classified. This does not exhaust our relationship to the natural world either. Something else seems to be going on in the full-blown totem complex that is also universal: a tendency to project our feelings and emotions onto the natural world. Whiting and Child found many societies in which animal spirits were thought to be either helpful or threatening.[8] All cultures have had their anxieties about nature or have "projected" their own anxieties onto nature. Natural categories are not only "good to think" and "good to forbid"; they are, perhaps, "good to feel." True, all these attitudes to nature need not coincide in every society, *but a society that does not apply interdictions to totemic classifications will apply them to some other;* if it does not have deep feelings about totem animals, it will have them about those with cloven hooves, or something such.

We seem, then, to have at least two fundamental processes going on here, both universal, but not necessarily isomorphic. There is the urge to classify—the intellectual process—and the urge to interdict—the emotional. The "rational" use of nature implied in the utilitarian theory (that concern with the food supply is at issue) verges on the intellectual anyway, while the "projective" use of nature is obviously emotional. These, in a sense, intersect when it is the totemic *classifications* that are the object of *interdiction* and *projection.*

"Good to eat," "good to think," "good to forbid," "good to feel"—need we oppose these?[9] Need we, like Lévi-Strauss, in the last chapter of *Totemism,* move "Toward the Intellect"? Or in any other particular direction? I don't think so. We only need to if we wish to preserve the mind versus nature distinction, and its associated dualities including intellect versus emotion. This is perhaps, as Lévi-Strauss might agree, a tendency that is as much a product of the mind's binary bias as of the true observation of reality.[10] Since in our view these must all be the products of related evolutionary processes, then perhaps we can resolve the self-imposed dilemma. The animal that evolved inhibition—equilibration—and so, rules, was not unmoved by the process. The intellect does not of itself motivate; it does not, literally move us to action. We have to *want* rules, we have to have some sense of unease or anxiety before we taboo; and the sense of anxiety, the motivations, the emotions are as much evolutionary products as the categories and rules we are moved to produce. And there lies the central question: *Why are we so emotive about concepts, categories, rules, and classifications?*

Toward the Emotions

Why do we have emotions at all? The answer is that like all animals we must act, and we have to be *moved* to act. The question then becomes, why do we have the particular emotions we have? We must pay as careful attention to these in our evolutionary assessment as to the intellectual functions of mind, because they are more basic, they are older—part of our reptilian and mammalian heritage—and they are what sets the mind in motion. But older theories that separated cortical activity from the "emotional" or "lower" brain have long since been discredited. The cortex is as much concerned with emotion as with memory or perception or any other of the "higher" functions. The whole brain is involved in all behaviors.[11]

Hamburg has put it very simply: *We learn easily those things that have had survival value.*[12] This includes emotional responses, as well as intellectual functions like language. Indeed, this is the essence of the Chomskian position. We are equipped with a "language acquisition device"—the LAD. This enables us to learn any natural language, since it programs us with the principles of universal grammar that are the basis for such learning. As with language, so with other aspects of behavior. We are geared to learn some things much more readily than others—given the right input of information—and some things scarcely at all. And the motivations (or emotivations) that we learn most easily are those that have got us here.[13] Thus we easily learn fear, aggression, love, language, incest avoidance, attachment, and altruism. We also learn to categorize, interdict, exchange, and make rules—to employ that whole range of mental activities, whether we dub them intellectual or emotional, that we can see are the outcome of our evolution—our *own* evolution, with its totally unique mix of straightforward mammalian functions and all the consequences of the hunting revolution and the acquisition of language. In the argument between Lévi-Strauss and the other schools, the matter at issue is a dichotomy between an emotional concern with the environment—with nature—on the one hand and the human propensity to indulge in taxonomic activity with the use of language on the other. In the perspective urged here, we must see these as joint products of natural selection that are combined in human behavior.

Evolution Revisited

And here we must pause and run briefly again over some features of that very unique path of evolution. Clearly the turning point was the advent of tools and hunting, and so we must have in mind at least the last two or three million years. Man's earliest excursions onto the dry savannas meant a radical change even in the absence of tools, for we must constantly recall that he was not, at this point, a very successful animal. Compared with the ancestors of the baboons and chimpanzees, he must have appeared, to an impartial observer, destined for failure. Very little about the earliest of our Australopithecine-like forebears could have inspired confidence, save the binocular vision—not the stature, the speed, the strength, the ferocity, or even the mental equipment. And the answer to his ultimate success can only lie in the very helplessness of the original creature.

It is unlikely to have forsaken the forests altogether; rather, like baboons and chimpanzees, it must have exploited a wide range of habitats. But it did so, more and more successfully, by making meat a regular part of its diet rather than a sporadic addition as with the other primates. The propensity to hunt and to digest animal food was there, but it was our ancestor who made this particular bid and left the rich vegetable world to its rivals. I say the "rich" vegetable world deliberately. The ancestral chimpanzees undoubtedly continued to dominate the forest and forest fringe, and even though they used the savanna, it is obvious from their continued semibrachiating, knuckle-walking adaptations that they preferred to make their headquarters the forests. The ancestral baboons, meanwhile, capitalizing on quadrupedal speed with a concomitant manual dexterity and a capacity for agonistic social organization,[14] had taken over the grasslands and the seeds and berries, roots and fruits that were sufficient for their nutritional needs.

And the ancestors of man? They must have been wandering about on the fringes of all this success looking for niches that were still open. Their gait, as we know, improved. And again, the tools. Robert Ardrey insists they were weapons, and perhaps they were, although they seem to me less efficient as such than a well-aimed rock. It doesn't matter. As many anthropologists have recognized, and recognized rightly, from Engels onward, this was the fulcrum, the turning time. At this point, with the brain poised for its dramatic takeoff, the intensity of selection for the lateralization of functions—the "split brain"—must have been enormous considering the costs of such a step.[15] Had our ancestors known what the gamble was, they might not have taken it. But tools imply handedness, imply lateralization of brain functions, imply speech of however rudimentary a kind. Tool-making is not a lone activity: It implies cooperation. And the cooperation was to do with the division—the butchering—of animals either killed or scavenged. These earliest tools are much more likely to be butchering instruments than anything else. And again it does not matter much how the meat was come by. The essential thing was the systematic introduction of meat into the diet, which provoked an organization to acquire it and divide it. And talk about it, as Engels said in 1876.[16]

What men (and women) had to say, and what they had to be very concerned about and hence able to learn quickly and easily, was to do with this continual discovery of "unknown properties in natural objects." Our ancestors were at a disadvantage compared with their better-equipped animal rivals. They did not have millions of years of carnivore history to help them out. Their guts were not adapted to a pure meat diet, but neither could they have lasted without the meat since their other rivals monopolized the richer vegetable areas, and until the advent of fire and cooking, many vegetables were unusable.[17] They compensated by developing genetic skills that would reduce this disadvantage if they were to stay in the game. It was not just language but *the things one had to do with language* that developed in response. In other words, it was those components of mind we have been discussing.

Take the taxonomic urge. If you are having to diversify your vegetable diet (the gorilla eats a narrow range of shoots, etc., the baboon largely seeds, and so on) and at the same time increase your range of meat consumption and, throughout, having to keep on the move and improvise, then it would pay to have an inbuilt tendency to classify the things you are dealing with—and a tendency that would be applicable to *anything,* since one never knew what might turn up. Given this, one could code information and pass it on to others, thus increasing by many powers the flexibility with which one could handle new environmental demands. To have available such categories as poisonous versus non-poisonous, edible versus inedible, dangerous versus harmless, medicinal versus non-medicinal, etc., must have been of enormous use in dealing successfully with expanding diet and expanding experience in expanding the diet. Concepts and categories, in other words, must have been as important a part of the eventual adaptive success of our unpromising ancestor as the pelvis, the ankle bone, the striding walk, and the tools. And the ever-expanding brain at one and the same time is being "pressured" by an extreme *emotional* concern with the environment and by the urge to control that same environment conceptually. It has to develop, therefore, *both the right emotions and the right conceptual processes at the same time* and as complements—even as functions of—one another.

This can be seen most clearly in the connection between memory processes and the "emotional" brain. In non-human animals, the majority of the memory is emotional: things are stored as pleasurable or painful, dangerous, harmful, and so on. In the higher primates, memory storage in the frontal lobes—the "thinking" brain—comes to be important too, but the connections with the limbic system (the "emotional" brain) are not lost at all. "If, for example," say Mark and Ervin, "both the hippocampi are injured, a man may literally be unable to remember what happens from one minute to the next."[18] This is because the hippocampi connect the cingulate gyrus and the frontal lobes to the hypothalamus (via the fornix), which in turn connects to the thalamus and back to the frontal lobes, as the highly simplified diagram in figure 6 shows.

It is as though memories, including rules and taxonomies, have to pass from the "thinking" areas of the brain through the "emotional" areas in order to be fully and thoroughly "lodged." The outstanding work of Jonathan Winson[19] is showing how exactly this operates during sleep, when "neural gateways" open to let recently learned material into the hippocampus and mix it with experience already stored there to produce those extraordinary events we have traditionally called dreams and nightmares. These are associated with REM sleep and species-specific theta rhythms and appear "late" in evolution—with the monotremes and mammals. Had they not appeared, Winson argues, to act as

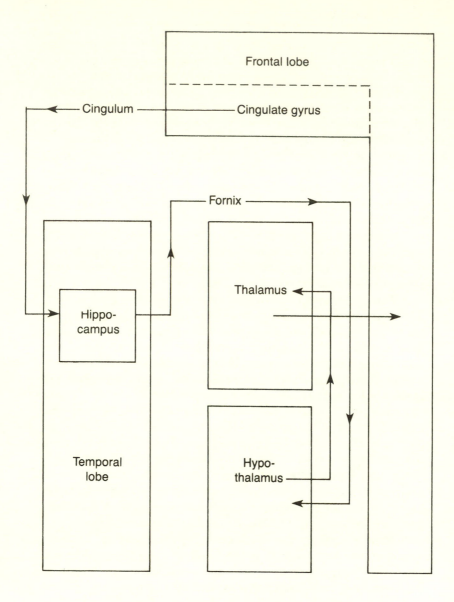

Schematic representation of human memory circuit
after Mark and Ervin, who note that it shows how
"many anatomical structures subserving memory are
also important in controlling emotion"

Figure 6

"filters" and selectors of memory, then impossibly huge forebrains would have been needed to store and retrieve *all* information coming in through the senses. The evolution of the brain, then, was dependent on the evolution of dreaming. (This makes dreams central to the mind, as Freud again saw, but for reasons he could not have anticipated.) Species-specific memory processing is what dreams are about, and this processing involves mixing the recent experiences (the causal memory) with the deepest emotional memories of the species (the phyletic memory). Taxonomy, then like habit, and the following of rules, while in a strict sense "cerebral," is far from "unemotional"—quite the contrary: *It has to be emotionally tagged and selected before it can operate at all.*

But this only tells half the story, for at the same time as the somatic, conceptual, and emotional capacities were developing, there was a development of *social* skills with *their* concomitant anxieties and their own taxonomies. The "mutual support and joint activity" of which Engels spoke, and which helped give people something to talk about, was making its own demands as well. But the growing social system was a system that grew to cope with exactly those environmental factors that provoked the anxieties and taxonomies we have been discussing! It is impossible to separate out arbitrarily here the "social," "mental," and "emotional" developments. They were all functions of one another.

Thus, the social system that was gradually emerging was based on the development of exogamy, itself an outcome of the change in tactics concerning the relationships between the sexes, itself an outcome of the division of tasks and the need for alliances, which itself exacerbated the old-male versus young-male quarrel inherent in the primate heritage and made more intense with the advent of weapons, which in turn provoked the systems of control and exchange that grew to meet the various challenges.

All this required its own taxonomies. While one can imagine primitive alliances forming in the absence of language, perhaps, and even the beginnings of initiation, it is inconceivable that exogamy can have so operated. Systematic exogamy cannot operate without the identification of "ours" and "theirs" and some rules about exchange and its consequences. The basis for the division of the world into such groupings and the thrust toward outbreeding, as we have seen, lay in the primate—even mammalian—heritage; but rules and classifications gave it its peculiarly human twist. The macaque male or female chimpanzees, who change groups to mate, do not do so because they classify the other group as "marriageable" and because of rules requiring such a mating. The human being does it precisely for the "rule and taxonomy" reasons and often in the teeth of motivation to the contrary. The rules have to be enforced, for not only are we rule-making animals but also inveterate rule-breakers. Our taxonomic-cum-rule systems can expand complexly, while our capacity to live with such complexity is limited. If the sociobiologists are right, then the detection of "cheating" may be another root cause of mental evolution. Cheaters, after all, are a great source of anxiety in any system based on rules.[20]

Sometimes, the rules and taxonomies that emerged served to amplify and underscore basic primate trends; in other cases, they deviated in new directions. But they were always concerned with controlling the access of young males to the breeding system, and with gathering allies: alliance and constraint. And in all this there was anxiety, just as there was in the relation of man and environment. The social system at first must have dealt only shakily with the problem of adjustment to the tools-and-hunting complex. Primate groups in the open savanna simply split apart when they are too big. The macaques are able to maintain relationships because they are close together in the forest. The ancestral hominids overcame the tendency simply to split by maintaining claims to common descent on the one hand ("we are all descended from the same ancestor") and by perpetuating alliances on the other ("we'll give you our women if you'll give us yours").

This shaky beginning, then, created its own anxieties, some having to do with purely internal matters, such as "cheating," and others with food supply and defense. It was one of those remarkable evolutionary trajectories that once started seem to have their own momentum. And whatever it was that was succeeding became *built into the cortical processes*. This included the intellectual and emotional apparatus that we have been discussing and, in the particular case of the social system, both a tendency to classify on a kinship basis and a tendency to make rules about the "objects" so classified. This went together with an *anxiety* about the whole process; both the internal—social—process of exchange and the relations between the social process and the environment that it was developed to exploit.

Good to Mean

If we try now to put this together, we see that the classifications and anxieties that were being built into the creature's mental structures are all part of the same process. The concern with the environment was certainly a concern with "goodness to eat"; but this good eating could only be achieved by the tools-and-speaking complex that had arisen in the first place to achieve it. We developed deep concerns with the world of nature, classified it and made rules about it: Concomitantly, we were aware of the inextricable connection between the social world we had evolved and the natural world that was its ecological context. We acted on the natural world as we classified it through the social world as we classified it and, in a sense, vice versa. Our ancestors would have been unable, as Yeats said of the dancer and the dance, to tell the hunter from the hunt. The categories of "social" versus "natural" were late-comers on the scene. Our ancestors were surely under no illusions about their separation from nature. That delusion came later with theologians and anthropologists.

One of the profoundest anthropological truths of our time is that kinship groups are natural groups—they are at the very core of the evolutionary process. That our ancestors saw no difference between the "herd" on the one hand and the "clan" on the other, that they classified their kinship groups in terms of groups of animals, and that they ordered the animal universe in terms of their notions of moiety and descent, should not surprise us. It did not surprise them.

Lévi-Strauss has, with his insistence on the unity of the human mind through the classificatory process, left the way open for us to set it in its evolutionary context. For as we have already remarked, whatever else they might or might not classify, *there is no known human group that does not classify its universe of kin.* This is a truth at once so trivial and so profound that we have known it for a century without seeing its significance. It is not only *that* we classify, but *what* we classify. And we classify kin. And if those of us still close to nature and the hunt classify them more readily in terms of emus or eaglehawks than in terms of, say, architecture or hair styles, this is not surprising.

Neither is our obviously easily learned anxiety over the natural/social world so classified. Once it became the case that we acted on the world *as we classified it,* that is, that our actions took on "meaning" in the fully human sense, then our anxieties could fix—had to fix—on the *stability and reliability of our categories and rules.* We were anxious about the world so we classified it, then we became anxious about our classifications. This double-layered anxiety is a typical human invention, because the expanded neocortex is a human invention. And it explains why we issue interdictions about food supply and categories generally and why we impose taboos.

Thus, whatever else humans do, one can be sure that they will classify and make rules about kin and the food supply, confuse the two, and be anxious about the whole process: either the "real" process (good to eat) or the "intellectual" process (good to think), because in fact the intellectual process is not a thing apart from the real process but is just as real, just as wired in, and just as anxiety-provoking.

A number of social anthropologists, like Douglas and Leach for example, have agreed that we see the world through our "social" classifications of it but, interestingly, add that what we often taboo or regard as "dirty," or even obscene, is that which offends against these classifications.[21] Dirt is matter in the wrong place, just as a weed is a flower in the wrong place. The categories of "pollutants," so important in many social systems, at first appear arbitrary, but are united, according to Douglas, in being "category mistakes." Thus cloven-hooved animals and shellfish, on the one hand, and domestic animals, on the other, become items of pollution and verbal abuse.

This can be used to show that "man is different" in that, unlike animals, he acts on the world according to "meanings" he attributes to it through his socially imposed categories, etc., etc. And indeed this is true. But what is not true is that this sets him apart from the evolutionary process in some way and in principle, for it is a product of the evolutionary process as surely as the brain that carries it all out is a product. But it is, in the view expounded here, also a producer. And we must return to that point. Social anthropology only errs when it uses this example to strengthen the "nature-versus-culture" distinction—to treat these human attributes as somehow pure invention, in principle different from the ankle bone.

If these tendencies that we have described are truly universal, like the categories of the universal grammar—if, this is to say, they are species-specific tendencies—then they exist in the human mind for the same reason the bones exist in the human body and the cells in the brain. They are aspects of the activity of an evolved organ—the brain and central nervous system—that is peculiar in its functions to man because of his peculiar evolution. But they are products of that evolution nonetheless. Mind is no more mysterious in principle than the ankle bone, although we are always less sure where we stand with mental anatomy. But until a social system is discovered that does not classify kin, I shall remain unconvinced that this universal feature is an accident of the imagination that has somehow or other reproduced itself everywhere. The same holds for the other universals we have discussed. Like language itself (and music too, if we are to believe Leonard Bernstein[22]), these aspects of mind are the products of a specific history of selection pressures.

The Social Mind

We have strayed from bridging the seeming abyss between the four "good to's" into reconciling the division between nature and culture, which was inevitable if too ambitious. We must probe it a little further, though, since there must be lingering doubts that suggest that man's concern with misclassification really is just intellectual discomfort and not a primitive evolutionary fear. But the distinction between intellect and emotion is as hard to maintain, particularly in an evolutionary perspective, as that between nature and culture. More tricky, even, is the distinction between the "social" and the "natural" that in one way or another runs through the thought of Durkheim and Mauss and is inherited by Lévi-Strauss and all those influenced by the ever-influential Durkheim. For Durkheim and Mauss, conceptual thought distinguished man from nature, but the origins of concepts were social rather than individual.[23] Durkheim, as it were, pushed Kant's categories of mind one step further back. He agreed that notions of time, cause, etc., were *a priori* and not primarily gained through individual experience. But this was not, he argued, because they were "innate," but because, rather than being lodged in the individual mind, they were lodged in the collective mind, the mind of society.

The individual derived his way of classifying and thinking about the world from the conceptual apparatus lodged in social traditions and institutions. Thus, notions of class, order, cause, time, hierarchy, and even space, were absorbed by the individual—implicitly or explicitly—from the collective wisdom of society. Durkheim and Mauss easily "proved" this by showing how all such categories and notions differed considerably from society to society—that one society's ideas of cause and time were not another's, etc. But there was an embarrassment: The categories, however different from culture to culture, had to fit "nature," or the result might be disastrous. They could not stray too far from natural reality and, indeed, were pretty constrained by it.

Durkheim was not unaware of the paradox this presented, but his attempt at a solution foundered on the set of dichotomies he had himself invented to establish the autonomy of sociology, in particular, his insistence on the strict separation of the "individual" and the "social." This distinction is fine, but a lot then hangs on what one equates with each of the items so separated, especially when one is discussing the origins of categories. If the categories are truly grounded in the *varied* experiences of social groups, then there is no reason why they should not be endlessly variable. But this they could not be, since the "nature" they have to deal with is uniform for all societies. Durkheim tries to solve this problem by declaring the societies from which the categories derive to be themselves "natural" phenomena. Since nature cannot contradict itself, societal and natural categories are bound to coincide. The categories are then, in a sense, implicit in nature; society "makes them more manifest." And, "if a sort of artificiality enters into them from the mere fact that they are constructed concepts, it is an artificiality which follows nature very closely."[24]

One wonders, therefore, why he found it necessary to erect the "society-versus-nature" dichotomy in the first place—with its elaborate demonstration of the "artificiality" of the categories of thought—if we are then forced to conclude that the artificiality is natural! The answer lies in Durkheim's ongoing quarrel with Herbert Spencer and the necessity to preserve the individual/socal distinction. The "evolutionary" view of Spencer he saw as essentially "individualistic" in that although it recognized that "experience" could accumulate through heredity, it still saw all this experience as individual. Durkheim, therefore, could only see this "hereditary" store of experience as a property of individuals, not of societies. Hence, he had to dismiss the possibility of the categories being "innate" in an evolutionary sense, because he had made the equation "innate=accumulated by heredity=individual." Since society had to be preserved as a "thing in itself," it could not be reduced to "individual experience," hence not to "accumulation by heredity," hence not to "nature" (itself equated with "biology"). But as we have seen, he insists that society *is* natural! What he does not do is to challenge Spencer's assumptions and make the next logical leap—as Darwin and philosophers like F. H. Bradley had done—to the view that experiences could accumulate by heredity (i.e., natural selection) *in society itself;* that is, in populations and species.[25] We have not the same excuse, in the light of modern knowledge, and we should not be inhibited by a slavish acceptance of Durkheim's dichotomies. Once we read into his insistence that "society is natural" the full Darwinian implications of "natural," then the paradox is resolvable, and Spencer and Durkheim can be reconciled as easily as we reconciled Freud and Westermarck. If we can analyze society itself as a natural product of natural selection, then the categories arising from it are themselves products of the same process, deriving, certainly, not from "individual experience" but from the collective genetic experience of the group—its gene pool. They are thus at once both "social" and "innate."

This reluctance to reduce the social to the natural runs also through the work of Lévi-Strauss, who creates the "intellect versus emotion" gulf to add to the others, and on the way, criticizes Durkheim and Mauss for embracing too "emotive" a theory of classification! He presents us then with another perplexing problem. He posits, as we have seen, "universal" categories of mind—the ones we are exploring—but when he deals with the issue (*Elementary Structures,* chapter seven) he goes out of his way to embrace a Durkheimian position and to reject Piaget's notion of inbuilt and unfolding stages of mental development. This is because he wants to avoid the Piagetian suggestion that the savage is "stuck" at a childlike level of development. He rejects this as he rejects the Freudian identification of children and savages. So, he opts for a social-developmental theory borrowed from Susan Isaacs, whereby the categories of thought develop from the child's original attempts to distinguish "self" and "other" and, hence, "own" and "other's": in other words, from social interaction and, hence, from "society." Thus, the categories are universal, but the Durkheimian position is saved because they are not "innate" but learned through social interaction.

Again there is a danger of erecting false dichotomies. We do not have to posit rigid, inbuilt mechanisms versus socially learned ones. Piaget's own position is not this, properly understood, however he may have misrepresented savages. What exists in man, as in all higher animals, is a *program* for learning. Nature is economical about matters that might otherwise overload the genetic code. What she develops is an animal (in this case man) with certain, but few, propensities to interact with others in certain ways at certain stages of growth *in such way as to fix the categories into the growing brain.* (Neoteny—the prolongation of the growth period and infant dependency—which we have already discussed, can best be understood as contributing to this whole process.) "Exchange" behavior as such is not inborn like the sucking response; but the basic equipment for developing it is there. The very structure of the brain demands an "exchange" of information from one hemisphere to another; and from the use of this capacity in social situations that are universal and inevitable in the species' experience, the emotional power of the exchange motive and the cognitive power of the exchange motif are developed. There really is no conflict here if the process is understood in this way, as there is no deep conflict between Piaget and Chomsky, despite their differences in surface opinion.[26]

Where does all this stand in our evolutionary perspective? It has been such an influential strain of thought in the social sciences, and one that has stood so firmly in the way of a biological perspective, that we ought to try to settle the matter in a preliminary fashion. The answer, of course, is that in our perspective there is no such set of dichotomies in the first place and, hence, no paradox. Culture and society are natural phenomena, and concepts and categories, rules and emotions, have all developed together as interconnected responses to recognizable selection pressures. Conceptual thought and language, inhibitions by obedience to rules, emotional responses to objects of social and environmental classification, all developed together. If we look at the "contemporary" situation, then we have to rule against the Durkheimian position about the relation of collective representations to individual. As Needham perceptively points out, Durkheim and Mauss really only show that the *content* of classificatory schemes, notions of time, etc., are "social" in their terms—that is, are derived by the individual from the collective cultural wisdom of the society. They do nothing to prove, as he sees, that the processes involved in assimilating this content, are not innate in the individual and species-specific.[27] In fact, the universality of the notions, despite their differing content, would argue for the latter, Kantian position. The model of language recurs. While the specific content differs from language to language, the principles of the universal grammar do not. They are there to start with, and they are what enable us to assimilate particular languages. Similarly, the categories of thought are there to start with and enable us to assimilate particular conceptual schemes. Notions, for example, of time, may differ between lineal and cyclical and, in each case, correspond to differences in social structure (the ossified social experience of the group), but the notion of time itself is universal, as is cause, etc.

But here is another beautiful paradox. Durkheim and Mauss may be wrong to locate the processes of conceptual thought in society in the sense that the individual acquires them through socialization, but in an evolutionary perspective, they may be right. That is, in the *evolution* of conceptual thought via language, pressures toward social classification may have been supremely important, and these would have become true "selection pressures" demanding mental equipment that could cope with them. But these conceptual processes concerned with the ordering of social relations were being programmed into the hominid individuals by natural selection over time, not induced by socialization in each succeeding generation.

How would this have worked? Some primate systems are what I have described as "only a naming system away" from human kinship systems—well, a naming system plus a rule or two perhaps: For example, the macaques who had two groups each with its ranked lineages and in which the males moved between groups, are familiar enough. If we named one group eaglehawk and the other crow and named the lineages after natural phenomena (bear, wolf, salmon, etc.) and then added a rule that excluded mating within each group and set up preferential mating with a lineage of the opposite group (or any variation thereon), we would have something approaching an "Iroquois" kinship system. (To make it easier, we could start with "group marriage"—this would lessen the number of rules to one.) Names, and one rule. But contained here are the notions of hierarchy, identity, opposition, exchange, class, part, whole, rule, reciprocity, time (consecutiveness), and even an incipient notion of space and cause. This can perhaps best be seen diagrammatically, as in figure 7.

The two diagrams are much oversimplified and intended only as a rough example of the trends I am talking about. In the first, the society ("people"—those outside would probably be classed as non-people or even animals unless incorporated through alliance) is classified into two groups, each group divided into smaller groups (lineages, clans), and there exists (a) a ranking between the groups (both between the moieties and within) and (b) a rule of exogamy such that one must mate in the opposite "moiety." The groups are then named. This structure can then be applied to "nature," not directly in any mechanical way, but *through the logical processes that have been generated from it.* These processes are fundamental logical processes that are inherent in the structuring of the group categories. They can be listed briefly and not necessarily exhaustively:

The idea of rule.

The ideas of relationship and identity.

The concept of part and whole.

The related concept of class and sub-class.

The notions of hierarchy and reciprocity.

The idea of sameness and opposition.

The ideas of time and (social) space.

A rudimentary idea of causation (deriving from time?).

A notion of dimensionality, since categories would crosscut (thus in the classification of animals "male" versus "female," "solitary" versus "pack," etc., cut across the division on the diagram).

I do not see how the conclusion can be avoided that there were powerful pressures to lock these "innate ideas" into the structures of the brain. Natural phenomena are first named and then incorporated into a system of social classification, being aranged in classes that correspond to the classes of phenomena in society. Thus, the Durkheimian formula can be rewritten to say that the mental processes of individual humans derive from collective social experience *as a result of natural selection.*

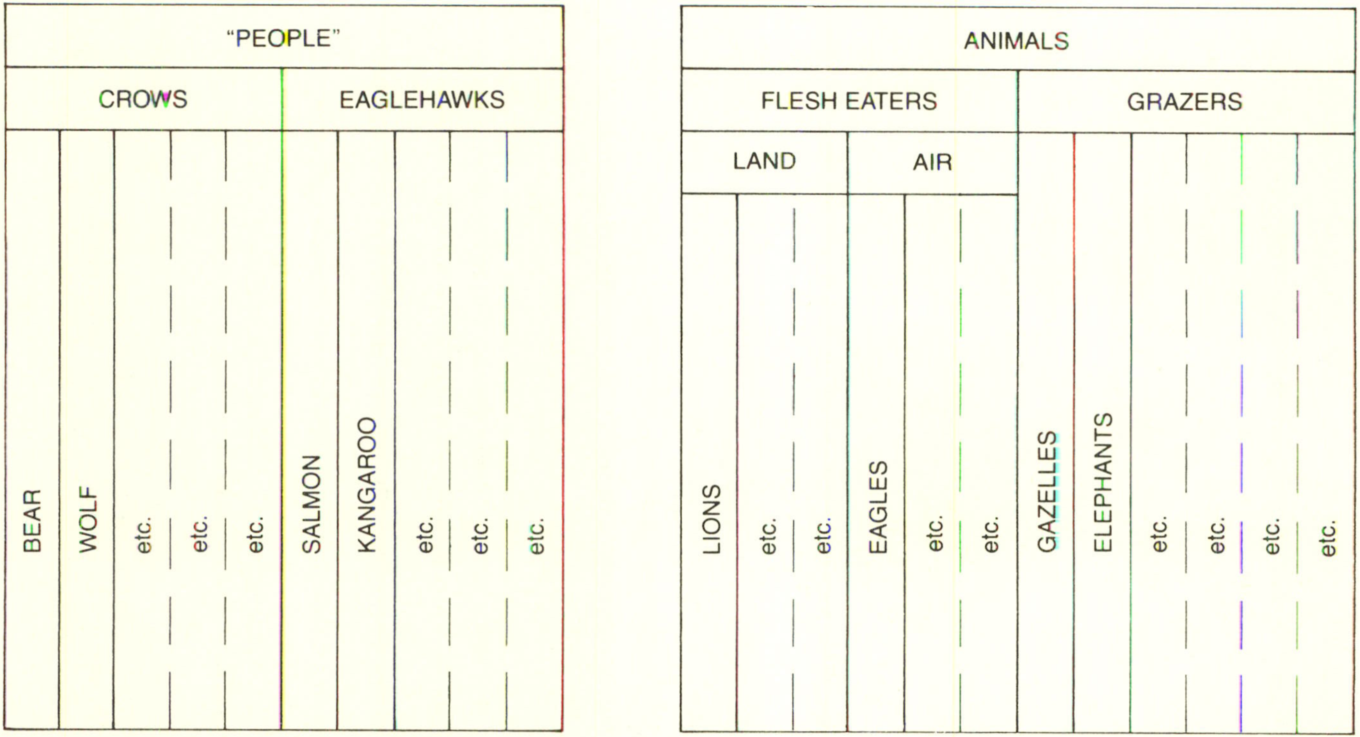

Figure 7

BEAR		
WOLF		
etc.	CROWS	
etc.		
etc.		"PEOPLE"
SALMON		
KANGAROO		
etc.	EAGLEHAWKS	
etc.		
etc.		

LIONS			
etc.	LAND	FLESH EATERS	
etc.			
EAGLES			
etc.	AIR		ANIMALS
etc.			
GAZELLES			
ELEPHANTS			
etc.		GRAZERS	
etc.			
etc.			
etc.			

If we reinterpret the quotation by the two brain scientists at the beginning of this chapter, we can say that insofar as our social environment over long stretches of time exerted selection pressures to produce the kind of brain functions we have, then *we can expect that same brain to reproduce the most significant aspects of that past sociological environment in its operations today.* Mark and Ervin were speaking of relatively short stretches of memory—within a human lifetime—but this same principle can easily be extended to the species and its lifetime. What the mind *does* now, in all societies, is an index of what the selection pressures on its development must have been.[28] That it classifies kin—or anything for that matter—makes rules, exchanges things, sets up relationships, and invests all this with emotion, is universally true at the most general level, and even in more specific detail. The mind does this because it has to. We have no choice but to be human.

The Elementary Forms of Speech

I have said that all this required language, but I am loath to get into a debate on the origins of speech. The Linguistic Society of Paris was perhaps right to ban such speculation. But the issue has been taken up again with vigor, and we must briefly address ourselves to it.[29] Let us take a deductive approach and ask "In order to run the most utterly simple of hominid social systems, what kind of language would have been needed?" We should first clear up two points. One is to get out of our heads any notion that rudimentary language would resemble modern speech. When Ogden and Richards invented Basic English, they reduced it to a vocabulary of 850 words. With these, they were able to rewrite Churchill's speeches without ever sacrificing intelligibility. The speeches weren't very elegant, but they were more than adequate. Chimpanzee sign-language experts are now well on the way to such vocabulary levels, so clearly they were not beyond even our very remote ancestors. *Homo erectus,* it seems to me, had a brain size well within the human range, and this would put speech, very conservatively, at one-and-a-half-million years old, give or take a few hundred thousand.[30] I doubt that it was the advent of tools and low-level hunting or scavenging *per se* that led to the development of speech. Many animals hunt and scavenge in coordinated groups without it, and very elementary tools can be handled by imitation and gesture. Rather it was the evolution of new social structures—marginally new to be sure, but new nonetheless—that was the necessary and sufficient condition for the emergence of language as such.

We need not go into the complicated question of what essentially differentiates human speech from animal "language," since that has been exhaustively dealt with; I am only concerned with the logical problem, "What must they have been able to do?"[31] The first attribute of language obviously is the power to *name*.[32] It is not surprising that the mere naming of things continues to have magical overtones or to give an unreal but satisfying sense of control over nature itself, as was the case with poor doomed Pincher Martin on his rock that he so desperately endowed with names. What do we need to add to this to get language? I would suggest that if our model is correct, then commands and injunctions must have come next. You cannot have rules without them. These might at first have been general "process words," which would include what we now think of as adverbs, adjectives, and verbs; but we must remember that these are not the best of distinctions. It is hard to decide whether chimp learners, for example, are using "eat" and "drink" as nouns or verbs, and the distinction is unnecessary at this stage. Process words could soon, however, from their origins in perhaps the warning cries of primates, produce command words and evaluative words. Thus, we can progress quite rapidly to such possible combinations as "noun plus process word plus command or evaluative word": the primitive sentence.[33] For example, starting with "mating eaglehawk," we can move to "mating crow bad," to "mating eaglehawk good," to "mating eaglehawk yes," "mating crow no." The simple invention of a negative (from a negative warning noise) would take care of these interdictions (negative commands). Thus, we might get "not eat green fruit," "eat yellow fruit," and so on. All I am maintaining here is that a structure of language at this level of utter simplicity would be enough to handle our primordial "Iroquois" system and the natural world of which it was a part, for a long time, and very successfully. It should be possible to show how, logically, the fundamentals of universal grammar would have emerged from this beginning, and the way in which the fundamental categories of thought would have become built into it.[34]

The selection pressures then were for better cerebral equipment to make the acquisition of language possible (the LAD), more complex taxonomic ability, and the ability to apprehend types of relationships between classes; also toward greater equilibration, for the control of emotions and the obedience to rules. This pressure was wholly "natural"—by definition, it was natural selection that was at work; but it was at work as much through "social selection" as it was through the effects from the non-social environment. We can conceptually separate these two types of environment (social and non-social), but we cannot separate either from "nature" without getting ourselves into Durkheim's dilemma. Hence, the categories of mind may well be social in origin, but this is a true phylogenetic origin and not a culturally learned ontogenetic origin. Thus we carry society within our minds, as Durkheim saw, but not simply because we incorporate it through socialization: It is in us to start with.

EIGHT

Past Imperatives: Present Discontents

In pious times ere priestcraft did begin
Before polygamy was made a sin
When man on many multiplied his kind
Ere one to one was cursedly confined . . .
Dryden
Absalom and Achitophel

Whatever lives long is gradually so
saturated with reason that its
irrational origins become improbable.

Nietzsche
Ecce Homo

In "Clonk Clonk," the second story of his Scorpion God trilogy, Golding introduces us to a society more ancient than the primitive Nile kingdom of Pretty Flower and the Liar. It is a hunting society at the dawn of time. (How marvelously unspecific the fabulist may be.) The story's eponymous hero, Clonk Clonk, is named for his limp—except that names in this society are ephemeral and change as whim and status change. Even so, being that precious commodity, personal nouns, they are originally in the keeping of She-who-

names-the-women—the leader of the female half of the group, or
Bee Women. Men's names, more volatile than those of the women,
are conferred by the Elder of Elders on aspiring males from the
men's half of the tribe, the Leopard Men. The men are hunters
and practice the cult of the leopard, whose skulls decorate the
Place of the Men (forbidden to women of course). The women tend
the children, gather vegetable food, fish, and live in the Place of
the Women (forbidden to the men). The men are childlike dreamers, babblers of inconsequential and poetic talk, but brave and
skilled in the hunt—when they can concentrate on it and not on
finery, eloquence, squabbling, singing, and killing leopards for cult
purposes. The women are practical, plainspoken, concerned with
the survival of their young; collectively, as a body. They have their
own rituals, practiced while the males are hunting, which include
drinking potent mead made from honey. They are the Bee
Women. At such times, they desecrate the Place of the Men and
drink from the sacred leopard skulls. They hold the men in some
contempt as impractical dreamers and incorrigible cultists. But
they know that they need the men to bring meat and make babies.
They choose from the men those that shall come to their huts, and
Golding makes his story turn on the apparently unlikely choice by
Palm (She-who-names-the-women), the aging leader of the Bee
Women, of Clonk Clonk himself. The men do not know that intercourse makes babies—Sky Woman does it. The women know, as
they know so many other things, but they do not tell the men. And
Palm wants another baby before it is too late.

The Leopard Men have been out hunting. Their first attempt
failed because Clonk Clonk, a younger male, did not close the line
quickly enough and the animal escaped. He is driven off and con-
temptuously renamed Chimp, thus relegating him to the category
of "not-men." He returns to the camp and finds the women at their
drunken orgy. (Homosexuality is normal within the two unisexual
groups.) He is raped by the women—during which he is mortally
afraid of the *vagina dentata*—then seduced by Palm, privately. Finally the Leopard Men return. The women are happy; they need
meat for the children. Palm goes to watch for the men:

> She blinked in the light, shaded her eyes more closely. She saw that
> two of the hunters carried a pole between them. A burden hung
> from the pole. She examined the size of the burden, the color—"Oh
> changeless Sky Woman! Not *another* leopard!"

But she regains her composure, suppresses her anger. The men's egos are frail, they weep and are easily hurt. If the women want them to perform, they must support and not knock. She greets them:

> "So go to your secret place mighty Leopard Men. Take the awful power of the leopard with you, while we women wonder, and cower; and humbly prepare you a feast of nourishing termite soup, and of dried fish, roots and fruit, and cool clear water."

"Rah! Rah! Rah!"

The fabulist has license to create at will, but the good one creates on the basis of a reality we know but that lies below appearances, below consciousness. Myths do this, as Lévi-Strauss so pertinently shows, of their own accord. They "think themselves out through us." They are accretions through time of collective wisdom, and in that sense no one man's creation. The fabulist taps the same sources; he is the myth creator, and in an oral culture his stories would also gather encrustations of collective wisdom through time. In our literate age, the myth maker has to do a once-for-all job — the collective mind will not help him; only the critics and commentators will render up their burnt offerings. The amazing thing about Golding is his sense of accuracy. He does not go simply straight to the archetypes (easy enough) but to the deep structures themselves. If we respond as directly to *Lord of the Flies*, *The Inheritors*, or "Clonk Clonk" as we do to myth, it is for the same reason in each case: There is an immediate recognition of a complex message about social order — immediate in that it strikes us whole, as a gestalt. We recognize the picture — even though it is set in a fabulous time and place — as being, in some sense, of ourselves. But an analysis of ourselves at which we could hardly otherwise have arrived.

Unless, that is, we have been patiently sifting through a lot of evidence for the evolution of our own capacity to make myths in the first place. To the reader who has made the voyage through the previous chapters, there will be a double sense of recognition: the immediacy of recognizing the mythic message, but also the lively awareness of having had the argument of this book brought vividly to life in the fabulary setting of the plains, ravines, hills, and human habitations of Golding's story — even to an encounter between the hunters and a band of chimps on the forest edge!

It is not quite complete. We have to go to *Lord of the Flies* for
the elements of order and violence and to *The Inheritors* for totemism, cannibalism, and the stirrings of guilt. But the ingredients are
there. This is society once the Rubicon of humanization has been
passed: They have speech, although for the men it is still largely
phatic rather than rational. They hunt silently, like good carnivores; talk is for before and after. They have a base camp and the
art of fermentation. But advanced as they are beyond the thresh-
old, their society is still based on the profound division of the
sexes—each a mystery to the other—and on the necessary transactions that hold between them. The men are at once the dreamers
and those-who-go-beyond; brave and cruel; fragile and vain. The
women know them and manage them. They select from the men
the ones they want as mates, and Palm selects the limping flautist
with his artistic credo, because Golding obviously prefers him. But
also because she senses perhaps that best genes in this society on
the verge of change (like all Golding's fabulous kingdoms) might
well lie in something other than hunting prowess alone:

> *Song before speech*
> *Verse before prose*
> *Flute before blowpipe*
> *Lyre before bow.*

Darwin's "female choice" and Atkinson's "maternal intervention"
are exaggerated here—although recent arguments might suggest
that Palm's selection of a handicapped male was well within sexual
selection expectations![1] But it is the business of the fabulist—the
myth maker—to show us graphically how the topological rubber
sheeting can be stretched in extreme ways while leaving the diagram intact. And this is why the great creator of fables is so valuable to us—and why women such as Palm did well to pick artists as
well as warriors and hunters.

We recognize the scene because the equipment with which we
recognize—our mind—is itself the memory of the pattern. The
pattern—the diagram on the rubber sheet of hominid evolution—
is what produced the mind, and the mind not only recognizes the
pattern of which it is the product, but it continues to produce it. As
Freud saw so vividly when he brilliantly combined science and
fable at precisely the point where they most naturally meet, in

generation after generation, we re-create the deeds of the primal
horde. The sheet is stretched and twisted—we even try in myth
and ritual, and even sometimes in creating utopian social orders, to
escape the pattern. And we fail. The ritual of disorder, of liminality and marginality, is of its nature temporary. By inverting the
pattern, we only serve to emphasize it.[2] Orgies remind us that
mating is ordered; egalitarian communities, that hierarchy is the
rule; celibacy, that sex is normal. Those who come close to the pattern through science rather than fable are not immune from the
desire to escape it. Marx dreamed of a society without hierarchy
and exploitation; Freud, of one without repression and guilt; Lévi-
Strauss, of one without history. Darwin was, notably, silent on this
issue, perhaps because he penetrated to the deepest pattern of all
from which there is no escape. And this brings us back to where we
started—to nature's one imperative: Reproduce. And to the only
basic question this leaves us to ask of any species: "How?"

It is not by inventing incest taboos, although the reasons behind our tabooing incest so freely and frequently are embedded in
the answer, but through the process of sexual selection and the
pressure for greater and greater powers of equilibration. Lodged in
the brain itself, these powers are the secret. They both facilitate
our sexual and aggressive responses to the opposite sex and our
elders and at the same time enable us to control these responses.
We are creatures primed to learn readily the things that helped us
to survive in our evolutionary past and to reproduce the drama of
that past in each generation in some form or other, lodged in whatever institutions are forged from the basic drives and the exigencies
of history.

That we learn easily to be uneasy about incest and categories
and throw ourselves readily into the business of exogamy and exchange is not because of a fear of dire consequences or reprisals or
even because of rational foresight or anything but that we are the
kind of creature that evolved to do these things because these
things were the pattern of our evolution, and our bodies, minds,
and social behaviors *are* these things—are the living, physical
memory of them. We reproduce what produced us; there is no
other way.

Immediately comes the cry: Determinism! But of course.
Strange, when from the fusion of sperm and ovum eventually there
emerges a human being with a completely predictable anatomy

and physiology, no one cries determinism in protest. Nor is there protest when this organism goes through a totally predictable life cycle triggered by predictable hormonal changes; nor when it ceases at some point and dies. However painful that may be, no one cries "determinism!" Yet, when this same creature produces predictable behavior and when colonies of the creatures produce recognizable, species-specific societies, there is—dare I use the word?—instinctive horror!

The idea that we must do as we are bid is repulsive enough to be sure, and equilibration theory would predict that there is an in-built revulsion to it. No child accepts it freely, neither does any little primate—neither did the sons of the primal horde, nor do they today (the daughters neither for that matter). This is one of the tricks: by overcoming the resentment the identification can occur. If our children do not resent our constraints, they will not end up being like us. But resentment of constraint and the power to dream and babble about dreams will always give us the opportunity to create, at least in our heads, situations the opposite of those that constrain us. But freedom in the end is, alas, the recognition of necessity; for the myth of the opposite—the unconstrained state—is as predictable as the constraint itself. There is no culture that does not have its share of such myths, although most primitive cultures are content to recognize them as myths and leave it at that. Only civilized dreamers strive to produce them on earth from the turmoil of history, and usually at a terrible cost. For we are free to try. We are free to flap our arms and try to fly. The Icarus complex is as rooted in us as the oedipus.

The illusion of freedom comes because, as I have said (to excess) in the first chapter, nature does not care what bizarre scenarios we write for ourselves—how desperately we strain the topological sheet—so long as we observe the ground rules; so long as the sheet stays intact. We have plenty of leeway—but ultimately we have none. That is a kind of freedom, and a generous one. We can experiment with our limits—even the physical limits of the life cycle. We do not do this consciously, as a rule, because we have not known what the real limits were, and we often prefer to think there are none. Or we invent some to suit ourselves, like the will of God, fate, original sin, the transmigration of souls, or race, or witchcraft, or the eternal struggle of good and evil. As long as we do not overstretch the basic pattern, we can live with almost anything—our capacity to do so is truly frightening. But that does not mean we can live well, and mostly, we live badly and for reasons beyond our control. But if the basic pattern is that of the hunting society that produced and governed us for 99 percent of our existence, what hope is there of living closely to it at all? Perhaps more than we think; but we are straining at the bounds in many ways, not the least of which is sheer numbers.

And here I must pass to some remarks about the contemporary scene. Reluctantly. I must do it because there is an obligation to point out the relevance of all this to the reader's quotidian concerns. What follows, then, is simply my interpretation—informed but personal. The reader might be interested to look at the various exercises in social doomsaying from *The Lonely Crowd* through *The Affluent Society* to *The Culture of Narcissism* and see how the structure of this argument helps to illuminate these diagnoses. For all of them depend on an explicit or implicit theory of "human nature," which is more or less wanting, lacking as it does an evolutionary framework. On the other hand, there are many issues that cannot be illumined by our lofty theory, any more than the learning of foreign languages can be helped by knowing the principles of universal grammar or phonology. A good language teacher who knows nothing of these things will be more help. Neither do ready-made solutions for social problems follow from knowing what we know. Sometimes, the best we can do is show why we have the problem.

There is, however, one thing that we might establish first and use it to ask some questions at least. The topological structure of hominid society, I have suggested, rests on the evolution of strategies of accommodation between the three basic "blocks": the building blocks of the hominid social/breeding structure. The issues of incest and exogamy turn on these strategies and accommodations, but so does much else. It might be objected that this pertains only to the ancient hunting society and not to more advanced or, certainly, more civilized societies. "No," I would stubbornly answer. "It is just society."

The first society I studied as an anthropologist was that of the Keresan Indians of New Mexico (particularly the Cochiti tribe).[3] These are one of the Pueblo group that live in settled towns—the oldest on the continent. They are the still intact descendants of the oldest settled agricultural tribes in North America. They live in little, autonomous "city states," with a complex, theocratic government and elaborate ceremonialism. Their social system revolved around three basic institutions: the matrilineal clans, which owned the land and arranged marriages; the matrilocal extended households, consisting of related women with loosely attached husbands; and the *Kivas,* or ceremonial moieties, which were patrilineal in recruitment for men (women joined their husbands') and which organized the ceremonial and governmental functions. These were complemented by several "medicine societies," largely male in membership.

Before European inroads, the pattern of society divided the men from the women: the men to their Kivas and societies and the women to their households. It brought them together in the clans to arrange marriages and adoptions and cures, and in the households for domestic purposes and reproduction. Girls stayed in their households all their lives, while boys stayed with their mothers until old enough to join the informal youth culture in its games and practices for adult male life. After initiation, the boys joined the Kiva and could, if they wished, try for membership in a society. They then had to work their way up through the various grades and degrees of the ceremonial and governmental hierarchy.

Marriage was officially monogamous (rare in North America), but there was considerable premarital sex, extramarital sex, and what I chose to call a "high turnover of spouses," since "divorce" has the wrong connotations. There was much differential reproductive success, especially between the various female households but also between males who moved around a lot. While the men ran the "public" side of things, there was a high status accorded women both in custom and in religion (the major deities were female), and women were very influential in the affairs of the clan and pretty much in charge of the households and the produce of the clan lands. The nuclear family was not much in evidence, except insofar as Catholic and Anglo influences had tended to make separate housing and at least a show of monogamy more prominent. But even today the basic pattern shows through.

These Indians were among the most "advanced" of the North American aboriginals, but are they an ethnographic exception perhaps? One could go on citing hundreds of examples to show that they are not, but I will be satisfied with a quote from Sir Edmund Leach, who must count as an independent observer if only because he is highly critical, not to say abusive, toward any such approach as this. In response to a point of my own he said:

> We have no need to suppose that all human societies can be broken down into simple nuclear bricks of the same kind which we can call families. On the contrary, empirical ethnography suggests that there are at least two kinds of basic brick. There are nuclear units which consist of mothers and their young children and there are other nuclear units which consist of groups of adult males.[4]

By extension, there must be a group of sub-adult males. But you might say that "ethnographic" evidence primarily concerns the "simpler peoples," even if they are more advanced than hunters and gatherers. Leach is as familiar with the civilization of Ceylon, for example, as the tribal society of the Kachin of Burma, and I am sure did not mean his remarks to apply solely to tribal and peasant society. We can clinch the matter by appeal to a completely independent source. Philippe Ariès is an historian who reeducated us all with his brilliant *Centuries of Childhood*. Here is his summary of the structure of human relations in preindustrial Europe.[5]

> In the traditional societies that existed before the industrial revolution, the entire organization of rural society, of a small community, of a district, or even of a single street in a town, was based on, I was going to say, the separation of the sexes, but that isn't altogether true. It was based on a separation into three groups: the group of married men, the group of married women with their children, and the group of young people, which consisted mainly of boys. These groups were separated; sometimes the girls went with the married women, sometimes with the boys. We can assume that each group had its favorite places: the tavern for the men, the washhouse for the women, for instance. In any case, it was not the home, for in traditional society the home played only a very small role, with the exception of the great bourgeois houses, where it was the custom for neighbors to spend the winter evenings. The woman was indeed the mistress of the house, but the house did not play a very great role, and the woman was out of the house almost as much as was the man. Each of these three groups, on the other hand, had a specific role in everyday life and in social life. The young men acted the part of the vice squad; it was their job to supervise the married couples. They were fairly indulgent toward adultery when com-

mitted by men, but not at all toward female adultery. Furthermore, the group of young men intervened when a married woman
either did not play her role, or exceeded it; when she "wore the
trousers," for instance, and ordered her husband about. So the
husband who allowed this situation to come about would be ridiculed by what was called the "charivari." This group of young men
had many functions apart from that of sexual policing, as for instance the organization of festivals. The group of married men was
the only one that had any money, which at the time was a very
precious monopoly. The group of women had many functions, one
of which is all the more interesting in that it is little known, and
that is the role of the pacifier. When there was a brawl, or a conflict
between the men, the women intervened when things were beginning to get serious. This division into three groups .vas not in con-
tradiction with monogamy, which separated the groups and united
husband and wife in the home. But the three groups all got together on certain occasions. For example, in the tavern, which we
imagine as being uniquely masculine, because of the nineteenth
century. But certain contracts needing the presence of women, such
as betrothals, were signed at the tavern—and Dutch iconography
gives us many illustrations of these special occasions at the tavern—in the presence of women and children. The real meeting
place of the sexes and of the three groups was outside the church,
after Sunday Mass. It was here that decisions affecting the whole
community were taken. According to the countries or regions studied, we find slightly more integration or slightly more segregation,
but always a certain type of strategy between these three groups.

The reader can perhaps imagine my astonishment at hearing
these words from Ariès' own lips—at a conference; from a scholar
who knew nothing of these theories of mine and who had not read
my work, but who described, almost in my own language, the basic
pattern in one of its variants: that of preindustrial Europe. His
final sentence is the theory in a nutshell. The various strategies between the groups have to do with the dynamics we have explored:
the female management of choice, and the male attempt to control
the marriage choices of the young men in order to control their initiation and membership in the male groups, with the concomitant
of youthful male resistance/identification. What Ariès describes is
very, very close to the basic structure and dynamics if we add that
marriages were arranged by the older males, with the connivance
of their females, since, as Ariès puts it bluntly, they had the money.

The charivari was also directed at older men who married young girls—not uncommon, given the power of the purse. If these old husbands were cuckolded then there were gleeful celebrations among the young men.

The whole picture is uncannily close to expectations and is not peculiar to western Europe by any means. I do not intend to bore you with lengthy quotes from the Asiatic literature to show this, or from African ethnography, etc. You already have the Australian Aboriginal example from chapter six. But is it, even so, no longer true of our societies in the modern technological, postindustrial age? We have certainly done some pretty serious tampering, but the basic pattern shows through in extraordinary ways—at least that is my interpretation of some of our present discontents. Let us pose ourselves some questions about these, trying to look beneath the obvious and accepted.

THE NUCLEAR FAMILY. Edward Shorter—possibly the best historian of the family since Ariès himself—documents beautifully the rise of "family obsession" in society-at-large during the twenties and thirties of this century.[6] The social scientists obediently went along. Having selected the nuclear family (its very name begs the question of its importance) as the cornerstone of society, they could proceed to lament its downfall and invent a huge industry of "family sociology" to research its "problems" and a huge profession of "social work" to put them right. If we see the nuclear family as simply one kind of compromise between the blocks—one outcome of their dynamics—then there is no cause either to rejoice or mourn. It will serve, like monogamy, as long as it works—more or less. Much of the concern with incest and incest taboos has been a by-product of the nuclear family obsession. If laws, architecture, and economics force us into nuclear-family living, then all the burden of the equilibrational conflicts between the blocks is placed on the shoulders of this compromise institution. The young male only has the "father" on whom to try out his skills of aggression and inhibition, and the mother and sisters are his only objects of sexual possessiveness—at first. He will soon move out into the wider society and find other targets for both—principally and disastrously at school. But at first, he is claustrophobically shut into *la bienfaisante chaleur animale et tropicale* of the family. It is small wonder we have problems for all concerned, but they are peculiar to these circumstances, as we saw in chapter two. Psychoanalysts who take the family as given often write of male hostility to authority outside it as "unresolved oedipus conflict." They may have the analytic cart before the proverbial horse. This is where the oedipal hostility *should* be.[7]

MONOGAMY. We have mentioned monogamy as itself a compromise, which it must be if our contention of "natural polygamy" is correct. Here, the confusion noted in chapter six must be cleared up again. The evidence is overwhelming that the trend across human societies is polygynous and that even where polygyny is officially banned, it flourishes clandestinely in various forms. But we are not maintaining that all men have an equal inclination to polygyny. It is the nature of the thing that they should not. The whole point of polygyny is that some do better than others. The other point is that it is a property of a social system, not of all the individuals in it. In terms of our theory, it is one of the more likely outcomes of the basic dynamics inherent in the hominid breeding pattern, for the obvious reason that it is the pattern that produced the pattern. Thus, left to themselves, human societies tend to sort themselves out into some form of mating system in which some men—usually the oldest, richest, and most powerful—will do better at the mating game than the young males who want to get into the system, to say nothing of the young women who are anxious to select among them. "Straight" polygyny is one obvious and widespread answer to this problem of the accommodation between the blocks, given their by-no-means-identical interests. It is one of the commoner strategies that emerge. But we must not forget that such straightforward polygyny is only one possible outcome of the more basic struggle of the older males to control the young ones by controlling their access to the breeding system. It can go other ways, and indeed, usually there is a mixture of strategies, sometimes of all of them. The only consistent one is adultery, which occurs in all societies; and it does not require refined analysis to suggest that sexual variety is preferred among a large subsection of any human population.

    The variety of strategies within a system can be illustrated by an exotic example, again from an ethnographer who had no intention of illustrating this thesis. Nur Yalman, in his elegant account of Ceylonese kinship and marriage and its relationship to the kin-

ship systems of south India,[8] finds three forms of marriage occurring together: polyandry, polygyny, and monogamy. Polyandry—
one woman with several men—is primarily a strategy of the poor.
It is often the only way very poor men can get a wife at all—by
sharing one. It is often brothers who do this. Monogamy characterizes the middle strata and goes with nuclear families. The upper
stratum and the rich practice polygyny, although some poorer men
will try to emulate this if they can, polygyny being a sign of status.
Here is a system in which there is no straight battle for wives
among equals as in northern Australia, with the weakest going to
the wall, but a variety of strategies open to men and women according to their economic means. The polyandry of the poor here
corresponds to the young Australian's bagging of a few old women
to start his entourage. The reproductive success of neither will be
high, but it is a foot on the ladder. The polyandry of the poor is
balanced at the top by the polygyny of the powerful and the aspirants to power. What this shows is the way the basic pattern can
result in a series of accommodations—not just one rigid outcome.
The "circulation" of old women to young men, young women to
old men in the Australian system will not work here, because the
society is not *simply* gerontocratic. That is why I have preferred the
"polygyny of the powerful" to the "polygyny of the old." The origin of class or caste society meant that old age alone did not ensure
success: It was power. The strategies changed in consequence; the
sheet was stretched a different way.

We can see from this how little it helps to try to lump human
monogamy (one possible strategy in societies striving for or stuck
with "equality") under some heading like "pair bonding" and to
confuse this with "falling in love." A more simpleminded piece of
nonsense has rarely been perpetrated. Sexual and personal preferences in mating occur in all systems, but few systems except our
own try to make this the basis for mate assignment. On the contrary, most systems of family law, even in the most primitive societies, exist to protect the institution of marriage from the volatile
emotional whims of individuals. There is no need to institute laws
to promote promiscuity. But any restrictions on sexual proclivities
need social sanctions, and monogamy, in large-scale societies,
comes under this rubric.

Here we must be careful to distinguish what has been called
"ecological monogamy" from "socially imposed monogamy."[9]

Under harsh conditions where, for example, constant wandering for food is necessary, the only viable reproductive unit may be the nuclear family and *de facto* monogamy exists. In large, settled, urban societies, polygyny could exist, so if it does not, this must result from the social imposition of monogamy. The reasons for this imposition are usually similar to those for the state's interference in kinship matters generally. The state bureaucracy is the natural enemy of kinship groups, and it tries to cut down their power. Imposing monogamy (and unigeniture among other things) helps to cut down on the growth and power of large lineages.

Thus, we have three types of system. The natural and most frequent one allows polygyny and whatever other strategies the less successful males can find to enable them to breed (as in Ceylon). The other two, both monogamous, are unnatural in that monogamy is imposed by law or circumstance. In our case, it is law aided and abetted by religion—always a ready handmaid of the state once institutionalized itself. But does this work? Has the western European, Christian, legally monogamous system ever been more than an approximation to the ideal? The evidence of history and the developments in our own society tell us that it has not. If older and more powerful men have not always had access to multiple wives, they have tried to monopolize access to the best; that is, the young and nubile. The young and less powerful males have always resisted this. A rereading of Denis de Rougement's marvelous *Passion and Society* with this in mind would be rewarding.[10] His opening myth, from which he reckons all the Western tradition of romantic love hails, shows the young Tristan stealing Isolde from the old King Mark (his uncle at that). Albeit, this was under "compulsion" and was frustrated, but as de Rougement shows, it sets the tone. Romantic love was at first adulterous and seen as totally incompatible with marriage. In its troubadour form, it exquisitely embodies the agonies of the underprivileged males from whom the "ladies" had been taken by the hard old warrior knights. He traces the "degeneration" of the myth—as he sees it—into the comedies of cuckoldry and low farce in the seventeenth and eighteenth centuries and, finally, with the nineteenth into Hollywood's "romantic love." But in so many of these sagas of adultery, one sees again and again the theme of the sexual revolutionary who challenges the established monopoly over the young women and threatens to overturn it. Don Juan, de Sade, Casanova, and the maliciously delightful plotters of Laclos' *Les Liaisons Dangereuses* are all engaged in the fight against the system that is implicit in the system itself. The young women, too, protest, sometimes through a male intermediary as in Brian Merriman's bawdy and brilliant "The Midnight Court."[11] But the old and powerful have not been idle. Systems of institutionalized mistresses, secondary wives and concubines, strategic adultery, prostitution, *droit de seigneur,* exploitation of servant girls (even in large peasant families—or daughters-in-law in Russia), and for the fortunate women, the lovers, gigolos, and cicisbei, have always been more or less rampant. Even within the supposedly celibate church, outbreaks of promiscuity in cult form, or even ritual polygyny (to say nothing of the proclivities of cardinals) have not been unknown.[12] That throughout this—and throughout the widespread victory of adultery over fidelity—some couples have remained in lifelong, loving monogamy, is perhaps more surprising than its opposite. Humans bond closely in many relationships, and marriage is no exception: but neither is it necessarily the rule.

This all seems to me so commonplace that it is scarcely worth comment. Left to ourselves, we will organize our sex relatively promiscuously and our mating around some variant of polygyny, whatever the official rules. But it is a conclusion strangely resisted by those who want monogamy to be "natural"—usually the same people who are claiming that we have no inbuilt tendencies at all! I see no escape from the conclusion, however—nor do I find many challenging it in private. One does not need the theory of evolution presented here to verify it, but given that theory, it makes sense of it; it is the natural outcome of the basic design and its dynamics.

DIVORCE. It is a system that only works well under certain demographic circumstances, and we are straining these. As well as increasing our sheer numbers, we are doubling our life-span—on average. In the world at large, people still die on average in their mid-thirties, as they always have. In the industrialized world, they live on average beyond seventy. The effect of this, combined with official monogamy, is to face a young couple, again on average, with the prospect of fifty years of monogamous marriage. This is unprecedented on a large scale.

Think of the consequences of this. The growing divorce rate in the U.S.A.—nearing 50 percent annually—has been pointed to by the "family sociology and social work" doomsayers as a major contribution to social degeneracy. But if we look at the *average length of marriage* now and, say, 100 years ago, I suspect that we would find it much the same: about fifteen to twenty years. The difference is that the marriage was then terminated by the death of one spouse, and this was followed by remarriage. What the frequency of divorce and remarriage does, then, is to restore this "normal" state of affairs (with divorce substituting for death) when medical science throws the system out of whack.

As long as we can view this calmly and adjust, there is no reason why the new "serial monogamy" or serial polygyny, if you like, should not make for a rich and viable system of kin relationships, breaking down the isolation of the nuclear family. After all, in this system the parent still lives. The point here is that we are too rigid—even those of us proclaiming our "freedom" most loudly. There are many ways in which the blocks can accommodate to each other as our Ceylonese, Indian, and Australian examples have shown. We have not exhausted these ways, and we are free to try new ones now that the daily food quest and yearly childbearing have been abolished. If we don't try them consciously, the collective wisdom of society will try them out for us, as it usually does, and is doing right now.

FEMALE LIBERATION. Even without yearly childbearing, the women's block still has to pursue its basic strategies. Since someone has to generate its children, it still has to select males, unless it renounces childbearing altogether. (Only a few seem to take this route—postponement is more common.) Never, perhaps, has choice been so free, either of sexual partners or mates. But ironically, this comes at one of those annoying demographic times when the choice is hardest to exercise: a shortage of marriageable males. These shortages are periodic, and after the imbalance has begun to be felt, women periodically demand emancipation from a system that only allows them to tap the economy via marriage. They demand direct access and all that goes with it—although their perception of what this is varies from period to period. There are now demands for sexual satisfaction, ending the double standard, freedom from the "drudgery" of housework, equal access to jobs, constitutional amendments, etc. These demands are, of course, a luxury of affluent industrial societies.

It is not only the demographic imbalance that forces women onto the job market. War, by eliminating males and recruiting females, hastens this process, but so does reduction in family size. It is a myth that inflation is responsible for the growth of "two-income families." Most families, except the very affluent, have always needed two incomes or more, but the second income in the past has come *from the children.* The wife produced and reared children who at a relatively early age (progressively raised in each decade of this century) went out to work and contributed to the family income until they in turn married. With the drastic reduction in family size, the pattern has changed: Wives, no longer producing children to put on the job market, have to move onto it themselves once their children are out of school age (or before). This aggravates the problem for women, driving more and more of them to seek jobs in areas where they have not traditionally competed. Male resistance to these moves escalates the female demands.

It is commonly assumed that the current wave of demands is either a pathological symptom of our times or a sign of expanding consciousness or something such. What can our perspective tell us? That it is neither of these things. The core of its assertions—that women are exploited and must band together to protect their interests—represents, in its way, an eternal truth, since the interests of men and women—the male and female blocks—are not happily coincident. Each wants something from the other, but there is a profound imbalance of interests. As we have seen, they come together in a series of accommodations, in which women generally have to play the underdog, because they have to bear the children (and commonly bear one a year while men can father hundreds), and this means many more compromises.[13] The accommodations they make are usually best when they cooperate as kin groups to exploit male vanity and gain their own ends—as Palm and the Bee Women knew. This they often do quite successfully as long as their aims are defined as the welfare of their offspring—a mighty leverage.

It seems to me that the current movement is somewhat confused over this. What it is objecting to, in essence, is what I have been objecting to for the last fifteen years—the tyranny of the nuclear family and the ideology of lifelong monogamy.[14] But these are not "natural," and it is not clear that they are altogether in the male interest either. What the militant women are objecting to, then, is the *role of wife* as it has been defined by the nuclear family ideologues. Our analysis tells us that this is quite in order since that role as defined is quite abnormal. For one thing, it robs women of precisely what they are asserting, namely *sisterhood*. In starting up their cooperative movements and asserting that as women they have interests to be protected from male exploitation, they are returning to normal. Where they get confused, because of the close links established by recent history, is to think that their protest is also against the *role of mother*. Since this has been defined as part of the role of wife in a monogamous nuclear family, they lump the whole lot together and attack it all. They imagine that what they really want (the more fanatical wing that is) is dominating male jobs in a male world. What they do not realize is that this is playing right into male hands, just as the so-called sexual revolution presented male chauvinists with a nirvana of sexually available women for whom they had to assume no responsibility. This is suicidal for women. True "sisterhood" is the sisterhood of comothers, and mothers and daughters, as many Irish, French, and Indian feminists realize. The only solid anchor for female solidarity is in the protection of their rights as mothers against males, and against the "family," and against the state and religious apparatus that threatens the absolute sanctity of the mother-child bond. The Irish mothers recognize this, for example, but the American lunatic fringe seems obsessed with the problem of access to the job market, which is the least of their problems in the long run. It leads to absurd philosophical and biological positions that can only do harm since they are false and not therefore a basis on which to make a movement claiming to be rational. Doctrines of essential sameness of the sexes are self-defeating and, more importantly, beside the point. The strength of women as a group, as a block of the social system, has always rested on their difference. This is what gives them their power and their dignity. If they turn to the men and say, "We want to abandon our children, or not have any, and we want to compete with you on equal terms for positions in the world you have created," then they will only succeed in either antagonizing—or in North America, if Lasch and the psychiatrists are correct, of terrifying and rendering impotent—the males. Palm would have understood. As long as they continue to bear the children, as they must, then their place in the system will be defined primarily by what they do about that, and their particular contribution should stem from the peculiar power that this position gives them. As Tiger and I pointed out, they could be the greatest power for peace in the world, if they exercised that power as *mothers* or potential mothers.[15] This is perfectly compatible with the basic pattern that says nothing about the subjugation of women, but a lot about their basic contribution in humanizing the males, as Ashley Montagu has always insisted to his credit.[16] What gets lost in all the noise—and this is a kind of Marxist objection, I suppose—is that the movement is a dupe of late capitalism. Rather than truly reforming society to bring it back closer to the basic pattern in which, in my opinion, women were equal and important, the militants are simply demanding to play male roles in a capitalist consumer society that both physically and mentally exploits men as well as women. Taken to its extreme, the militant position seems to suggest that if Hitler and his cronies had all been women, Nazism would have been just fine. Their concerns are elitist and parochial, and in the coming shift in world power and the turmoil that will ensue, they are going to be a minor irrelevance. As the greatest living woman novelist, Doris Lessing, puts it:

> I don't think that women's liberation will change much though— not because there is anything wrong with their aims, but because it is already clear that the whole world is being shaken into a new pattern by the cataclysms we are living through: probably by the time we are through, if we do get through at all, the aims of Women's Liberation will look very small and quaint.[17]

Another reason for my reluctance even to deal with such ephemera.

CONTRACEPTION. This is an issue that crosscuts all the others. In some ways, although it seems to be in fundamental opposition to it, it combines with increased population to have the most devastating effect on the pattern. Up until now, however, this has had a limited impact in the world at large. Affluent, middle-class women in industrial societies have been the major beneficiaries—if we can call it that—of chemical or any other contraception. We have really very little idea of the social and behavioral consequences.[18] Typically, we have concentrated on the physical effects, which are bad enough. But oral contraceptives essentially kid the body that it is pregnant, and pregnant bodies do not get pregnant. The result is that we have a lot of pseudopregnant women about in the world. At least with primates we know that pregnant females are not attractive to males sexually and that unpregnant ones treated with "the pill" are also ignored.[19] A small but disturbing clue. At the same time, in the traditional system, the possibility of pregnancy was a powerful control that the males could exercise over the behavior of the females and a powerful lever that the females could employ in dealings with the males. This is lost to both sides now. The old, in the U.S.A. at least, have more or less given up the struggle to control the sexuality or the mate choice of their young. The former is not so serious—there have been plenty of societies that have allowed youthful promiscuity. But the latter is the cornerstone of old-male power. To lose that control is to lose the last strategy short of sheer physical intervention, particularly if the system of initiation is also breaking down, as it seems to be in the school system. That all this happened at the same time as a whole generation of middle-class males refused to obey the authoritarian command of the old males to fight in a national (read "tribal") war, might just be coincidence. But it is unprecedented on this scale, and these subterranean connections are just what our knowledge of the pattern lead us to seek out. (It is also connected to increasing life-span, which leaves old males in power much longer.) If our schools are in turmoil and our colleges completely unsure about what they are doing, it cannot be unrelated to the decline of control over initiation and mate choice by the older males. The failure of nerve of the older generation in the sixties had a frightening Freudian air about it. It may, however, right itself once the initial hysteria dies down. The pattern holds. The young still want to enter the adult world, and economic sanctions, after the period of affluence, are still there and becoming severe. But the young have lost many of their former functions. They are no longer contributors to the family income or heirs to family fortunes. As someone observed, they are more like very expensive pets. But the pattern does hold, and the males and females still come together and make implausible sacrifices of time, wealth, and patience to produce them. Her will be done.

TEENAGE PREGNANCY. The pattern holds. A survey of those same North American "liberated" women, for example, shows that in choosing sexual partners they employ much the same criteria they would use in choosing potential fathers for their children—what the author calls the male's "resource accrual ability."[20] Some, however, seem enthusiastic to do this without such a benefit—unless one assumes that the welfare state is seen as the best resource accrual system of all: The whole tribe looks after its children! In the U.S.A., one million girls each year become pregnant without benefit of spouse. "Epidemic of teenage pregnancy," chants the headline, and the doom and gloom merchants rush to pronounce on the latest "social pathology." What can we expect with the nuclear family on the downgrade and divorce rampant, etc.? Curiously though, this coincides with the advent of universal knowledge of, and availability of, contraceptives. Explanations abound. The psychiatrists, as always, have a beauty: The girls do this to assert their independence from their mothers! Meanwhile, the girls continue doggedly to have their babies, and one survey showed, at least a third of them *actually expressed a desire* to have them. They actually wanted them.[21]

No one, it seems, sees that for healthy, fertile, active, postadolescent females of childbearing age to have children is the *normal* situation. What is really strange is how we have managed to prevent them for all these years. Now *that* needs explaining. We can easily turn the question on its head—after all, it is what they are supposed to be doing. For all human history, and in most of the world today, it is what they did and are doing. As an easy exercise, take the *United Nations Demographic Year Book* (I have 1976) and look up table 11. This shows live births per thousand females in each five-year age category. Under twenty is treated as one category. (Age at first pregnancy would be a better statistic, but this will do.) Divide the world roughly into "developing" and "developed" countries (this is very rough), and work out the figures for the under-twenty category. The averages are 91.05 for developing countries, and 39.47 for developed. In the huge rural, tribal-peasant, rest of the world, girls under twenty are producing more than twice as many babies on average as their counterparts in the industrialized world. The U.S.A. at 59.3 is much higher than the industrial average. (The U.K. is 38.4, the eastern European countries hover in the 70s, while Switzerland hits a low 15.1. Japan's amazing 4.1 is aided by an aggressive abortion policy.) The U.S.A. can then be seen, among the advanced industrial nations, as once more leading the way back to normality; that is, first pregnancy being teenage. This was always so until very recently in the world's history, and for obvious reasons—most obviously the short life-span and hence short breeding period, combined with high infant mortality. The earlier, in these circumstances, the better. The human race knows this, but the U.S.A. must institute studies to prove that teenage mothers are the best mothers if they have the right care.[22] (The possibility of spontaneous abortions, for example, is much lower in teenagers than older women.[23]) I make this point against those who claim that these girls are not "ready" to have children. If this is so, it is we who have rendered them inept. But on one point I agree with Konner, who claims that since the age of menarche has become artificially low in industrial countries, we are forcing eleven and twelve year olds to become mothers before their time.[24] This is true. (The curious phenomenon of the drop in age of menarche over the last hundred years is probably not due to nutrition but to the effect of artificial lighting on the pineal gland, which controls the onset of adolescence.[25]) My argument concerns fifteen year olds on.

None of this helps deal with the social inconveniences that ensue. I never promised solutions. But my point is that *we* create these inconveniences, not the teenage mothers—or rather, the changed circumstances of our time create them. The girls are not pathological, just human, young, and female. The time is out of joint. And the answer, whatever it may be, is surely not a pogrom against unborn babies.

We are going through a rocky time. The pattern is taking a lot of stretching. But it persists, and the paradox is, as I have tried to show, that many of our so-called social pathologies that keep the social science industry in business are more probably signs that the pattern is reasserting itself: decline of the nuclear family, increasing divorce, increasing female solidarity and choice, premarital sexuality, teenage pregnancy. Other things, like the decline of initiation and control of mate choice, are probably more pathological and help to account for Christopher Lasch's "Narcissistic Personality of Our Time." But it holds. If it does not, then we will not. I could have been writing this at another time in history, and I would have been plagued with questions about priestly celibacy, original sin, salvation by grace, dispensations for the marriage of third cousins, courtly love, rioting students, Albigensianism, royal concubines, chastity belts, unruly apprentices, love potions, and the shocking increase in the cost of dowries. Who knows what, in ten years, will appear to be the pressing problems?

All I know, ultimately, is that the pattern must hold, with all its flexibility. Because it not only constrains us, it is us. It emanates from us like the web from the spider and is our sustenance and our cocoon. It is, like the spider's web, both fragile and unbelievably resilient—to other spiders and their unfortunate flies. It cannot, however, stand a blow from an alien source. So far, we have not become sufficiently alienated from ourselves to destroy the web of our existence. No spider would do it. Will we be as wise?

There are many other particular things on which I could touch, but these few are enough. Tiger and I dealt with many in *The Imperial Animal,* and what we said mostly stands. The argument of this book does not stand or fall by these comments on the passing scene, for I am quite likely to be misapplying my own theory. We are too close to our times to be certain. But there is a last word that must be said.

Incest Today

Back into the feeble shadow cast by Prévert's red lantern. I have argued that in our evolutionary history it was dealing with the problems inherent in the "primal horde" situation that, in conjunction with hunting, made us human. Thus, evolving the capacity to inhibit sexual and aggressive responses in the context of related older males and the females they controlled led to selection for improved brains and all that followed. The need for alliances, aided by the capacity to equilibrate, made necessary and possible the beginnings of exchange of spouses and, hence, exogamy and truly human systems of kinship and marriage. Our bodies, minds, and behaviors are outcomes of the process, and from them, we create our societies which in turn reflect this history.

The consequence is that we have several inbuilt mechanisms that lead us to avoid incest (mother-son and brother-sister) and a readiness of males to inhibit incestuous impulses where they occur toward women controlled by other males or toward women they themselves control (father-daughter). Breakdowns are more likely between brother-sister and father-daughter, but throughout the population as a whole, they are likely to be relatively few.

That is where we stand; what of the future? It looks as though less and less control by the older males is going to be the order of the day in many societies. If this is so, then the need for strict incest laws will probably be less felt and they will perhaps wither away. It is noticeable that the first real sign of withering is in Sweden, the home of sexual permissiveness. Sweden's example is interesting. The only real opposition to the proposed (and as yet unimplemented) changes, came from those who were afraid of genetic defects. Against them, this argument was made: purely legally. "You are not saying that incestuous marriages *per se* should be banned, but marriages that are likely to produce defective offspring. But there are thousands of such marriages every year among unrelated people. In equity, then, we should ban those as well. Since we cannot do this, it is inequitable to single out brothers and sisters." For father and daughter marriages, the same reasoning would apply. For cases of sexual relations outside marriage, it was argued, these came under the general laws of such relationships. Thus a father's liaison with an underage daughter was covered by the laws against sexual abuse of minors and needed no special statute. No one ever seemed to think it worth considering mother and son! The general attitude to adult incest is that what adults choose to do in the privacy of their bedrooms has nothing to do with the state. The state, as Pierre Trudeau said, has no place in the bedrooms of the nation. Not now perhaps; but it has only reluctantly relinquished its powers over our most personal intimacies.

My prediction? That even if the special laws against incestuous sex and those against incestuous marriages were removed, there would be no great rush to do either—sex or marriage. If Sweden takes such laws from its books, it will be an interesting test case. As we established in chapter one, we don't really want to do it all that much—we are primed not to. Many of the old conditions are now changed, however. The huge populations in which we live make a delicate balance of kinship alliances meaningless, and such incest as there might be would be a drop in the genetic ocean for the population at large and not affect it at all. But I still suspect that there would not be much in the long run. In the rest of the world (outside the industrial nations), the pattern holds more firmly. And unless some unprecedented redistribution of wealth occurs, the rest of the world will persist for a long time as it is. Not much room for maneuver there.

Have we then extinguished the lamp? Not at all. We were always right to ask why it burned for us at all, for as Freud and the other seekers knew, somehow it held the secret of our humanity. And it did. But having got us so far, it can only light our way to the one eternal truth: We are a species among all the others, rather a special one, but one that will be judged, in the long run, like the others. We have no dispensation from nature; we are not cut loose from the requirements of natural selection; intelligence is not peculiar to us nor does it guarantee our superiority or our success; we must measure up or join her list of interesting but extinct experiments in living and reproducing. Our only uniqueness is that if we go, it will be in full consciousness of what we do; which is no compliment to our uniqueness.

Notes and Bibliography

I have tried where possible to refer to summary or review articles or to books that have their own bibliographies. If I had put in a full bibliography, item by item, it would have been longer than the book. In some cases, however, I have had to spell out the references for lack of an easily available summary source or because a particular point needed documenting. Also, because I so often present a summary of findings myself, I feel it necessary to indicate the sources for what may appear cursory judgments in the text. The edition of a book referred to is the one actually consulted, but with books of historical importance, I have given the date of first publication. Similarly, with foreign books, I have given the first foreign edition as well as the English translation.

I am deeply grateful to Linda Marchant for her help with this bibliography and, for specific items, to Tony Pfeiffer, Jay Callen, Richard Diener, and Henry Kranzler. Karen Colvard coped with a difficult manuscript.

A Note on the Main Sources of the Text

This book, which is based on the various things I have written on this theme since 1959, is a kind of Cook's tour through the anthropology in these two decades. Various influences are apparent. The earliest article, which forms the basis of chapter two, was "Sibling Incest" (*British Journal of Sociology*, 13, 128–150, 1962). Most of this was written from 1957 to

1959 at Harvard, under the influence of John Whiting and B. F. Skinner, and illustrates the contributions of both psychoanalysis and learning theory to anthropological ideas. But its stubborn attempt to reconcile Freud and Westermarck was my own, and so was the sense of dissatisfaction it left. Some of this was resolved in *"Totem and Taboo Reconsidered,"* E. R. Leach, ed., *The Structural Study of Myth and Totemism* (London: Tavistock, 1966). This has a curious history. The symposium of which it was a part was supposed to be on Lévi-Strauss, and Leach asked me to contribute something on myth and totemism from my Pueblo work, since Lévi-Strauss had used Pueblo material in his study of myth. I responded that what was engaging me was the gap that his theory left: It did not explain why the totem was so often taboo; Freud at least tried. Leach offered to include something on Freud—since he agreed about the lack—and I wrote this piece. This essay forms the basis of chapter three—again much modified. It shows the strong influence of social anthropology in the British style and the attempt to reconcile this, Freud, and the "culture and personality" research of the Yale-Harvard variety, with Whiting again in evidence.

But yet again, there was both a kind of resolution and a profound dissatisfaction. Some issues were resolved, but a lot of questions about totems, myths, and mind—and hence about Lévi-Strauss—were left open. So, also, were the questions about the origins of incest taboos *in time*—in history and evolution. The next excursion was what became chapter two of *Kinship and Marriage: An Anthropological Perspective* (London and Baltimore: Penguin Books, 1967)—with a title borrowed from Lévi-Strauss. Some of this material—written largely from 1962 to 1966—is incorporated in chapter one here, but with considerable revisions in retrospect. The basic idea, however, persists: that any explanation must be lodged in evolutionary processes—but not in an "anti-incest instinct," rather in the *readiness to learn* anti-incest behavior. This was expanded in the Malinowski Memorial Lecture for 1967 ("In the Beginning: Aspects of Hominid Behavioral Evolution," *Man* (n.s.) 2, no. 3, 415–33, 1967). This was where I first tried to effect a synthesis between Freud's ideas of the "primal horde" and my own interpretation of the theories of Michael Chance.

Everything since then has been a commentary on this basic theory. The influence here of the staggering findings of primatology, particularly the work of Washburn and Hall, is obvious, as is the effect of the burst of archaeological findings in East and South Africa. I confess also to the strong influence of that much maligned but remarkable amateur Robert Ardrey, who turned so many of us to the primates, the past, and the animal world at a crucial time. I here render him thanks and homage. Whether we agree or disagree with them, we need these questing amateur spirits to keep professionalism from killing curiosity. A paper

written for a Wenner-Gren Foundation symposium at Burg Warten-
stein in Austria called "Incest, Inhibition and Hominid Evolution"
(1969) became eventually "Alliance and Constraint: Sexual Selection in
the Evolution of Human Kinship Systems," B. Campbell, ed., *Sexual Selection and the Descent of Man 1871–1971* (Chicago: Aldine/Atherton,
1972). Here, I was returning firmly to Darwin and sexual selection and,
appropriately, on the hundredth anniversary of the Great Book.

Much of the general theory and the detail of these articles had
found its way into *The Imperial Animal* (with Lionel Tiger, New York:
Holt, Rinehart and Winston, 1970). The growing influence of ethology
becomes more and more evident here. Most of what we had to say still
stands, although some modifications have obviously become necessary
in the light of later evidence. Most of our propositions hold, however,
and it is amusing to note how many of them have been "discovered"
later, often with great fanfare, e.g., that neonates and mothers suffer
from being separated at birth; that it is the quality of crowding not the
quantity that affects aggression; that heightened sensitivity at ovulation
is the most obvious vestige of estrus in human females; that busing is as
likely to be detrimental as beneficial to the students involved; that
quotas will be needed to facilitate female entry into male-dominated
professions, etc., etc., etc.

In "Primate Kin and Human Kinship," R. Fox, ed., *Biosocial Anthropology* (New York: Halsted; London: Malaby, 1975), I expanded the
theme of primate and human kinship broached in the 1972 article. This
plus the previous two articles form the basis of chapters four, five, and
six, considerably rearranged, rewritten, and brought up to date. They
show the growing influence of the brain sciences and population genetics. The second half of "Alliance and Constraint" was an attempt to
demonstrate to biologists some of the complexities of human kinship
systems as systems of exchange. Most of this technical material has been
omitted here. Some of it will appear in a second edition, in preparation,
of *Kinship and Marriage.*

The chapter "The Matter of Mind" was delivered as a lecture at
the University of New Mexico and has not been published before, neither has the last chapter. But some of the ideas in the latter were derived
from "La selection sexuelle et le rôle du choix féminin dans l'évolution
du comportement humain," E. Sullerot, ed., *Le Fait Féminin* (Paris:
Fayard, 1978). The recently christened "sociobiology" (New Improved
Variety) makes an appearance here. Since this "new synthesis" puts
kinship at the center of evolutionary processes, its relevance is obvious.
It is a late marriage between the work of Lorenz and Fisher that should
have been made in the thirties. It needed the work of Hamilton (included in my 1975 book) and the midwifery of Wilson (among others)
to bring it together. Better late than never. It adds an important di-

mension—Hamilton's "inclusive fitness"—to our analytical tool kit but adds little to the basic issues that have been debated for many years previously, except to restore Darwin's central notion of individual selection.

Another article that has had an influence on various parts of the text is "On the Genetics of Being Human," Arnold R. Kaplan, ed., *Human Behavior Genetics* (Springfield, Illinois: Charles C. Thomas, 1976). This deals particularly with the problem of "universals." Various other articles that have contributed something are mentioned in the notes.

One: The Lighting of the Lamp

1. Peter Kropotkin, *Mutual Aid* (London: Heineman, 1902).

2. R. D. Alexander and T. E. Moore, *The Evolutionary Relationships of 17-Year and 13-Year Cicadas, and Three New Species (Homoptera, Cicadidae, Magicicada)*, (Miscellaneous Publications: Museum of Zoology, University of Michigan, No. 121), Ann Arbor (Museum of Zoology, University of Michigan), 1962.

3. J. S. Huxley, "The Courtship Habits of the Great Crested Grebe *(Podiceps cristatus)*: with an addition to the Theory of Sexual Selection," *Proceedings of the Zoological Society of London* (1914): 491-562.

4. J. F. McLennan, *Primitive Marriage* (Edinburgh: Black, 1865); idem *Studies in Ancient History* (London: Macmillan, 1876); L. H. Morgan, *Ancient Society* (New York: World, 1877); idem *Systems of Consanguinity and Affinity of the Human Family* (Washington: Smithsonian, 1870).

5. E. B. Tylor, "On a Method of Investigating the Development of Institutions; Applied to Laws of Marriage and Descent," *Journal of the Royal Anthropological Institute* 18 (1888): 245-69.

6. The classic "extensionist" position is summed up in G. P. Murdock, *Social Structure* (New York: Macmillan, 1949), ch. 10.

7. Among the most recent major studies are Murdock, *Social Structure,* and Claude Lévi-Strauss, *Les Structures Elémentaires de la Parenté* (Paris: Presses Universitaires de France, 1949). English translation: *The Elementary Structures of Kinship,* trans. J. H. Bell, J. R. von Sturmer, and Rodney Needham, ed. (Boston: Beacon, 1969). This edition will be referred to throughout.

8. Russell Middleton, material presented at seminar, Institute for Advanced Study, Palo Alto, California. See his "Brother-Sister and Father-Daughter Marriage in Ancient Egypt," *American Sociological Review* 27(5) (1962): 603-11.

9. Lars-Göran Engström, "New Penal Provisions on Sexual Offenses Proposed in Sweden," *Current Sweden* (1976): 118.

10. Yehudi A. Cohen, "Ends and Means in Political Control: State Organization and the Punishment of Adultery, Incest, and Violation of Celibacy," *American Anthropologist* 71(4) (1969): 658-87.

11. The literature on incest taboos, etc., is vast, but several critical articles and books have summaries and bibliographies of the main theories, e.g., the works of Murdock and Lévi-Strauss already cited, and those of Bischof, Goody, Slater, and Kortmulder to follow, as well as my *Kinship and Marriage* (chapter two). The references are cumulative since most authors are attacking some point or other in the "established" theories. Lord Raglan, in *Jocasta's Crime* (1933), is marvelously witty in dismissing other theories, but then advances a completely crackpot one of his own. Most textbooks list the established theories in the standard remarks on the incest taboo.

12. S. K. Weinberg, *Incest Behavior* (New York: Citadel, 1955). Sensible studies of consummated incest are rare. There has been a spate of recent popular books with obvious axes to grind and not much serious enlightenment.

13. The literature on inbreeding and its consequences is again large and contradictory. For a good summary of some of the arguments see F. B. Livingstone, "Genetics, Ecology and the Origins of Incest and Exogamy," *Current Anthropology* 10 (1969): 45-61.

There is a lot of literature on inbreeding per se, but not much of it is helpful. A good summary exists in L. L. Cavalli-Sforza and W. F. Bodmer, *The Genetics of Human Populations* (San Francisco: Freeman, 1971). Since data over hundreds of years on real populations are lacking, simulation by computer is resorted to, as in *Computer Simulation in Human Population Studies,* Bennett Dyke and Jean W. MacCluer, eds. (New York: Academic Press, 1973). The question they ask is the opposite of the usual one: What is the *cost* to a population of incest/exogamy restrictions? They limit, it seems, the number of possible matings, and in extreme cases can lead to extinction. But the simulations are themselves limited by the restrictions in their own assumptions. They do not seem able, for example, to include polygyny (plural wives) in the models, although it is allowed that this makes a difference. As we shall see, it makes *all* the difference. The first detailed evidence for inbreeding depression in a natural population is: P. J. Greenwood, P. H.

Harvey, and C. M. Perrins, "Inbreeding and Dispersal in the Great Tit," *Nature* 271 (1978): 52-54.

14. W. D. Hamilton, "Extraordinary Sex Ratios," *Science* 156 (1967): 477-88.

15. One theory trying manfully to hitch the genetic wagon to the Freudian horse, hit on the perfect solution to the "problem of incest taboos": thus, inbreeding (close) has indeed bad consequences, yet we all crave (Freud) to commit incest; therefore, we have to have severe taboos to stop ourselves bringing about the bad consequences! This really displays a low opinion of natural selection: It is as though it had produced a species of Gadarene swine that wanted nothing more than to rush over cliffs and had to build elaborate fences to stop itself. Gardner Lindzey, "Some Remarks Concerning Incest, the Incest Taboo, and Psychoanalytic Theory," *American Psychologist* 22(12) (1967): 1051-59.

16. Norbert Bischof, "The Comparative Ethology of Incest Avoidance," *Biosocial Anthropology,* R. Fox, ed. (New York: Halsted Press; London: Malaby Press, 1975). For a similar approach, but without the "variation" argument: K. Kortmulder, "An Ethological Theory of the Incest Taboo," *Current Anthropology* 9 (1968): 437-49.

17. G. C. Williams, *Sex and Evolution* (Princeton: Princeton University Press, 1975). Williams makes the telling point that theoretically sexual reproduction is a problem, since the more efficient asexual reproduction should win in a competitive situation. Sexual species, therefore, can be seen as struggling to *avoid* close inbreeding, since inefficiently inbred organisms would lose to asexual mutants.

18. The much quoted D. Aberle, et al., "The Incest Taboo and the Mating Patterns of Animals," *American Anthropologist* 65 (1963): 253-65, starts in a similar direction, but too readily dismisses asexual imprinting and ends with the usual "favorite disaster" theory. But their point—that animals have ways of avoiding inbreeding that don't work for us, so we have the incest taboo instead—is on the right lines: It recognizes inbreeding as the *ultimate* problem.

19. Mariam K. Slater, "Ecological Factors in the Origin of Incest," *American Anthropologist* 61 (1959): 1042-59.

Two: Between Brother and Sister

1. Gordon Rattray Taylor, *Sex in History* (New York: Vanguard, 1954).

2. William Golding, *The Scorpion God* (New York: Harcourt, Brace, Jovanovich, 1972).

3. E. Westermarck, *A Short History of Marriage* (New York: Macmillan, 1926), p. 80. Havelock Ellis, *The Psychology of Sex* (London: Davis, 1901) shared Westermarck's opinion on this issue.

4. S. Freud, *Introductory Lectures on Psychoanalysis* (London: Allen and Unwin, 1922), p. 177.

5. Westermarck, *A Short History*, p. 86.

6. J. Goody, "A Comparative Approach to Incest and Adultery," *British Journal of Sociology* 7 (1956): 286-305.

7. F. A. Beach, "Comparison of Copulatory Behaviour of Male Rats Raised in Isolation, Cohabitation and Segmentation," *Journal of Genetic Psychology* 60 (1942): 137-42; J. Yanai and G. E. McClearn, "Assortative Mating in Mice and the Incest Taboo," *Nature* 238 (1972): 281-82.

8. D. C. McClelland, *Personality* (New York: Sloane, 1951), ch. 13.

9. Melford E. Spiro, *Children of the Kibbutz* (Cambridge, Massachusetts: Harvard University Press, 1958).

10. In this, as in all ethnographic examples to follow, page numbers are placed after each quotation for ease of reference.

11. M. Opler, *An Apache Life Way* (Chicago: Chicago University Press, 1941).

12. B. Malinowski, *Sexual Life of Savages*, 3rd ed. (London: Routledge, 1932), ch. 14.

13. M. Fortes, *The Web of Kinship among the Tallensi* (Oxford: Oxford University Press, 1949).

14. B. Malinowski, *Sex and Repression in Savage Society* (New York: Meridian Books, 1955).

15. M. Hunter, *Reaction to Conquest* (Oxford: Oxford University Press, 1936).

16. M. Mead, *Sex and Temperament in Three Primitive Societies* (New York: Mentor Books, 1950).

17. R. Firth, *We the Tikopia*, 2nd ed. (London: Allen and Unwin, 1957).

18. Arthur P. Wolf, "Adopt a Daughter-in-Law, Marry a Sister: A Chinese Solution to the Problem of the Incest Taboo," *American Anthropologist* 70(5) (1968): 873.

19. A. P. Wolf, "Childhood Association, Sexual Attraction, and the Incest Taboo: A Chinese Case," *American Anthropologist* 68(4) (1966): 883-98.

20. A. P. Wolf, "Childhood Association and Sexual Attraction: A Further Test of the Westermarck Hypothesis," *American Anthropologist* 72(3) (1970): 503-15.

21. Y. Talmon, "Mate Selection on Collective Settlements," *American Sociological Review* 29(3) (1964): 491-508.

22. J. Shepher, "Voluntary Imposition of Incest and Exogamic Restrictions in Second Generation Kibbutz Adults" (Ph.D. Thesis, Rutgers University, 1971); idem, "Mate Selection among Second Generation Kibbutz Adolescents and Adults: Incest Avoidance and Negative Imprinting," *Archives of Sexual Behavior* 1 (1971): 293-307.

Three: The Primal Horde

1. S. Freud, *Totem und Tabu* (Vienna: Hugo Heller, 1913). The first English translation was by A. A. Brill, 1918. For this book, I have used James Strachey's authorized translation, *Totem and Taboo* (New York: W. W. Norton and Co., 1952).

2. Ernest Jones, *Sigmund Freud: Life and Work,* vol. 3 (London: Hogarth, 1957), pp. 346–7.

3. Claude Lévi-Strauss, *Structural Anthropology* (New York: Basic Books, 1963), p. 217.

4. A. A. Goldenweiser, "Totemism: An Analytical Study," *Journal of American Folklore* 23 (1910): 179-293. Reprinted with modifications in A. A. Goldenweiser, *History, Psychology and Culture* (London: Kegan Paul, 1933).

5. A. L. Kroeber, *"Totem and Taboo:* An Ethnologic Psychoanalysis," *American Anthropologist* 22 (1920): 48-55; idem, *"Totem and Taboo* in Retrospect," *American Journal of Sociology* 55 (1939): 446-451.

6. J. R. Goody, "A Comparative Approach to Incest and Adultery," *British Journal of Sociology* 7 (1956): 286-305.

7. E. R. Leach, *Rethinking Anthropology* (London: Athlone Press, 1961), ch. 1.

8. E. R. Leach, "Virgin Birth," *Genesis as Myth* (London: Cape Editions, 1969).

9. E. Jones, "Mother Right and the Sexual Ignorance of Savages," *International Journal of Psycho-Analysis* 6 (1925): 109-130.

10. J. J. Atkinson, *Primal Law* (together with A. Lang, *Social Origins*) (London: Longmans, 1903).

11. One of the more entertaining of these, which drew heavily on Atkinson, was a feminist version by C. Gasquoine Hartley, *The Position of Women in Primitive Society* (London: Eveleigh Nash, 1914).

12. J. W. M. Whiting, "Totem and Taboo: A Re-Evaluation" (manuscript, Laboratory of Human Development, Harvard University, no date).

13. S. Freud, *Totem and Taboo*, p. 131.

14. J. W. M. Whiting, R. Kluckhohn, and A. S. Anthony, "The Function of Male Initiation Ceremonies at Puberty," in E. E. Maccoby et al., eds., *Readings in Social Psychology* (New York: Henry Holt, 1958).

15. E. R. Leach, *Rethinking Anthropology*, p. 7.

16. For a balanced discussion of these points see: Robert A. Paul, "Did the Primal Crime Take Place?," *Ethos* vol. 4, No. 9 (1976). A sensitive commentary on *Totem and Taboo* can be found in René Girard, *La Violence et le sacré* (Paris: Grasset, 1972).

Four: The Monkey Puzzle

1. T. H. Huxley, *Man's Place in Nature and other Anthropological Essays* (originally published in 1863) (London: Macmillan, 1900).

2. We are fortunate to have available as a comprehensive reference *The Great Apes,* David A. Hamburg and Elizabeth R. McCown, eds. (Menlo Park, California: Benjamin/Cummings, 1979). The descriptions that follow have been brought up to date from this source, and readers are referred to its bibliography for specific references.

3. A. L. Kroeber, "Totem and Taboo: An Ethnologic Psychoanalysis," *American Anthropologist* 22 (1920): 48-55.

4. Derek Freeman, "Totem and Taboo: A Reappraisal," in W. Muensterberger, ed., *Man and His Culture* (New York: Taplinger, 1970).

5. G. B. Schaller, *The Mountain Gorilla* (Chicago: Chicago University Press, 1963).

6. Hamburg and McCown, eds., *The Great Apes,* part two.

7. Jane Goodall, *My Friends the Wild Chimpanzees* (New York: Na-

tional Geographic Society, 1967). See Hamburg and McCown, eds., *The Great Apes* for a summary of later findings.

8. For example, A. Zihlman and N. Tanner, "Gathering and the Hominid Adaptation," L. Tiger and H. Fowler, eds., *Female Hierarchies* (Chicago: Beresford, 1978).

9. Hamburg and McCown, eds., *The Great Apes,* part three.

10. See Richard W. Wrangham, "Sex Differences in Chimpanzee Dispersion," Hamburg and McCown, eds., *The Great Apes.*

11. Full references for material up to 1975 can be found in my "Primate Kin and Human Kinship," R. Fox, ed., *Biosocial Anthropology* (London: Malaby Press; New York: Halsted Press, 1975).

12. On the relevance of ecological "grades" or "niches" to evolution and adaptation, one of the best references is still J. H. Crook and J. S. Gartlan, "Evolution of Primate Societies," *Nature* 210 (1966): 1200-3.

13. Multi-male systems have been noted for the following: *Cercocebus albigena; Cercopithecus aethiops; C. sabaeus; C. talopin: Macaca fuscata; M. mulatta; M. silenus; M. radiata; M. uris; Papio anubis; P. cynocephalus; P. papio; P. ursinus.* In the late fifties and early sixties, reports on multi-male systems came in from N. Bolwig, "Study of the behavior of the chacma baboon, *Papio ursinus,*" *Behaviour* 14 (1959): 136-63; K. R. L. Hall, "Numerical Data, Maintenance Activities, and Locomotion of the Wild Chacma Baboon, *Papio ursinus,*" *Proc. Zool. Soc. Lond.* 139 (1962): 181-220; idem, "Sexual, Agonistic and Derived Behaviour Patterns of the Wild Chacma Baboons, *Papio ursinus,*" *Proc. Zool. Soc. Lond.* 139 (1962): 283-326; S. L. Washburn and I. DeVore, "Social Life of Baboons," *Scientific American* 204 (1961): 62-71; P. E. Maxim and J. Buettner-Janusch, "Field Study of the Kenya Baboon," *Amer. J. Phys. Anthrop.* 21 (1963): 165-79; K. Imanishi, "Social Behaviour in Japanese Monkeys, *Macaca Fuscata,*" *Psychologia* 1 (1957): 46-54; idem, "Social Organization of Subhuman Primates in Their Natural Habitat," *Current Anthropology* 1 (1960): 393-407.

Throughout the fifties the Japanese workers had been publishing their data on macaques, largely in the journal *Primates.* The early volumes being in Japanese, the circulation was at first restricted. S. A. Altmann published a welcome set of translations, *Japanese Monkeys: a Collection of Translations* (Atlanta: published by the editor S. A. Altmann, 1965), and subsequent volumes in English have continued the flow of data. Various compilations by I. DeVore, ed., *Primate Behavior: Field Studies of*

Monkeys and Apes (New York: Holt, Rinehart and Winston, 1965); S. A. Altmann, *Social Communication among Primates* (Chicago: University of Chicago Press, 1967); and P. Jay, ed., *Primates: Studies in Adaptation and Variability* (New York: Holt, Rinehart and Winston, 1968), among others, gathered together much of the material. Struhsaker demonstrated this form of organization for the vervet monkeys: T. T. Struhsaker, "Behaviour of Vervet Monkeys," *Univ. Cal. Pub. Zool.* 82 (1967); "Social Structure among Vervet Monkeys (*Cercopithecus aethiops*),"*Behaviour* 29 (1967): 83-121; idem, "Ecology of Vervet Monkeys (*Cercopithecus aethiops*) in the Masai-Amboseli Reserve, Kenya," *Ecology* 48 (1967): 891-904; idem, "Behaviour of Vervet Monkeys and Other Cercopithecines," *Science* 156 (1967): 1197-1203; idem, "Auditory Communications among Vervet Monkeys (*Cercopithecus aethiops*)," S. A. Altmann, ed., *Social Communication among Primates* (Chicago: University of Chicago Press, 1967); idem, "Correlations of Ecology and Social Organization among African Cercopithecines," *Folia Primatologia* 11 (1967): 80-118, but other *Cercopithecus* species seem to be one-male.

Chimpanzees and gorillas, as we have seen, have multi-male groups. Reynolds' notion of chimpanzee "open groups"—contrasting markedly with the "closed groups" of baboons, for example—rests on a confusion about the nature of the group: V. Reynolds, "Open Groups in Hominid Evolution," *Man n.s.* 3 (1966): 209-23. Because the chimpanzee "group" is spread out in the forest, with its bands of roving males and matrifocal units of females, this does not make it any less a total group—a multi-male group, in fact. Baboons in the forest do not have such "closed" groups (see T. E. Rowell, "Forest-dwelling Baboons in Uganda," *J. Zool.* 149 (1966): 344-64)—macaques never did anyway—while chimpanzees in open country have a group structure quite like the norm for multi-male savanna species. See J. Itani and A. Suzuki, "The Social Unit of Chimpanzees," *Primates* 8 (1967): 355-81. This holds only for this dimension of social structure—kinship and the breeding system—and does not mean that there are not significant differences in other dimensions between, say, chimpanzees and baboons. See M. R. A. Chance, "Social Cohesion and the Structure of Attention," R. Fox, ed., *Biosocial Anthropology*.

14. J. Itani and A. Suzuki, "The Social Unit."

15. J. Vandenbergh, "The Development of Social Structure in

Free-ranging Rhesus Monkeys," *Behaviour* 29 (1967): 174-94; A. Wilson, "Social Behavior of Free-ranging Rhesus Monkeys with an Emphasis on Aggression" (Ph.D. thesis, University of California, Berkeley, 1968).

16. This very condensed account of female rank in multi-male systems is based largely on the following: S. Kawamura, "Matriarchal Social Ranks in the Minoo-B Troop: A Study of the Rank System of Japanese Monkeys," *Primates* 1 (1958): 149-56; S. A. Altmann, ed., *Japanese Monkeys* (Atlanta: the editor, 1965), pp. 105-12; K. Imanishi, "Social Organizaton of Sub-human Primates in Their Natural Habitat," *Current Anthropology* 1 (1960): 393-407; J. Itani, K. Tokunda, Y. Furuya, K. Kano, and Y. Shin, "The Social Construction of Natural Troops of Japanese Monkeys in Takasakiyama," *Primates* 4(3) (1963): 1-42; M. Yamada, "A Study of Blood Relationship in the Natural Society of the Japanese Macaque," *Primates* 4(3) (1963): 43-65; C. B. Koford, "Rank of Mothers and Sons in Bands of Rhesus Monkeys," *Science* 141 (1963): 356-57; D. S. Sade, "Some Aspects of Parent-Offspring Relations in a Group of Rhesus Monkeys, with a Discussion of Grooming," *Amer. J. Phys. Anthrop.* 23 (1965): 1-17; J. H. Kaufmann, "Behaviour of Infant Rhesus Monkeys and Their Mothers in a Free-ranging Band," *Zoologica* 51 (1966): 17-28; idem, "Social Relations of Adult Males in a Free-ranging Band of Rhesus Monkeys," S. A. Altmann, ed., *Social Communication among Primates;* J. Vandenbergh, "Development of Social Structure"; H. M. Marsden, "Agonistic Behaviour of Young Rhesus Monkeys after Changes Induced in the Social Rank of Their Mothers," *Animal Behaviour* 16 (1968): 38-44; N. Koyama, "On Dominance Rank and Kinship of a Wild Japanese Monkey Troop in Arashiyama," *Primates* 8(3) (1967): 189-216; idem, "Changes in Dominance Rank and Division of a Wild Japanese Monkey Troop in Arashiyama," *Primates* 11 (1970): 335-90; B. K. Alexander and E. M. Roth, "The Effects of Crowding on Aggressive Behaviour of Japanese Monkeys," *Behaviour* 39 (1971): 73-90; T. W. Ransom and T. E. Rowell, "Early Social Development of Feral Baboons," F. E. Poirier, ed., *Primate Socialization* (New York: Random House, 1972); J. Loy, "The Effects of Matrilineal Relationships on the Behaviour of Juvenile Rhesus Monkeys" (*Abstracts of the 71st Annual Meeting of the American Anthropological Association,* 1972). M. H. Miller, A. Kling and D. Dicks, "Familial Interactions of Male Rhesus Monkeys in a Semifree-ranging Troop," *Amer. J. Phys. Anthrop.* 38 (1973): 605-611.

17. D. S. Sade, "Inhibition of Son-Mother Mating among Free-ranging Rhesus Monkeys," *Science and Psychoanalysis* 12 (1968): 18-37; E. Missakian, "Genealogical Mating Activity in Free-ranging Groups of Rhesus Monkeys (*Macaca mulatta*) on Cayo Santiago," *Behaviour* 45 (1973): 224-40.

18. The data we now have show that a social system based on one-male groups is characteristic of the following species: *Cercopithecus ascanius; C. campbelli; C. cephus; C. diana; C. erythrotis; C. l'hoesti; C. mitis; C. mona; C. nictitans; C. pogonias; C. preussi; Erythrocebus patas; Colobus badius; Papio hamadryas; Theropithecus gelada; Presbytis johni; P. pileatus;* (on *C. mitis,* A. Omar and A. Devos, "Annual Reproductive Cycle of an African Monkey (*Cercopithecus mitis kolbi,* Neumann)," *Folia Primat.* 16 (1971): 206-215; on *P. johni,* F. E. Poirier, "Niligri langur (*Presbytis johni*) of South India," L. A. Rosenblum, ed., *Primate Behavior,* vol. 1 (New York: Academic Press, 1970).

    The first modern report (langurs were written about as early as 1902: J. F. G., "Habits of the Lungoor Monkey," *J. Bombay Nat. Hist. Soc.* 14 [1902]: 149-151), was by H. Kummer and F. Kurt, "Social Units of Free-living Populations of Hamadryas Baboons," *Folia Primat.* 1 (1963): 4-19. See also H. Kummer, *Social Organization of Hamadryas Baboons* (Chicago: University of Chicago Press, 1968). The patas monkey was reported on by K. R. L. Hall, "Behaviour and Ecology of the Wild Patas Monkey, *Erythrocebus patas,*" *J. Zool.* 148 (1965): 15-87, and the gelada baboon by J. H. Crook, "Gelada Baboon Herd Structure and Movement," *Symp. Zool. Soc. Lond.* 18 (1966): 237-58. See also J. H. Crook and P. Aldrich-Blake, "Ecological and Behavioral Contrasts between Sympatric Ground-dwelling Primates in Ethiopia," *Folia Primat.* 8 (1968): 192-227. Indian langurs received attention from Y. Sugiyama, "Group Composition, Population Density and Some Sociological Observations on Hanuman Langurs (*Presbytis entellus*)," *Primates* 5 (1964): 17-37; idem, "Behaviour Development and Social Structure in Two Troops of Hanuman Langurs (*Presbytis entellus*)," *Primates* 6 (1965): 213-47; "On the Social Change of Hanuman Langurs (*P. entellus*) in Their Natural Condition," *Primates* 6 (1965): 381-418; idem, "Social Organization of Hanuman Langurs," S. A. Altmann, ed., *Social Communication among Primates.* See also Y. Sugiyama, K. Yoshiba, and M. D. Parthasarathy, "Home Range, Breeding Season, Male Group and Inter-troop Relations in Hanuman Langurs," *Primates* 6 (1965): 73-106. Struhsaker's series of reports on various *Cerco-*

pithecus species showed that many had one-male groups. The colobus monkey appears to have this form of organization. See P. Marler, *"Colobus guereza:* Territory and Group Composition," *Science* 163 (1969): 93-5, and T. Nishida, "Note on the Ecology of the Red Colobus Monkeys *(Colobus badius tephrosceles)* Living in the Mahali Mountains," *Primates* 13 (1972): 57-64.

The work of Zuckerman on hamadryas baboons, although it showed clearly that a harem structure existed, was flawed because it studied monkeys in overcrowded zoo conditions. See S. Zuckerman, *The Social Life of Monkeys and Apes* (London: Routledge and Kegan Paul, 1932). Unfortunately, it may be impossible to obtain further material on Ethiopian hamadryas and gelada baboons because the political situation in that country is making research impossible.

19. Forest species—cercopithecine and colobine—prefer relatively solitary families, while the savanna and desert species tend (with the exception of patas) to encapsulate the harem in a larger herd. The latter system *could,* then, have ancient roots and represent species that were *ab origino* one-male in the forest and adapted this to a "one-male group plus herd structure" in the dry open country.

20. Susan M. Cachel, "A New View of Speciation in *Australopithecus,"* R. H. Tuttle, ed., *Paleoanthropology, Morphology and Paleoecology* (The Hague/Paris: Mouton, 1975).

21. Sarah Blaffer Hrdy, *The Langurs of Abu* (Cambridge, Massachusetts: Harvard University Press, 1977).

22. R. Curtin and P. Dolhinow, "Primate Social Behavior in a Changing World," *American Scientist* 66(4) (1978): 468-75.

23. There are clear differences between the genera in preferences for one or the other form of organization, suggesting that phylogeny, as well as ecology and ontogeny, is important. In *Cercopithecus,* only three species are multi-male while twelve are one-male; in *Macaca,* five are multi-male and none are one-male; *Papio* has four multi-male and one one-male. But we should also note that there are "mixed" systems in which animals of the same species in different habitats gravitate toward one or other structure; for example, *Colobus guereza, Mandrillus leucophaeus, Nasilis larvatus, Presbytis cristatus, Presbytis entellus.* (On *C. guereza,* see P. Marler, *"Colobus guereza"; M. leucophaeus,* J. S. Gartlan, "Preliminary Notes on the Ecology and Behavior of the Drill, *Mandrillus leucophaeus,* Ritgen, 1823," J. R. and P. H. Napier, eds., *Old World Monkeys* (New York: Academic Press, 1970); *P. entellus,* P. Jay, "Aspects of Maternal Behavior

among Langurs," *Ann. N.Y. Acad. Sci.* 102 (1962): 468-76; idem, "Indian Langur Monkey (*Presbytis entellus*)," C. H. Southwick, ed., *Primate Social Behaviour* (Princeton: Van Nostrand, 1963; idem, "Mother-Infant Relations in Langurs," H. Rheingold, ed., *Maternal Behavior in Mammals* (New York: Wiley, 1963); idem, "Common Langur of North India," I. DeVore, ed., *Primate Behavior.*

There are several evolutionary possibilities. The "basic" primate group could be the nuclear family, which evolved into the one-male group and eventually into the multi-male group in the savanna; that is, by adding first more females and then more males. Alternatively, the multi-male group can be seen as basic and going in two directions: the shedding of males to produce the one-male group structure or the shedding of both males and females to produce nuclear families. Various possibilities are discussed in J. Eisenberg, N. A. Muckenhirn and R. Rudran, "The Relation between Ecology and Social Structure in Primates," *Science* 176 (1972): 863-74, and J. D. Goss-Custard, R. M. Dunbar, and F. P. G. Aldrich-Blake, "Survival, Mating and Rearing Strategies in the Evolution of Primate Societies," *Folia Primat.* 17 (1972): 1-19.

24. These differences are illustrated graphically in my "Primate Kin and Human Kinship," R. Fox, ed., *Biosocial Anthropology.*

25. N. Koyama, "On Dominance Rank and Kinship"; Y. Furuya, "On the Fission of Troops of Japanese Monkeys. II. General View of Troop Fission of Japanese Monkeys," *Primates* 10 (1969): 47-69; J. Cheverud, J. Buettner-Janusch, and D. Sade, "Social Group Fission and the Origin of Intergroup Genetic Differentiation among Rhesus Monkeys of Cayo Santiago," *Amer. J. Phys. Anthrop.* 49 (1978): 449-56; and B. D. Chepko-Sade and D. S. Sade, "Patterns of Group Splitting within Matrilineal Kinship Groups," *Behav. Ecol. Sociobiol.* 5 (1979): 67-86.

26. This would be an example of "kin selection" aiding sexual selection. We shall take up kin selection briefly in chapter six, with the appropriate references.

27. Ralph Linton, *The Study of Man* (New York: Appleton, 1936), ch. 9. An extraordinarily perceptive chapter given the paucity of knowledge at the time.

Five: Sex in the Head

1. J. Napier, "The Evolution of Bipedal Walking in the Hominids," *Arch. Biol* 75 Suppl. (1964): 673-708 and "The Antiquity

of Human Walking," *Scientific American* 216 (4): (1967): 56-66. *The Roots of Mankind* (Washington, D.C.: Smithsonian Institution Press, 1970).

2. Verne Grant, *The Origin of Adaptations* (New York: Columbia University Press, 1963), pp. 206-11. The "conservative" nature of adaptations is known also as "Romer's Rule" after A. S. Romer, *Man and the Vertebrates* (Chicago: Chicago University Press, 1933).

3. There is a large and growing literature on sexual selection. The classic source is Darwin's own *The Descent of Man and Selection in Relation to Sex* (London: Murray, 1871). The work of R. A. Fisher in the thirties carried this forward and is now being rediscovered. See *The Genetical Theory of Natural Selection,* originally published in 1930 (New York: Dover, 1958). The centennial celebratory volume contained many new approaches and applications: B. Campbell, ed., *Sexual Selection and the Descent of Man 1871-1971* (Chicago: Aldine, 1972). See also Gordon Orians "On the Evolution of Mating Systems in Birds and Mammals," *American Naturalist* 103 (1969): 589-603.

4. Gordon R. Stephenson, "Social Structure of Mating Activity in Japanese Macaques," *Symp. 5th Cong. Int'l. Primat. Soc.* (Nagoya, Japan, August 1974).

5. On mating success of dominant females see L. C. Drickamer, "A Ten-year Summary of Reproductive Data for Free-ranging *Macaca mulatta,*" *Folia Primat.* 21 (1974): 61-80.

6. Chance's basic writings on equilibration are contained in: M. R. A. Chance and A. P. Mead, "Social Behavior and Primate Evolution," *Evolution: Symposium of the Society for Experimental Biology* 7 (New York: Jonathan Cape, 1953); M. R. A. Chance, "Nature and Special Features of the Instinctive Social Bond of Primates," in S. L. Washburn, ed., *Social Life of Early Man* (London: Methuen, 1962); "Social Behaviour and Primate Evolution," in Ashley Montagu, ed., *Culture and the Evolution of Man* (New York: Oxford University Press, 1962). His later writing has been largely about the concept of "attention" as the basis of primate rank and dominance. I have not gone into this in great detail here, but its relevance is obvious. See: M. R. A. Chance, "Attention Structure as the Basis of Primate Rank Orders," *Man, n.s.* 2(4) 1967: 503-18; M. R. A. Chance and C. J. Jolly, *Social Groups of Monkeys, Apes, and Men* (New York: E. P. Dutton, 1970); M. R. A. Chance and R. R. Larsen, *The Social Structure of Attention* (London: Wiley, 1977); M. R. A. Chance, "Social Cohesion and the Structure of Attention" in

R. Fox, ed., *Biosocial Anthropology* (New York: Halsted Press; London: Malaby Press, 1975).

7. The most graphic description of this is Paul MacLean's, in his picture of the "triune brain." In chapter seven (note 11) I point out that this *is* a description, not an adequate theory, but for our purposes it remains a good description. See: "Man and His Animal Brains," *Modern Medicine* (February 3, 1964), among many other articles.

8. Eugene Marais, *The Soul of the Ape* (New York: Athenaeum, 1969).

9. On the role of the amygdala and the social deficits experienced when it is damaged or removed, see: A. Kling, "Effects of Amygdalectomy on Social-Affective Behavior in Nonhuman Primates," in B. E. Eleftheriou, ed., *The Neurobiology of the Amygdala* (New York and London: Plenum Press, 1972); A. Kling and H. D. Steklis, "A Neural Substrate for Affiliative Behavior in Nonhuman Primates," *Brain, Behavior and Evolution* 13 (1976): 216-38.

10. J. N. Spuhler, "Somatic Paths to Culture," in J. N. Spuhler, ed., *The Evolution of Man's Capacity for Culture* (Detroit, Michigan: Wayne State University Press, 1959).

11. I will provide here, since no other such summary exists, a bibliography of reports pro and con the relationship of dominance and breeding. Those favoring the relationship are, chronologically:

> Maslow, 1936a and 1936b; Maslow and Flanzbaum, 1936; Carpenter, 1942; Yerkes, 1943; Carpenter, 1954; Kawai, 1960; Chance, 1961; Itani, 1961; Altmann, 1962; Hall, 1962; Jay, 1963; Koford, 1963; Etkin, 1964; Miyadi, 1964; DeVore, 1965; DeVore and Hall, 1965; Hall and DeVore, 1965; Miyadi, 1965; Simonds, 1965; Kaufmann, 1967; Struhsaker, 1967; van Lawick-Goodall, 1968; Bernstein, 1970; Crook, 1970; DeVore, 1971; Drickamer, 1974; Richards, 1974; Stephenson, 1974; Struhsaker, 1975; Southwick (in Kolata, 1976); Dunbar and Dunbar, 1977; Popp and DeVore, 1979.

Those doubting the relationship are as follows (some authors equivocate and so appear twice):

> Kummer, 1957; Reynolds, 1963; DeVore, 1965; Hall and DeVore, 1965; Kaufmann, 1965; Simonds, 1965; Southwick, et al., 1965; Jolly, 1966; Jolly, 1967; Baldwin,

1968; DuMond, 1968; Yoshiba, 1968; Conaway and Ko-
ford, 1969; Rahaman and Parthasarathy, 1969; Loy, 1970;
Loy, 1971; Saayman, 1971; Jolly, 1972; Missakian, 1972;
Alvarez, 1975; Hausfater, 1975; Loy, 1975; Kolata, 1976;
Slatkin and Hausfater, 1976.

Altmann, S. A.
1962 "A Field Study of the Sociobiology of Rhesus
      Monkeys, *Macaca mulatta.*" *Ann. N.Y. Acad. Sci.*,
      102:338-435.
Alvarez, Fernando
1975 "Social Hierarchy Under Different Criteria in
      Groups of Squirrel Monkeys, *Saimiri sciureus.*" *Pri-
      mates* 16(4):437-55.
Baldwin, J. D.
1968 "A Study of the Social Behavior of a Semi-free-
      ranging Colony of Squirrel Monkeys (*Saimiri
      sciureus*)." *Folia Primat.* 9:218-314.
Bernstein, I. S.
1970 "Primate Status Hierarchies." *Primate Behaviour:
      Developments in Field and Laboratory Research*, vol. 1.
      Edited by L. A. Rosenblum. New York: Academic
      Press.
Carpenter, C. R.
1942 "Sexual Behavior of Free-ranging Rhesus Mon-
      keys, II: Periodicity of Estrus, Homo and Autoero-
      tic and Nonconformist Behavior." *J. Comp. Psychol.*
      33:147-62.
1954 "Tentative Generalizations on the Grouping Be-
      havior of Non-human Primates." *The Non-Human
      Primates and Human Evolution.* Edited by J. A.
      Gavan. Wayne University Press: Detroit, Michi-
      gan.
1964 "Societies of Monkeys and Apes." *Naturalistic Be-
      havior of Non-human Primates.* Edited by C. R. Car-
      penter. University Park: Pennsylvania State Uni-
      versity Press.
Castell, R. V. and Ploog, D.
1967 "Zum sozialverhalten der totenkopf-affen (Saimiri
      sciureus): Auseinandersetzukg zwischen zwei ko-
      lonien." *Z. f. Tierpsychol.* 24:625-41.
Chance, M. R. A.

1961 "The Nature and Special Features of the Instinctive Social Bond of Primates." *Social Life of Early Man.* Edited by S. L. Washburn. Chicago: Aldine.

Conaway, C. H. And Koford, C. B.
1965 "Estrous Cycles and Mating Behavior in a Free-ranging Band of Rhesus Monkeys." *J. Mammal.* 45:577-88.

Crook, J. H.
1970 "The Socio-ecology of Primates." *Social Behaviour in Birds and Mammals.* Edited by J. H. Crook. New York: Academic Press.

DeVore, I.
1965 "Male Dominance and Mating Behavior in Baboons." *Sex and Behavior.* Edited by F. A. Beach. New York: Wiley.
1971 "The Evolution of Human Society." *Man and Beast: Comparative Social Behavior.* Edited by J. F. Eisenberg and W. S. Dillon. Washington, D.C.: Smithsonian Institution Press.

DeVore, I. and K. R. L. Hall
1965 "Baboon Ecology." *Primate Behavior: Field Studies of Monkeys and Apes.* Edited by I. DeVore. New York: Holt, Rinehart and Winston.

Drickamer, L. C.
1974 "A Ten-year Summary of Reproductive Data for Free-ranging *Macaca mulatta.*" *Folia Primat.* 21:61-80.

DuMond, F. V.
1968 "The Squirrel Monkey in a Seminatural Environment." *The Squirrel Monkey.* Edited by L. A. Rosenblum and R. W. Cooper. New York: Academic Press.

Dunbar, R. I. M. and E. P. Dunbar
1977 "Dominance and Reproductive Success among Female Gelada Baboons." *Nature* 266:351-52.

Etkin, W.
1964 "Types of Social Organization in Birds and Mammals." *Social Behavior and Organization among Vertebrates.* Edited by W. Etkin. Chicago: University of Chicago Press.

Hall, K. R. L.
1962 "The Sexual Agonistic and Derived Social Behavior Patterns of the Wild Chacma Baboon *Papio ursinus.*" *Proc. Zool. Soc. London* 139:283-327.

Hall, K. R. L. and DeVore, I.
1965 "Baboon Social Behavior." *Primate Behavior, Field Studies of Monkeys and Apes.* Edited by I. DeVore. New York: Holt, Rinehart & Winston.

Hausfater, Glenn
1975 *Dominance and Reproduction in Baboons* (Papio cynocephalus): *A Quantitative Analysis.* Karger, Basel: Contributions to Primatology, vol. 7.

Hrdy, Sarah and Hrdy, Daniel
1976 "Hierarchical Relations among Female Hanuman Langurs (Primates: *Colobinae, Presbytis entellus*)." *Science* 193:913-15.

Itani, J.
1961 "The Society of Japanese Monkeys." *Jap. Quart.* 8:10.

Jay, P.
1963 "The Indian Langur Monkey (*Presbytis entellus*)." *Primate Social Behavior.* Edited by C. H. Southwick. Princeton: Van Nostrand.

Jolly, A.
1966 *Lemur Behavior.* Chicago: University of Chicago Press.
1967 "Breeding Synchrony in Wild *Lemur catta.*" *Social communication among primates.* Edited by S. A. Altmann. Chicago: University of Chicago Press.
1972 *The Evolution of Primate Behavior.* New York: Macmillan.

Kaufmann, J. H.
1965 "A Three-year Study of Mating Behavior in a Free-ranging Band of Rhesus Monkeys." *Ecology* 49:500-12.
1967 "Social Relations of Adult Males in a Free-ranging Band of Rhesus Monkeys." *Social Communication among Primates.* Edited by S. A. Altmann. Chicago: University of Chicago Press.

Kawai, M.
1960 "A Field Experiment on the Process of Group Formation in the Japanese Monkey (*Macaca fuscata*) and the Releasing of the Group at Ohirayama." *Primates* 2:181-253.

Koford, C. B.
1963 "Group Relations in an Island Colony of Rhesus Monkeys." *Primate Social Behavior.* Edited by C. H. Southwick. Princeton: Van Nostrand.

Kolata, G. B.
1976   "Primate Behavior: Sex and the Dominant Male."
        Science 191:55-56.

Kummer, H.
1957   "Soziales verhalten einer mantel pavian-gruppe."
        Schweiz-Z. Psychol. Beih. 33:1.
1973   "Dominance versus Possession: An Experiment of
        Hamadryas Baboons." *Precultural Primate Behavior,*
        vol. 1. Karger, Basel: Sympt. IVth Congr. Primat.

Loy, J.
1970   "Peri-menstrual Sexual Behavior among Rhesus
        Monkeys." *Folia Primat.* 13:286-97.
1971   "Estrous Behavior of Free-ranging Rhesus Mon-
        keys (*Macaca mulatta*)." *Primates* 12(1):1-31.
1975   "The Descent of Dominance in *Macaca:* Insights
        into the Structure of Human Societies." *Socioecology
        and Psychology of Primates.* Edited by R. H. Tuttle.
        The Hague, Paris: Mouton Publishers.

Maslow, A. H.
1936a   "The Role of Dominance in the Social and Sexual
        Behavior of Infrahuman Primates: Observations at
        Villas Park Zoo." *J. Genet. Psychol.* 48:261-77.
1936b   "A Theory of Sexual Behavior in Infrahuman
        Primates." *J. Genet. Psychol.* 48:310-36.

Maslow, A. H. and Flanzbaum, S.
1936   "An Experimental Determination of the Behavior
        Syndrome of Dominance." *J. Genet. Psychol.* 48:278-
        309.

Missakian, E. A.
1972   "Genealogical and Cross-genealogical Dominance
        Relations in a Group of Free-ranging Rhesus
        Monkeys (*Macaca mulatta*) on Cayo Santiago. *Pri-
        mates* 13(2):169-80.

Miyadi, D.
1964   "Social Life of Japanese Monkeys." *Science*
        143:783-86.
1965   "Social Life of Japanese Monkeys." *Science in Japan.*
        Edited by A. H. Livermore. Washington, D.C.:
        Amer. Ass. Advan. Sci.

Popp, J. L. and DeVore, I.
1979   "Aggressive Competition and Social Dominance
        Theory: Synopsis." *The Great Apes.* Edited by D. A.
        Hamburg and E. R. McCown. Menlo Park, Calif.:
        Benjamin/Cummings.

Richards, S. M.
1974 "The Concept of Dominance and Methods of Assessment." *Anim. Behav.* 22:914.

Rahaman, H. and Parthasarathy, M. D.
1969 "Studies on the Social Behavior of Bonnet Monkeys (*Macaca radiata*)." *Primates* 10:149.

Reynolds, V.
1963 "An Outline of the Behaviour and Social Organization of Forest Living Chimpanzees." *Folia Primat.* 1:95-102.

Saayman, G. S.
1971 "Behaviour of the Adult Males in a Troop of Free-ranging Chacma Baboons (*Papio ursinus*)." *Folia Primat.* 15(1,2):36-57.

Simonds, P. E.
1965 "The Bonnet Macaque in South India." in *Primate Behavior: Field Studies of Monkeys and Apes.* Edited by I. DeVore. New York: Holt, Rinehart and Winston.

Slatkin, M. and Hausfater, G.
1976 "A Note on the Activities of a Solitary Male Baboon." *Primates* 17(3):311-22.

Southwick, C. H., Mirza Azhar Beg and M. Rafiq Siddiqi
1965 "Rhesus Monkeys in North India." In *Primate Behavior: Field Studies of Monkeys and Apes.* Edited by I. DeVore. New York: Holt, Rinehart and Winston.

Stevenson, G. R.
1974 "Social Structure of Mating Activity in Japanese Macaques." *Symp. 5th Int'l. Primat. Soc.,* Nagoya, Japan.

Struhsaker, T. T.
1967 "Behavior of Vervet Monkeys and Other Cercopithecines." *Science* 156:1197-1203.
1975 *The Red Colobus Monkey.* Chicago: University of Chicago Press.

Syme, G. J.
1974 "Competitive Orders as Measures of Social Dominance." *Anim. Behav.* 22:931-40.

Tuttle, R. H.
1975 "Quantitative Sociobiology." *Science* 191:939-40.

van Lawick-Goodall, J.
1968 "A Preliminary Report on Expressive Movements and Communication in the Gombe Stream Chimpanzees." *Primates.* Edited by P. C. Jay. New York: Holt, Rinehart & Winston.

Wilson, E. O.
1975   *Sociobiology: The New Synthesis.* Cambridge, Mass.:
        The Belknap Press of Harvard University Press.
Yerkes, R. M.
1943   *Chimpanzees: A Laboratory Colony.* New Haven: Yale
        University Press.
Yoshiba, K.
1968   "Local and Intertroop Variability in Ecology and
        Social Behavior of Common India Langurs." *Pri-
        mates.* Edited by P. C. Jay. New York: Holt, Rine-
        hart and Winston.

12. D. Suarez and D. R. Ackerman, "Social Dominance and Re-
    productive Behavior in Male Rhesus Monkeys," *Amer. J. Phys.
    Anth.* 35 (1971): 219-22.

13. Bernard Strehler, "Polygamy and the Evolution of Human
    Longevity," *Mechanisms of Aging and Development* 9 (34) (1979),
    shows in a computer study that polygynous mating of the kind
    described here *must* have happened to account for the rate of
    genetic change between primate and man. This is important
    supportive evidence for our basic thesis.

14. M. R. A. Chance, "Social Behavior and Primate Evolution,"
    Evolution: Symposium of the Society, p. 125.

15. Ibid.

16. Ibid., p. 128.

17. M. R. A. Chance, "Nature and Special Features of the Instinc-
    tive Social Bond of Primates," *Social Life of Early Man,* p. 32.

18. J. H. Crook and J. S. Gartlan, "Evolution of Primate Socie-
    ties," *Nature, London* 210 (1966): 1200-03; B. G. Campbell,
    Human Evolution: An Introduction to Man's Adaptations (Chicago:
    Aldine, 1966).

19. J. H. Crook, "Sexual Selection, Dimorphism, and Social Orga-
    nization in the Primates," in B. G. Campbell, ed., *Sexual Selec-
    tion.*

20. One of latest and best summary volumes, which has excellent
    bibliographies, maps, pictures, graphs, etc., is: G. Isaac and E.
    McCown, eds., *Human Origins: Louis Leakey and the East African
    Evidence* (Menlo Park, California: W. A. Benjamin, 1976).

21. In what follows, I have aimed at reaching a consensus from
    many sources on brain sizes and dates. The general question is
    discussed in H. J. Jerison, *Evolution of the Brain and Intelligence*
    (New York: Academic Press, 1973) and in Phillip V. Tobias,
    The Brain in Hominid Evolution (New York: Columbia, 1971).

The useful sources used in the survey include: C. Loring Brace, et al., *Atlas of Fossil Man* (New York: Holt, Rinehart and Winston, 1971); B. G. Campbell, *Human Evolution: An Introduction;* W. E. Le Gros Clark, *The Fossil Evidence for Human Evolution* (second edition) (Chicago: University of Chicago Press, 1964); R. L. Holloway, "Australopithecine Endocast (Taung Specimen, 1924): A New Volume Determination," *Science* 168 (1970): 966-68; "Australopithecine Endocasts, Brain Evolution in the Hominoidea, and a Model of Hominid Evolution," in R. Tuttle, ed., *The Functional and Evolutionary Biology of Primates* (Chicago: Aldine/Atherton, 1972); "Cranial Capacity of the Olduvai Bed 1 Hominine," *Nature* 210 (1966): 1108-10; "Cranial Capacity of the Hominine from Olduvai Bed 1," *Nature* 208 (1965): 205-6; M. H. Day, et al., "New Hominids from East Rudolf, Kenya 1," *Amer. J. Phys. Anthrop.* 42(3) (1975): 461-75; D. Pilbeam, "Early Hominidae and Cranial Capacity," *Nature* 224 (1969): 386; J. S. Aigner and W. S. Laughlin, "The Dating of Lantian Man and His Significance for Analyzing Trends in Human Evolution," *Amer. J. Phys. Anthro.* 39 (1) (1973): 97-109; R. A. Dart, "The Relationship of Brain Size and Brain Pattern to Human Status," *S. Afr. J. Med. Sci.* 21 (1956): 23-45; P. V. Tobias, "New Developments in Hominid Paleontology in South and East Africa," *Ann. Rev. Anthro.* 2 (1973): 311-34.

22. There were two main species of *Australopithecus: A. africanus*—the "gracile" form—and *A. robustus*—the larger, gorillalike form. Some of the latter probably continued in existence and overlapped with *erectus,* which strengthens the view that the graciles were the human precursors.

23. See P. V. Tobias, *The Brain in Hominid Evolution.*

24. The question of allometry—brain weight/body weight or brain size/body size or brain-surface area/body-surface area ratios—has been much discussed. H. J. Jerison had an early attempt in "Brain to Body Ratios and the Evolution of Intelligence," *Science* 121 (1955): 447-9, and several succeeding articles, culminating in the book cited in note 21. Also, ratios *within* the brain have been studied, such as that between the neocortex and the rest: R. E. Passingham, "Changes in the Size and Organization of the Brain in Man and His Ancestors," *Brain, Behavior and Evolution* 11 (1975): 73-90. S. J. Gould has made some interesting contributions in "Allometry and Size in Ontogeny and Phylogeny," *Biol. Rev.* 41 (1966): 569-640 and "Allometry in Primates, with Emphasis on Scaling and the Evolution of the Brain," in F. S. Szalay, ed., *Approaches to Pri-*

mate Paleobiology, Contributions to Primatology, vol. 5 (Basel: Karger, 1975) pp. 244-92. See also D. Pilbeam and S. J. Gould, "Size and Scaling in Human Evolution," *Science* 186 (1974): 892-901.

25. A problem in this progression has been posed by the discovery by R. Leakey of "Skull 1470," which he dated at 2.9 million years B.P. and gave a cranial capacity of at least 810 cubic centimeters. This was so far off the line of development that Leakey proposed it belonged to a distinct line of *Homo* with a separate and ancient origin. It now appears that the dating was wrong, it should be nearer 1.5 million, and so was the estimate of cranial capacity—more like 770 cubic centimeters. The more accurate figures fit into the Habiline curve, which makes sense. See: G. Curtis, et al., "Age of KBS Tuff in Koobi Fora Formation, East Rudolf, Kenya," *Nature* 258 (1975): 395-98; R. B. Eckhardt, "Observed and Expected Variation in Hominid Evolution," *Journal of Human Evolution* 5 (4) (1976): 467-75; R. E. Leakey and R. Lewin, *Origins* (New York: E. P. Dutton, 1977); R. E. Leakey, "Evidence for an Advanced Hominid from East Rudolf, Kenya," *Nature* 242 (1973): 447-50; M. H. Day, et al., "New Hominids from East Rudolf, Kenya, I," *Amer. J. Phys. Anthrop.* 42 (3) (1975): 461-76.

26. E. Caspari, "Selective Forces in the Evolution of Man," *Amer. Naturalist* 97 (1963): 5-14.

27. E. W. Count, Comment on "The Human Revolution" by C. F. Hockett and R. Ascher, *Current Anthrop.* 5 (1964): 156. For a recent estimate see: P. E. Lestrel, "Hominid Brain Size versus Time: Revised Regression Estimates," *Journal of Human Evolution* 5 (1975): 207-12.

28. The demands the brain makes are enormous: brain cells, for example, use up to 20 percent of the cell DNA compared with two to three percent in other organs (50 percent is the maximum that can be used).

29. Vitamin C can also be obtained from raw meat.

30. Jane Lancaster, "Carrying and Sharing in Human Evolution," *Human Nature* 1 (2) (1978): 82-9.

31. J. N. Spuhler, "Continuities and Discontinuities in Anthropoid-hominid Behavioral Evolution: Bipedal Locomotion and Sexual Receptivity," N. Chagnon and W. Irons, eds., *Evolutionary Biology and Human Social Behavior* (North Scituate, Massachusetts: Duxbury Press, 1979).

32. On "structural fats" see: M. Crawford and S. Crawford, *What*

We Eat Today (London: Spearman, 1972). On the amino acids: William A. Stini, "Evolutionary Implications of Changing Nutritional Patterns in Human Populations," *American Anthropologist,* 73 (5) (1971): 1019-30. On toxicity of raw vegetables: A. C. Leopold and R. Ardrey, "Toxic Substances in Plants and the Food Habits of Early Man," *Science* 176 (1972): 512-14.

33. Ralph Holloway has been the strongest exponent of this view. See: R. Holloway, "Cranial Capacity, Neural Reorganization, and Hominid Evolution: A Search for More Suitable Parameters," *American Anthropologist* 68 (1) (1966): 103-21; idem, "The Evolution of the Human Brain: Some Notes towards a Synthesis between Neural Structure and the Evolution of Complex Behavior," *Gen. Syst.* 12 (1967): 3-19; idem, "Cranial Capacity and the Evolution of the Human Brain," A. Montagu, ed., *Culture: Man's Adaptive Dimension* (New York: Oxford University Press, 1968); "The Evolution of the Primate Brain: Some Aspects of Quantitative Relations," *Brain Research* 7 (1968): 121-72; idem, "Some Questions on Parameters of Neural Evolution in Primates," *Ann. N.Y. Acad. Sci.* 167 (1) (1969): 332-40.

Tobias, Gould, Jerison and Passingham, in the works cited, have been more optimistic regarding what can be inferred from size about internal developments.

34. Holloway has modified his position a little in "Australopithecine Endocasts, Brain Evolution in the Hominoidea, and a Model of Hominid Evolution," R. Tuttle, ed., *The Functional and Evolutionary Biology of Primates* (Chicago: Aldine/Atherton, 1972). See also: R. E. Passingham, "Anatomical Differences between the Neocortex of Man and Other Primates," *Brain Behav. Evol.* 7 (1973): 337-59; "Changes in the Size and Organization of the Brain in Man and his Ancestors," *Brain Behav. Evol.* 11 (1975): 73-90; R. E. Passingham and G. Ettlinger, "A Comparison of Cortical Functions in Man and the Other Primates," *Int'l. Rev. Neurobiol.* 16 (1975): 233-99; J. W. Papez, *Comparative Neurology* (New York: Hafner, 1967).

35. V. I. Kotchetkova, "L'évolution des régions specifiquement humaines de l'écorce cérébrale chez les hominides," *Proc. 6th Int. Cong. Anthrop. and Ethnol. Sci. Paris* 1 (1960): 623-30.

36. On increase in number of neurons in the brain of *H. sapiens,* see works of Jerison already cited.

37. On Koobi Fora particularly see G. Ll. Isaac, J. W. K. Harris and D. Crader, "Archeological Traces of Early Hominid Activities, East of Lake Rudolf, Kenya," *Science* 173 (1971): 1129-34, and G. Ll. Isaac, "The Activities of Early African Hominids: A

Review of Archeological Evidence from the Time Span Two and a Half to One Million Years Ago," G. Ll. Isaac and E. R. McCown, eds., *Human Origins* (Reading, Maryland: Benjamin/Cummings, 1976). See also: G. Ll. Isaac, "The Diet of Early Man: Aspects of Archeological Evidence from Lower and Middle Pleistocene Sites in Africa," *World Archeology* 2 (1971): 278-99; idem, "Stratigraphy and Cultural Patterns in East Africa During the Middle Ranges of Pleistocene Time," K. W. Butzer and G. Ll. Isaac, eds., *After the Australopithecines* (Chicago: Aldine, 1975); idem, "Early Hominids in Action: A Commentary on the Contribution of Archeology to Understanding the Fossil Record in East Africa," *Yearbook of Physical Anthropology* 19 (1975): 19-35.

38. On Torralba see: F. C. Howell, "Observations on the Earlier Phases of the European Lower Paleolithic," J. D. Clark and F. C. Howell, eds., *Recent Studies in Paleoanthropology, American Anthropologist* 68 (special publication) (1966): 88-201; L. G. Freeman, "Acheulean Sites and Stratigraphy in Iberia and the Maghreb," in K. W. Butzer and G. Ll. Isaac, eds., *After the Australopithecines.*

39. P. S. Martin, "Africa and Pleistocene Overkill," *Nature* 21 (1966): 339-42; idem, "The Discovery of America," *Science* 179 (1973): 969-74.

40. Susan M. Cachel, "A New View of Speciation in *Australopithecus,"* R. H. Tuttle, ed., *Paleoanthropology, Morphology and Paleoecology* (The Hague/Paris: Mouton, 1975).

41. Phillip Thompson, *Rethinking Human Evolution* (Ph.D. Thesis, Rutgers University, 1979); idem, "The Evolution of Territoriality and Society in Top Carnivores," *Social Science Information* 17 (6) (1978): 949-92.

42. S. L. Washburn, "Speculation on the Inter-relations of the History of Tools and Biological Evolution," J. N. Spuhler, ed., *The Evolution of Man's Capacity for Culture* (Detroit: Wayne State University Press, 1959); idem, "Tools and Human Evolution," *Scientific American* 203(3) (1960): 62-75; idem, "An Ape's Eye View of Human Evolution," I. DeVore, ed., *The Origin of Man* (New York: Wenner-Gren Foundation, 1965).

Six: Alliance and Constraint

1. R. Fox, *Kinship and Marriage: An Anthropological Perspective* (Harmondsworth and Baltimore: Penguin, 1967), p. 70.

2. Karl Pribram, ed., *On the Biology of Learning* (New York: Harcourt, Brace, Jovanovich, 1969).

3. We have mentioned Spuhler on this, but C. S. Ford and F. Beach, *Patterns of Sexual Behavior* (London: Eyre and Spottiswoode, 1952) and F. Beach, ed., *Sex and Behavior* (New York: Wiley, 1965) make the same point forcefully.

4. C. E. Poletti and M. Sujatanond have announced this in "Evidence for a Second Hippocampal-Diencephalic Physiological Pathway Comparable to the Fornix System—A Unit Study in the Awake Monkey" (paper presented at: Society for Neuroscience Meeting, Anaheim, California, 1977). They point out that the hippocampal influence on the amygdala is *predominantly inhibitory,* thus providing "a limbic substrate for learning to modify aggressive behavior."

5. W. Etkin, "Social Behavior and the Evolution of Man's Mental Capacities," *American Naturalist* 88 (1954): 129-42.

6. The phrase was coined by D. Morris in *The Naked Ape* (London: Constable, 1967), although ideas of "natural monogamy," etc., are at least as old as Westermarck in the anthropological tradition. Other "pair bond" advocates are V. Reynolds, "Open Groups in Hominid Evolution," *Man, n.s.,* 3 (1966): 209-23; "Kinship and the Family in Monkeys, Apes and Man," *Man, n.s.,* 3(1968):209–223; and J. Shepher, "Reflections on the Origin of the Human Pair-bond," *J. Social Biol. Struct.* 1 (1978): 253-64. The latter, flatteringly, seems to think this is all my theory lacks! If one substitutes "regular mate allocation" where he has "pair bond," I would not quarrel with his interpretation.

7. S. Wright, *Statistical Genetics in Relation to Evolution* (Paris: Hermann, 1939). See also B. E. Ginsberg, "Breeding Structure and Social Behavior of Mammals: A Servomechanism for Avoidance of Panmixia," D. C. Glass, ed., *Genetics* (New York: Rockefeller University Press and Russell Sage Foundation, 1968).

8. E. O. Wilson, "On the Queerness of Social Evolution," *Bull. Entomological Soc. Amer.* 19 (1) (1972): 20-2, has revived Sir Arthur Keith's notions on this, *A New Theory of Human Evolution* (London: Watts, 1948), and "differential extinction" has had an airing in the literature of the new improved sociobiology: P. J. Darlington, Jr., "Non-Mathematical Models for Evolution of Altruism, and for Group Selection," *Proc. Natl. Acad. Sci. USA* 69 (1972): 293-7.

9. For a good summary of the range of modern information, see R. Lee and I. Devore, eds., *Man the Hunter* (Chicago: Aldine,

1968); for an excellent cross-cultural study, see C. R. Ember, "Myths About Hunter-Gatherers," *Ethnology* 17 (4) (1978): 439-48. See also N. Blurton-Jones, "Ethology, Anthropology, and Childhood," R. Fox, ed., *Biosocial Anthropology.*

10. F. Engels, "The Part Played by Labor in the Transition from Ape to Man," written in 1876 and first published in 1896, reprinted in *The Dialectics of Nature* (Moscow: Progess Publishers, 1934), pp. 170-83. Marx's concerns appear in the earlier writings, in particular the Paris manuscripts. The best analysis, as yet unfortunately unpublished, is Paul Heyer's "Marx and Darwin: A Related Legacy on Man, Nature and Society" (Ph.D. Thesis, Rutgers University, 1975). See also D. McLellan, *Karl Marx: The Early Texts* (Oxford: Basil Blackwell, 1971), also his excellent *Marx Before Marxism* (New York: Harper, 1970).

11. Lee's estimate of 80 percent vegetable food and 20 percent meat in the hunter's diet has been challenged (Eskimos have almost 100 percent meat!)—see Ember, "Myths About Hunter-Gatherers"—and something nearer 50 percent—50 percent is more likely, with males contributing somewhat more if "fishing" societies are included as hunters. My point here is more dependent on the logic of omnivorousness in our ancestors than on current data. This point also interlocks with "increased infant dependency," in creating greater dependency between the sexes. Thus, even if the role of vegetables is downgraded, "domestic services" still loom large.

12. I will take this up again in the final chapter. It is a point easily misunderstood, since promiscuity is a characteristic of individuals, while polygyny characterizes *systems* of assortative mating. There is much confusion here, since no one is suggesting that all men or women are *equally* promiscuous in sexual motivation. There is a tendency to prefer sexual variety, but like all other tendencies, this can be suppressed if it conflicts with other goals. Similarly, not all men have the same stamina for polygyny. But this is precisely the point: Some will do better than others. On the prevalence of polygynous systems, see G. P. Murdock, *Social Structure* (New York: Macmillan, 1949) and "World Ethnographic Sample," *American Anthropologist* 59 (1957): 604-87. Of the societies with sufficient information (187), Murdock found 77.5 percent to be polygynous, 21.4 percent to be monogamous, and 1.6 percent polyandrous. On the possible polygyny of *Australopithecus* see W. Leutenegger, "Sociobiological Correlates of Sexual Dimorphism in Body Weight

in South African Australopiths," *South African Journal of Science*
73 (1977): 143-4. See also R. Trivers on differential male-female reproductive strategies—"Parental Investment and Sexual Selection," B. Campbell, ed., *Sexual Selection.*

13. On puberty, testosterone, and aggression, see D. Hamburg and
D. Lunde, "Sex Hormones and the Development of Sex Differences in Human Behavior," in E. Maccoby, ed., *The Development of Sex Differences* (Stanford: Stanford University Press,
1966). Pubescent males secrete between ten and thirty times as
much testosterone as prepubescent males. Girls only double the
amount from a lower base.

14. I have not made as much as I might have of the importance of
neoteny and the consequent lengthening in neonate dependency and the rapid growth of the brain in the seven months
after birth. See G. Roheim, *Psychoanalysis and Anthropology* (New
York: International Universities Press, 1968); A. Montagu, *The
Human Revolution* (Cleveland: World Publishing Co., 1965); and
the works of S. Gould, already cited. This is not because I underestimate its importance, but because if selection was basically for improved equilibration, then it would have favored
neoteny anyway. Neoteny thus becomes a mechanism in the
equilibration process—there is otherwise no point to the selection of neoteny *eo ipso.*

15. The question of where and how memories are stored—particularly
linguistic ones—is still being explored. It seems to involve
either an alteration of the neural net or coding in macromole-
cules (RNA), or some combination of these. A study that ties
the neural net in with development and, hence, with neoteny
(see previous note) is J. Altman, "Postnatal Growth and Differentiation of the Mammalian Brain, with Implications for a
Morphological Theory of Memory," G. C. Quarton, T. Melnechuck and F. O. Schmitt, eds., *The Neurosciences* (New York:
Rockefeller University Press, 1967). The RNA theory was advanced by H. Hyden, "RNA—A Functional Characteristic of
the Neuron and Its Glia," M. A. B. Brazier, ed., *Brain Function*
(Berkeley, California: California University Press, 1964). See
also his excellent summary of possibilities in "Biochemical
Changes Accompanying Learning," Quarton, Melnechuck
and Schmitt, eds. On the role of synapses, see J. C. Eccles,
"Possible Ways in Which Synaptic Mechanisms Participate
in Learning, Remembering and Forgetting," D. P. Kimble,
ed., *The Anatomy of Memory,* vol. 1 (Palo Alto, California: Science
and Behavior Books, 1965). All in all, in terms of sheer

volume, I would stand by my contention that late *Homo erectus,*
at least, had a "human" memory storage capacity. This, of
course, cannot be proved, but it seems to me a reasonable infer-
ence.

16. The literature on inclusive fitness and kin selection is growing
daily. See the summaries in E. O. Wilson, *Sociobiology: The New
Synthesis* (Cambridge and Harvard: Belknap Press of Harvard
University Press, 1975); R. Dawkins, *The Selfish Gene* (New
York and Oxford: Oxford University Press, 1976); R. Fox and
U. Fleising, "Human Ethology," *Ann. Rev. Anth.* 5 (1976): 265-
88. The classic papers are W. D. Hamilton, "The Evolution of
Altruistic Behavior," *Am. Nat.* 97 (1963): 354-6; idem, "The
Genetical Evolution of Social Behavior," *J. Theor. Biol.* 7
(1964): 1-52, although J. Maynard Smith coined the term,
"Kin Selection and Group Selection," *Nature* 201 (1964): 1145-
47. For an extension of these ideas to human kinship behavior
see: N. Chagnon and W. Irons, eds., *Evolutionary Biology and
Human Social Behavior: An Anthropological Perspective* (North Scituate, Massachusetts: Duxbury Press, 1979).

17. See S. A. Boorman and P. R. Levitt, "A Frequency-dependent
Natural Selection Model for the Evolution of Social Coopera-
tion Networks," *Proc. Natl. Acad. Sci. USA* 70 (1973): 187-9, and
J. L. Brown, "Alternate Routes to Sociality in Jays—with a
Theory for the Evolution of Altruism and Communal Breed-
ing," *Am. Zool.* 14 (1974): 63-80.

18. These are: long lifetime, low dispersal rate, high mutual dependence.

19. See J. Kurland, *Kin Selection in the Japanese Macaque* (Contrib. to
Primatol., vol. 12) (Basel: S. Karger, 1977).

20. For some new improved sociobiological speculations on the relation of this to "paternity confidence," see R. D. Alexander,
"The Evolution of Social Behavior," *Ann. Rev. Ecol. Syst.* 5
(1974): 325-83; idem, "The Search for a General Theory of Behavior," *Behav. Sci.* 20 (1975): 77-100; and J. Kurland, "Paternity, Mother's Brother and Sociality," in N. Chagnon and W.
Irons, eds., *Evolutionary Biology and Human Social Behavior.* I doubt
that the existence of matrilineal institutions turns on this factor
for the same reasons put forward by Sydney Hartland—*Primitive Paternity* (London: David Nutt, 1909-1910)—but this will
have to be discussed elsewhere.

21. L. R. Hiatt, "Authority and Reciprocity in Australian Aboriginal Marriage Arrangements," *Mankind* 6 (10) (1967): 468-75.

22. See R. Fox, *Kinship and Marriage,* chapters seven and eight, also
R. Fox, "Alliance and Constraint: Sexual Selection in the Evo-

lution of Human Kinship Systems," Bernard Campbell, ed.,
Sexual Selection and the Descent of Man 1871-1971, pp. 315-24. See
K. Maddock, "Alliance and Entailment in Australian Marriage," *Mankind* 7 (1) (1969): 19-26; W. S. Shapiro, "The Exchange of Sister's Daughter's Daughters in Northeast Arnhem
Land," *Southwestern J. of Anthropology* 24 (1968): 346-53; idem,
"Miwuyt Marriage" (Ph.D. Thesis, Australian National University, Canberra, 1969); B. S. Lane, "Structural Contrasts Between Symmetric and Asymmetric Marriage Systems: A Fal-
lacy," *Southwestern J. of Anthropology* 17 (1961): 49-55; idem,
"Jural Authority and Affinal Exchange," *Southwestern J. of Anthropology* 18 (1962): 184-97.

23. See C. Lévi-Strauss, *The Elementary Structures of Kinship*, chapter
twenty-eight, and R. Fox, *Kinship and Marriage*, chapter eight.

24. See L. R. Hiatt, *Kinship and Conflict: A Study of an Aboriginal Community in Northern Arnhem Land* (Canberra: Australian National
University, 1965); M. J. Meggitt, *Desert People: A Study of the
Walbiri Aborigines of Central Australia* (Sidney: Angus and Robertson, 1962); C. W. M. Hart and A. R. Pilling, *The Tiwi of
Northern Australia* (New York: Holt, Rinehart and Winston,
1960); R. B. Lee and I. Devore, eds., *Man the Hunter*, part 4;
F. G. G. Rose, *Classification of Kin, Age-structure and Marriage
among the Groote Eylandt Aborigines: A Study in Method and a Theory
of Australian Kinship* (Berlin: Akademie-Verlag; London: Perga-
mon Press, 1960); J. Goodale, "Marriage Contracts among the
Tiwi," *Ethnology* 1 (1962): 452-65. For a graphic description of
differential reproductive success in a tribal society, see the articles by N. Chagnon in N. Chagnon and W. Irons, eds., *Evolutionary Biology and Human Social Behavior*.

25. See J. W. M. Whiting, R. Kluckhohn, and A. S. Anthony,
"The Function of Male Initiation Ceremonies at Puberty," in
E. E. Maccoby, et al., eds., *Readings in Social Psychology* (New
York: Henry Holt, 1958).

26. Reviews of male initiation procedures: Y. A. Cohen, *The Tran-
sition from Childhood to Adolescence* (Chicago: Aldine, 1964); S. M.
Eisenstadt, *From Generation to Generation* (Glencoe, Illinois: Free
Press, 1955); Mircea Eliade, *Rites and Symbols of Initiation* (New
York: Harper, 1965); H. Garfinkle, "Conditions of Successful
Degradation Ceremonies," *Amer. J. Sociol.* 61 (5) (1956): 420-4;
M. Gluckman, ed., *Essays on the Ritual of Social Relations* (Man-
chester: Manchester University Press, 1962); A. Van Gennep,
Les Rites de Passage (Paris: Nourry, 1909); *Rites of Passage*, M. B.
Vizedom and G. L. Caffee, trans. (Chicago: University of Chi-

cago Press, 1960); F. Young, *Initiation Ceremonies: A Cross-Cultural Study of Status Dramatization* (New York: Bobbs-Merrill, 1965). This is an interesting critique of the work of J. W. M. Whiting, et al., "The Function of Male Initiation Ceremonies." Lionel Tiger's *Men in Groups* (New York: Random House, 1969) remains the classic discussion of the internal dynamics of the male block and recruitment to it. What we are adding to his picture is the emphasis on the old males' attempts to control the breeding system, a powerful source of their control over the young males.

27. G. E. King, "Society and Territory in Human Evolution," *J. Hum. Evol.* 5 (1976): 323-32; idem, "Socioterritorial Units among Carnivores and Early Hominids," *J. Anthropol. Res.* 31 (1975): 69-87; P. Thompson, "A Cross-Species Analysis of Carnivore, Primate and Hominid Behavior," *J. Hum. Evol.* 4 (1975): 113-24; idem, "The Evolution of Territoriality and Society in Top Carnivores," *Social Science Information* 17(6) (1978): 949:992.

28. A. Rossi, "A Biosocial Perspective on Parenting," *Daedalus* 106 (1977): 1-33.

29. Earl W. Count, "The Lactation Complex: A Phylogenetic Consideration of the Mammalian Mother-Child Symbiosis, with Special Reference to Man," *Homo* 18 (1) (1967): 38-54; idem, "The Biological Basis of Human Sociality," *American Anthropologist* 60 (1958): 1049-85.

30. I am not implying that there can *never* be incestuous attraction between mother and son nor that a great deal of psychic energy does not go into the suppression or conversion of such attractions. But it is the very *incompatibility* of such thoughts with the "reverberations" of the nurturing experience that cause the anxiety where it occurs. This comes out acutely in the "madonna/whore" contrast on the one hand, and the "suppressed archetype" of the "mother-lover" on the other, as exemplified by the figure of Aphrodite. It is significant that while all kinds of simpleminded rantings make headlines in anthropology today, Paul Friedrich's exquisite study *The Meaning of Aphrodite* (Chicago: Chicago University Press, 1978) has gone totally unnoticed.

31. See a sensible review of some current literature by James W. Ramey, "Dealing with the Last Taboo," *SIECUS Report* 7 (5) (1979).

Seven: The Matter of Mind

1. But see my "Kinship Categories as Natural Categories," N. Chagnon and W. Irons, eds., *Evolutionary Biology and Human Social Behavior: An Anthropological Perspective* (North Scituate, Massachusetts: Duxbury Press, 1979).

2. N. Chomsky, *Syntactic Structures* (The Hague, Paris: Mouton, 1957); idem, *Aspects of the Theory of Syntax* (Cambridge, Massachusetts: M.I.T. Press, 1965); idem, *Cartesian Linguistics* (New York: Harper, 1966); idem, *Language and Mind* (New York: Harcourt, Brace, Jovanovich, 1968); idem, *Problems of Knowledge and Freedom* (New York: Pantheon, 1971); idem, *Reflections on Language* (New York: Pantheon, 1975).

3. Gilbert Ryle, *The Concept of Mind* (London: Hutchinson, 1949); Leslie White, *The Science of Culture* (New York: Grove, 1949). This is not to accept at all a behaviorist position on mind, since I am obviously going to defend *a priori* categories and do not think "mind" can be *simply* reduced to "brain." See J. R. Smythies, ed., *Brain and Mind: Modern Concepts of the Nature of Mind* (London: Routledge, 1965); P. A. Buser and A. Rougeul-Buser, eds., *Cerebral Correlates of Conscious Experience* (Amsterdam: Elsevier/North-Holland Biomedical Press, 1978); K. R. Popper and J. C. Eccles, *The Self and Its Brain* (Heidelberg: Springer-Verlag, 1977).

4. C. Lévi-Strauss, *Elementary Structures of Kinship,* trans., J. H. Bell, J. R. von Sturmer and Rodney Needham ed. (Boston: Beacon, 1969), p. 75.

5. Ibid., p. 84.

6. E. B. Tylor, "Remarks on Totemism with Especial Reference to Some Modern Theories Concerning It," *Journal of the Royal Anthropological Institute* 28 (1899): 138-48.

7. Meyer Fortes, "Totem and Taboo," *Proceedings of the Royal Anthropological Institute 1966* (1966): 5-22.

8. J. Whiting and I. Child, *Child Training and Personality* (New Haven: Yale University Press, 1953).

9. Rodney Needham, *Primordial Characters* (Charlottesville: University of Virginia Press, 1979), has added "good to imagine," which I accept but, since imagination can be seen as a function of thought and feelings, have not added it as a fifth dimension.

10. Lévi-Strauss, *Elementary Structures of Kinship,* preface. This is essentially the preface to the second French edition.

11. Some of the argument in the previous chapters may have sug-

gested a "visceral brain" or "triune brain" approach, but I regard that more as a graphic description than an accurate theory. For a good summary of "brain and emotion" problems, see David Glass, ed., *Neurophysiology and Emotion* (New York: Rockefeller University Press/Russell Sage, 1967), especially the paper by Karl Pribram. See also Pribram's *Languages of the Brain: Experimental Paradoxes and Principles in Neuropsychology* (Englewood Cliffs: Prentice-Hall, 1971), for his latest position.

12. D. Hamburg, "Emotions in Perspective of Human Evolution," P. Knapp, ed., *Expression of the Emotions in Man* (New York: International Universities Press, 1963).

13. See Konrad Lorenz, *Evolution and Modification of Behavior* (London: Methuen, 1966). This is the "ethological" position generally.

14. In the sense used by Chance to contrast with the chimpanzee "hedonic" mode, see his various articles and books on attention structure already cited.

15. "Evolution and Lateralization of the Brain," S. Dimond and D. Blizard, eds., *Ann. N.Y. Acad. of Sci.,* vol. 299 (1977).

16. F. Engels, "The Part Played by Labor in the Transition from Ape to Man," written in 1876 and first published in 1896, reprinted in *The Dialectics of Nature* (Moscow: Progress Publishers, 1934), pp. 170-83.

17. A. C. Leopold and R. Ardrey, "Toxic Substances in Plants and the Food Habits of Early Man," *Science* 176 (1972): 512-14.

18. Vernon H. Mark and Frank R. Ervin, *Violence and the Brain* (New York: Harper and Row, 1970), p. 142.

19. J. Winson, "Loss of Hippocampal Theta Rhythm Results in Spatial Memory Deficit in the Rat," *Science* 201 (1978): 160-3; J. Winson and C. Abzug, "Gating of Neuronal Transmission in the Hippocampus: Efficacy of Transmission Varies with Behavioral State," *Science* 196 (1977): 1223-5; idem, "Neuronal Transmission through Hippocampal Pathways Dependent on Behavior," *J. Neurophysiology* 41 (1978): 716-32; idem, "Dependence upon Behavior of Neuronal Transmission from Perforant Pathway through Entorhinal Cortex," *Brain Research* 147 (1978): 422-7.

On the role of the hippocampus in "stamping in" signals see: G. A. Ojemann, "Correlations between Specific Human Brain Lesions and Memory Changes: A Critical Survey of the Literature," *Neurosci. Res. Prog. Bul.* 4, Supplement (1966): 1-70.

20. R. Trivers, "The Evolution of Reciprocal Altruism," *Quarterly Review of Biology* 46 (4) (1971): 35-57.

21. Mary Douglas, *Purity and Danger* (London: Routledge, 1969); idem, *Natural Symbols* (New York: Academic Press, 1973); E. R. Leach, "Anthropological Aspects of Language: Animal Categories and Verbal Abuse," E. Lenneberg, ed., *New Directions in the Study of Language* (Cambridge, Massachusetts: M.I.T. Press, 1964).

22. Leonard Bernstein, *The Unanswered Question* (Cambridge, Massachusetts: Harvard University Press, 1976).

23. E. Durkheim and M. Mauss, *Primitive Classification,* originally published in 1903, Rodney Needham, trans. (Chicago: Chicago University Press, 1963).

24. E. Durkheim, *The Elementary Forms of the Religious Life,* originally published in 1912, J. W. Swain, trans. (London: Allen and Unwin, 1915), pp. 18-9 and conclusion.

25. For Durkheim's individual/social dichotomy, see *The Rules of Sociological Method,* originally published in 1895, S. Solway and J. Mueller, trans. (New York: Free Press, 1951). F. H. Bradley's extraordinary essay, which anticipated much of the work of G. H. Mead and the whole "status and role" school of social psychology, while at the same time being aware of the Darwinian implications, was "My Station and Its Duties," *Ethical Studies* (first published in 1876), second edition, Oxford: Clarendon Press, 1927. The whole discussion here is, of course, too brief to do justice to the complexities of "Durkheim's Dilemma" (first invoked in a footnote to L. Tiger and R. Fox, "The Zoological Perspective in Social Science," *Man, n.s.,* 1, no. 1 (1966): 75-86, and a more adequate account will have to wait. It has often been pointed out, for example, that while he banishes the biological from sociological explanation, when it comes to explaining the division of labor he invokes population growth as a causal principle. Population trends may be "social facts," but they are indisputably in some sense biological facts as well. The paradox is further confounded, since Durkheim claimed to have derived his basic notions from his teacher Alfred Espinas (*Des Sociétés Animales,* 1878), who unquestionably saw "society" as a prehuman, hence animal, hence biological phenomenon (Bradley's point). So strong is the Durkheimian influence, however, that even the demonstration by the ethologists—the logical successors of Espinas—that *social* behavior can be, in the words of Jaques Monod, "part of the species' genetic patrimony," has failed to make much impact on sociology proper.

The fatal connection made by Durkheim is, of course, that between the "individual" and the "biopsychological," thus leaving for sociology its autonomous, if untenable (and unnecessary), realm of "social fact."

26. For Lévi-Strauss on Durkheim and Mauss see his *Totemism*, trans., R. Needham (London: Merlin Press, 1964), p. 97. On Chomsky and Piaget, see Massimo Piattelli-Palmarini, ed., *Théories de langage: Théories de l'apprentissage* (Paris: Seuil, 1979).

   Lévi-Strauss has defended his position on emotions—especially anxiety—in a lively way in the final chapter of *L'homme nu* (Paris: Plon, 1971), even to the point of invoking physiological correlates (lactic acid, p. 588). I find myself much in sympathy with his position as against his critics, except that without the evolutionary perspective, it lacks a framework for *basic* explanation—why the "lactic acid-anxiety-category failure" connection? Such a complicated feedback system with such a "hard" physiological correlate must have its roots in a long-standing adaptive process.

27. R. Needham, "Introduction" to his translation of Durkheim and Mauss, *Primitive Classification*.

28. This was more or less the position arrived at by Herbert Spencer in his *Principles of Psychology* (1855), to reconcile *a priorism* and empiricism. It is also K. Lorenz's position in: "Kant's Doctrine of the A Priori in the Light of Contemporary Biology," L. Von Bertalanffy and A. Rapoport, eds., *General Systems, Yearbook of the Society for General Systems Research*, vol. 7 (New York: Society for General Systems Research, 1962), pp. 23-35 (originally published in German in 1941). See also his *Behind the Mirror* (New York: Methuen, 1977).

   As Donald Campbell has pointed out, some forty scholars since Darwin have held the same position without it ever becoming a "school." See his "Evolutionary Epistemology," P. A. Schilpp, ed., *The Philosophy of Karl Popper*, vol. 14, I and II, *The Library of Living Philosophers* (La Salle, Illinois: Open Court Pub., 1974, 413-63). All I am adding is an anthropological view of the *content, mechanisms,* and *origins.* This includes the overriding principle that the "content, mechanisms and origins" are *social* rather than individual—Lorenz's point—thus overcoming the Durkheimian objections to Spencer.

   The position taken in this chapter also has a lot in common with that of Charles D. Laughlin and Eugene G. d'Aquili, *Biogenetic Structuralism* (New York: Columbia University Press, 1974), and indeed the original version was written at much the same time, and presented at a meeting of the American Anthropological Association (1973).

29. S. Harnad, H. D. Steklis, and J. Lancaster, eds., "Origins and Evolution of Language and Speech," *Ann. N.Y. Acad. of Sci.,* vol. 280 (1976).

30. James Hamilton, "Hominid Divergence and Speech Evolution," *Journal of Human Evolution* 3 (1974): 417-24, summarizes evidence for and against "early" development of language. Much has been made, for example, of the supposed inability of Neanderthals to make certain vowel sounds. But small-range vocabularies can exist quite easily with two vowels; and one must not forget gestures.

31. The classical papers on human/animal language differences are still those of Charles Hockett. See: "Animal Languages and Human Language," J. N. Spuhler, ed., *The Evolution of Man's Capacity for Culture* (Detroit, Michigan: Wayne State University Press, 1959); idem, "The Origin of Speech," *Scientific American* (September 1960). See also C. F. Hockett and R. Ascher, "The Human Revolution," *Current Anthropology* 5 (1964): 135-68.

32. Jane Lancaster, "Primate Communication Systems and the Emergence of Human Language," Phyllis Jay, ed., *Primates: Studies in Adaptation and Variability* (New York: Holt, Rinehart and Winston, 1968). See also: E. H. Lenneberg, *Biological Foundations of Language* (New York: Wiley, 1967). The capacity to name seems to rest on the existence in man of the angular gyrus. This was the discovery of Norman Geschwind, "The Development of the Brain and the Evolution of Language," *Monograph Series on Language and Linguistics* 17 (1964): 155-69; "Disconnection Syndromes in Animals and Man," *Brain* 88 (1965): 237-94, 585-644.

33. Charles Osgood discovered three universal linguistic "affective factors," which he labeled (1) evaluative, (2) potency, and (3) activity, accounting for 60 percent of semantic loading. These can be roughly understood as dimensions including the properties of "good-bad," "strong-weak," and "slow-fast," for example. Osgood suggests that in evolution an estimation of "strength" and "activity," with an evaluation of these as good or bad, may have been a basic necessity of linguistic adaptation. See: C. E. Osgood, "Language Universals and Psycholinguistics," W. H. Greenberg, ed., *Universals of Language* (Cambridge, Massachusetts: M.I.T. Press, 1963); idem, "Semantic Differential Technique in the Comparative Study of Cultures," *American Anthropologist* 66 (1964): 171-200.

As for what may seem my rather arbitrary category of "process words" (which in some ways only adds to my overuse of the word process in this entire book), see the brilliant argument of G. Lakoff in his *Irregularity in Syntax* (New York: Holt, Rinehart and Winston, 1970), where he argues that verbs and adjectives, for example, should be assigned to the same lexical class.

34. In such a reconstruction, studies of child language will be crucial. See Jane Lancaster, "Primate Communication Systems," for a discussion of this. As important will be studies of neonate cognition—a rapidly growing and fascinating field. See: Jacques Mehler, "La perception du langage chez le nourrisson," *La Recherche* 9:88 (1978): 324-30; also, J. Mehler and Josiane Bertoncini, "Infants' Perception of Speech and Other Acoustical Stimuli," John Morton and John C. Marshall, eds., *Structures and Processes* (London: Paul Elek, 1979).

Eight: Past Imperatives: Present Discontents

1. See the debate between Zahavi and his critics: Amotz Zahavi, "Mate Selection—A Selection for a Handicap," *Journal of Theoretical Biology* 53 (1975): 205-14; John Maynard Smith, "Sexual Selection and the Handicap Principle," ibid. 57 (1976): 239-42; J. W. F. Davis and P. O'Donald, "Sexual Selection for a Handicap: A Critical Analysis of Zahavi's Model," ibid. 57 (1976): 345-54.

2. On marginality, liminality, etc., see Victor Turner, *The Ritual Process* (Chicago: Aldine, 1969). His concept of "communitas," as he recognizes, is tantalizingly "biological." This needs further exploration in our framework.

3. Robin Fox, *The Keresan Bridge: A Problem in Pueblo Ethnology* (L. S. E. Monographs on Social Anthropology No. 35) (London: Athlone Press, 1967).

4. In Katherine Elliott, ed., *The Family and its Future* (London: J. and A. Churchill, 1970), pp. 10-1.

5. In E. Sullerot, ed., *Le Fait Féminin* (Paris: Fayard, 1978), pp. 382-3; this passage translated by Barbara Wright.

6. Edward Shorter, *The Making of the Modern Family* (New York: Basic Books, 1975).

7. Margaret Mead, Comment on Hockett and Ascher, "The Human Revolution," *Current Anthropology* 5 (3) (1964): 160.

8. Nur Yalman, *Under the Bo Tree: Studies in Caste, Kinship and Marriage in the Interior of Ceylon* (Berkeley: University of California Press, 1971).

9. R. D. Alexander, J. L. Hoogland, R. D. Howard, K. M. Noonan and P. W. Sharman, "Sexual Dimorphisms and Breeding Systems in Pinnipeds, Ungulates, Primates and Humans," N. Chagnon and W. Irons, eds., *Evolutionary Biology and Human Social Behavior.*

10. Denis de Rougement, *Passion and Society* (London: Faber and Faber, 1940). Originally *L'Amour et l'Occident* (Paris: Plon, 1934).

11. Originally written in Irish Gaelic in about 1780, Merriman's great poem *Cúirt an Mheadhon Oidhche* is perhaps the most outspoken of the protests against the practice of marrying young girls off to wealthy old farmers. Even in the thirties, Conrad Arensberg and Solon T. Kimball—*Family and Community in Ireland* (Cambridge, Massachusetts: Harvard University Press, 1940)—showed how the inheritance system could delay a man's marriage until as late as forty, when he took over the farm. Until then, he was still a "boy." For an alternative Irish system with some curious variants on both the basic pattern and the Irish version of it, see Robin Fox, *The Tory Islanders: A People of the Celtic Fringe* (New York: Cambridge University Press, 1978).

12. See Jerzy Peterkiewicz's remarkable *The Third Adam* (London: Oxford University Press, 1975), for an account of a Polish polygynous cult. His chapter 7 is a thoughtful discussion of the problem of the church and sexual repression.

13. See the works of Robert Trivers, previously cited, for the best discussion of the asymmetry between male and female reproductive strategies. The major modifier of male promiscuity, he notes, is the need for male parental investment. This is the strongest female card.

14. I discuss this in *Encounter with Anthropology,* and it is evident in *Kinship and Marriage.*

15. In *The Imperial Animal,* chapter four.

16. Ashley Montagu, *The Natural Superiority of Women* (New York: Macmillan, 1953).

17. Doris Lessing, *The Golden Notebook* (New York: Bantam Books, 1973), pp. viii-ix.

18. There is an intriguing study by Kristin Luker, *Taking Chances: Abortion and the Decision Not to Contracept* (Berkeley: University of

California Press, 1975). She shows how often "taking chances" results from a seeming calculation of "costs and benefits" by the woman. Contraception does not, then, rule out female reproductive strategies, it simply modifies them. The whole issue of "risk taking" could profitably be looked at in the light of our theory and Trivers' theory of reproductive strategy.

19. A. Estrada, M. Alcaraz and C. Guzman-Flores, "Efectos de los estrogenos y progestagenos sobre la conducta social del mono verde" ("Effects of Estrogens and Progestins upon the Social Behavior of the Green Monkey"), *Bol. Estud. Méd. Biol. Mex.* 29 (1976): 250.

20. Heather Fowler, "Female Choice: An Investigation into Human Breeding System Strategy" (Paper presented at Animal Behavior Society Meetings, Pennsylvania State University, June 1977).

21. See Steven V. Roberts, "The Epidemic of Teenage Pregnancy," The *New York Times,* June 18, 1978. For a discussion of the social problem, see Frank F. Furstenberg, Jr., *Unplanned Parenthood* (New York and London: Macmillan, 1976).

22. The *New York Times* reported ("New Findings on Teen Pregnancy," April 29, 1979) that Dr. Brian Sutton-Smith, having studied 9,000 Danish mothers, concluded, "The younger the mother, the better the birth," given proper care.

23. C. T. Javert, *Spontaneous and Habitual Abortion* (New York: McGraw-Hill, 1957).

24. Mel Konner, "Adolescent Pregnancy," The *New York Times,* Sept. 24, 1977.

25. There is considerable literature on the pineal gland and its role in reproductive development. See: G. E. W. Wolstenholme and J. Knight, *The Pineal Gland* (London: J. and A. Churchill, 1971); On light and the pineal gland: D. P. Cardinali and R. J. Wurtman, "The Effects of Light on Man," A. Damon, ed., *Physiological Anthropology* (New York: Oxford University Press, 1975); N. A. Jafarey, M. Y. Khan, and S. N. Jafarey, "Role of Artificial Lighting in Decreasing the Age of Menarche," *Lancet* 2 (1970): 471.

INDEX